M. Siegrie[illegible]

BRINGING IT ALL TOGETHER

A Program for Literacy

BRINGING IT ALL TOGETHER

A Program for Literacy

Terry D. Johnson and Daphne R. Louis

Scholastic

Canadian Cataloguing in Publication Data

Johnson, Terry D., 1936-
Bringing it all together

1st Canadian ed.
Bibliography: p.

1. Language arts (Elementary). I. Louis, Daphne R.,
1949- . II. Title.
LB1576.J63 1989 372.6'044 C89-093529-7

ISBN 0-590-73356-7

This revised edition published by Scholastic Canada Ltd. by permission of Nelson Education (Australia). First published by Methuen Australia Pty Ltd in 1987.

6 5 4 3 2 Printed in Canada 1 2 3 4/9

I would like to dedicate my part of this book to my mother,
Madge Dawson Johnson, who introduced me to
a lifetime pleasure in language.
Terry D. Johnson

To David, in the hope that he will have teachers who will share
a love of language and literature.
Daphne R. Louis

CONTENTS

FOREWORD

This book is very much a continuation of our earlier *Literacy through Literature* (1987). Some issues we address again, with a new perspective, but if we already gave detailed explanations of a routine in *Literacy through Literature*, we simply make reference to it.

ACKNOWLEDGMENTS

We would like to express our appreciation to long-suffering colleagues who listened to us talk the theory out: Bob Anthony, Jim Field, Norma Mickelson, Lloyd Ollila and Alison Preece; to hundreds of diligent undergraduate students who brought so many stories to our attention; to the patient teachers who graciously lent their classrooms while we fumbled through half-formed ideas. In particular our thanks to Lorraine Travis (principal, Campus View Elementary School), Len Anderson, Maureen Archambault, Richard Boisvert, Diane Cowden, Pamela Elliott, Jan Hockin, Anne Kilduff, Sheila O'Brien, Margaret Sayles, Diane Symers and Frances Witt.

We would also like to thank Sue Miyake who knows not only a vast amount about children's books, but also where to find them.

The following people contributed specific ideas to the book:

John Durkin, Jim Field, Norma Mickelson, Lloyd Ollila and Alison Preece of the University of Victoria, (B.C., Canada) for prolonged and productive discussions of the materials in Chapter 5, Evaluation.

Anne Davies, School District No. 1, Yellowknife, Northwest Territories, Canada, for the letter reproduced in figure 5.13.

Gail Heald-Taylor, Faculty of Education, University of Windsor, for the examples of Michael's writing in figure 5.10.

Mrs. Jean Jordan, Saanichton Elementary School (British Columbia, Canada) contributed her idea for the story binding chart, page 102.

Graham Rice and the staff of Sidney Elementary School, (B.C.,Canada) for the materials from the program "Read With Me," described in Chapter 7.

Debby Wilson, Judith Terry and Karen Swanson for their parts in preparing the teacher's guide to *The Secret of NIMH* in Chapter 8.

We extend our thanks to Sarah Baylow, Sharon Kucey and Betty Obee for typing the manuscript.

And finally, our thanks to the ever open, ever optimistic children who made it worthwhile.

The publisher would like to thank the following for permission to use materials:

Magorian, Michelle. Excerpt from *Goodnight, Mr. Tom* by Michelle Magorian. Copyright © 1981 by Michelle Magorian. Reprinted by permission of Harper & Row, Publishers, Inc., New York and Deborah Rogers Ltd., London for Michelle Magorian.

Malam, Charles. "Steam Shovel" from *Upper Pastures* by Charles Malam. Reprinted by permission of Henry Holt and Company, Inc., New York.

Mare, Walter de la. "Autumn" from *Crystal Cabinet*, edited by H. Gregory and M. Zaturenska. Reprinted by permission of The Literary Trustees of Walter de la Mare and The Society of Authors as their representative, London.

Mark, Jan. "Nothing to be Afraid Of" from *Nothing to be Afraid* of by Jan Mark (Kestrel Books, 1980), copyright © Jan Mark, 1977, 1980. Reprinted by permission of Penguin Books Ltd., London. Specified excerpt from pages 3–5 in NOTHING TO BE AFRAID OF by Jan Mark. Copyright © 1980, 1981 by Jan Mark. Reprinted by permission of Harper & Row, Publishers, Inc., New York.

Morrison, Lillian. "The Sidewalk Racer or on the Skateboard" from *The Sidewalk Racer*. Text: Copyright © 1977 by Lillian Morrison. Reprinted by permission of Lothrop, Lee & Shepard Books (A Division of William Morrow & Co.) New York.

O'Neill, Mary. "My Fingers" from *My Fingers are Always Bringing Me News*. Reprinted by permission of the author, Mary O'Neill, Florida, U.S.A.

Roethke, Theodore. "The Bat" from *Collected Poems of Theodore Roethke*. Reprinted by permission of Faber and Faber Limited, London and Doubleday & Company, Inc., New York.

Silverstein, Shel. "Hug O'War" from *Where the Sidewalk Ends* by Shel Silverstein. Copyright © 1974 by Evil Eye Music, Inc. Reprinted by permission of Harper & Row, Publishers, Inc., New York and Jonathan Cape Limited, London.

Every effort has been made to clear permissions for world rights for the material in this book. However, in the event of any oversight, the publishers apologise and guarantee to make the due acknowledgement or amendment in a subsequent reprint.

INTRODUCTION

OUR PURPOSE: WHOLISTIC TEACHING

Teachers are busy people. Because teaching puts so many demands on their time and attention, they are often reduced to looking for quick fixes: sure-fire suggestions the children will enjoy, something practical and easy to prepare, something that develops useful skills, something that doesn't require too much marking. We sympathize: we've been there.

It's all too easy to presume that quick fixes will do for all — or at least most — teaching conditions. But teachers teach under an amazing diversity of circumstances, with many different sets of goals. The suggestions in this book come out of our own experiences, and the more detailed, specific and concrete they are, the fewer teaching situations they're likely to suit. Even as we described our experiences we knew that what we did and said in one time and place wouldn't necessarily suit others in quite different times and places.

So in addition to the practical suggestions we've included sections meant to help build an understanding of the principles of developmental literacy that underlie them. Why do we recommend wholistic methods and reject a skills-based approach? Why do we encourage the use of natural texts? Our beliefs grow out of our current understanding of the nature of language and language learning. The rest of this introduction outlines very briefly those basic beliefs, the first chapter describes the foundations of literacy, and the next four present specific teaching suggestions plus "Theoretical Reflections" that pull together our views about instructional procedures. The next chapter discusses evaluation. These chapters build toward a short chapter in which we combine theory and practice to put forward a few ideas about developing a literacy curriculum, again followed by Theoretical Reflections. The final two chapters discuss parental involvement, and present a sample teaching guide and both professional and children's bibliographies.

It's our hope that, armed with a set of understood principles, you'll take our ideas and modify and extend them to suit your own circumstances. The sense of ownership and creativity you gain from developing your own activities will far surpass any benefits you might derive from merely implementing our suggestions.

OUR PHILOSOPHY: DEVELOPMENTAL LITERACY

It's clear that human beings continue from birth through maturity to increase their control over both oral and written language. It's also evident that an accomplished language user has a large repertoire of language skills. From those observations the assumption has been that the acquisition of language skills can be developmentally sequenced: that we can identify basic skills which are easy for inexperienced learners to acquire and which will provide the foundation for learning more demanding skills.

However, literacy learning doesn't appear to proceed in that linear-additive manner. Rather, it seems to grow through a process of assimilation and accommodation, forming an increasingly rich associative net. The process of increasing the number and complexity of associative connections is general, but the making of specific associations is peculiar to each individual. While we can say in general terms what children must do to become literate, we can't specify what any given individual needs to do on a given day. Programs that arrange instructional activities in rigid, predetermined sequences are in conflict with the natural learning proclivities of children. Learning often happens without the learner being aware of it, and without it being directly evident to an observer.

Reading Development

Acceptance of an associative network view of literacy calls many traditional assumptions and practices into question — controlled vocabulary, for example. We don't know, and never will know, which words in which order a given child is ready to learn to read. Nor do we know the rate at which new vocabulary should be introduced, nor the number of repetitions each child needs for each word. We once heard an eminent scholar boast that some kindergarten children had learned to read *marshmallow* by acting out a poem that used the word. *Marshmallow,* he reminded us, is not a kindergarten word. Why not? What committee is authorized to allocate particular words to particular grades?

We can ask similar questions about predetermined skill sequences, and about the very concept of a discrete reading skill. Breaking reading down into skills involves a process of intellectual abstraction and may not result in a description of reading that has any psychological reality for the reader. It's like studying rabbits by looking at rabbit molecules. The actions of those tiny particles tell us nothing about the animal. Texts, like rabbits, are dynamic structures. Each word in a given text derives some of its meaning and function from its association with the others. If we reduce the text to single, separate words the nature of each word changes. We can learn little by the close examination of each word in isolation.

With respect to readability, we can refer to the level of difficulty of a text only in the broadest terms. If a child reading at a grade three level has an obsessive interest in a given topic, he or she will likely be able to read books on that topic at a much higher level. A readability assessment that reports levels of difficulty to one or two decimal places is a figment of a hand calculator's imagination. At best we can say that a book with a readability level of 5.0, for example, can normally be read by children with a reading ability somewhere between grades four and six.

It is best to select materials intuitively, guided by the content and presentation that seems to appeal to the children they're intended for, rather than by some linguistic characteristic supposedly appropriate for a learner at a given level. We can identify stories and poems that are suitable for children in a given year, but we simply can't justify a fixed, predetermined order for presenting them.

We should select activities on the same intuitive basis. By and large we know the kinds of activities six-year-old children like. We also know what changes we'd make if we were planning to teach nine, 14- or 27-year-olds. We couldn't, however, defend a particular sequenced set of activities. Almost any activity that requires children to interact meaningfully with written language will serve our purpose. Indeed, most activities don't fit into a developmental paradigm which makes them suitable for one age but not for another. People sing, chant, write, perform and discuss at all ages. The level of maturity and the complexity of these activities will increase over time, but in most cases those changes are under the control of the learner rather than the teacher.

Instructional implications

The notion that there are limits to the specificity with which we can describe language development has instructional implications. Instruction should parallel our knowledge of the learning process. If we can specify the general level of individual children's present capacity for language processing and can generally predict the direction in which it will develop, then our instructional procedures should reflect that generality. Instruction should *not* pretend that we know that today Jessica must learn the *ng* digraph and Joshua must work on an appreciation of symbol. Or, as is more likely, that today is the day the children are *all* "ready" to use three-syllable words or to pay attention to medial vowels.

All we can really say is that there are certain things readers need to be able to do — use context, for example. In that case we should use an activity that encourages the use of context, perhaps one that requires the children to identify the meaning of nonsense words embedded in the summary of a story. We can offer general guidance on how to approach tasks, but the specific tactics used and the specific learnings that result are controlled by the individual children.

Arguments are often raised against letting children control their own learning, especially when it seems that changes are regressive rather than progressive. The child who used *went* correctly at two years of age may say *wented* at three. But we can consider that change regressive only if we take a limited view of the child's language. The erroneous use of *wented* for the verb *to go* signals a new awareness of how the past tense is regularly formed; the child will soon come to understand regularities and their exceptions. Similarly, when learners who earlier were able to read/recite a familiar text fluently begin to read haltingly they've likely begun to realize the one-to-one correspondence between written and spoken words.

Such "regressions" are in fact signs of developmental change; raising them to support the argument that change isn't necessarily progress simply confuses the issue. Children may, through poor instruction, come to mistrust their linguistic instincts and artificially constrict their vocabularies, but by and large their language moves in the direction of the adult speech community in which they live.

This is not to suggest that the language of children is inherently inferior to the language of adults. We value the speech of a three-year-old as appropriate for that age. But we wouldn't value the same language expressed by a seven-year-old; we would label it "immature" and feel that some intervention was required. And if a teenager used the same language we might suspect limited mental capacity. We expect that children's language will progress toward adult norms, and value even apparently regressive changes that in reality indicate progress.

Writing Development

Writing development is analogous to reading development in that beginning writers must learn the conventions associated with written expression: letter formation, spelling, selection and sequencing of words on the page, sentence formation, grammar and appropriate usages. They must also learn to express themselves within the constraints of the numerous forms of written expression: stories, poems, plays, letters, posters, memos, shopping lists, forms, expository texts, editorials, political pamphlets, travel brochures, directions, rules and warnings. Each form has numerous sub-categories. Within narration, for example, children must learn about chronology and permissible ways for linear time sequences to be manipulated through flashbacks and parallel plot construction.

The procedures involved in writing, like reading, can be placed on a continuum between deep structure and surface realization. Deep structure includes the act of creation or inspiration, which is not communicable; the learning of surface structure is largely tacit. Most speakers and writers are unaware of most of the rules that govern their selection and ordering of words. So writing instruction, like reading instruction, should be approached through a range of mid-level strategies that are readily available to the conscious mind and that can be demonstrated, analyzed, discussed and modified.

The early writing of young children, like much of their other behavior, is egocentric — but that doesn't last. Graves (1981) has documented some of the changes towards increased conventionality that occur as children, realizing that others can't understand what they've written, proceed to make the necessary elaborations. As writers mature, elaboration is seen in longer and more complex T-units/sentences (a T-unit is a written construction that an adult writer would have punctuated as a sentence), as demonstrated by Hunt (1965) and O'Donnell, Griffin and Morris (1967). But further research casts up an interesting anomaly. Although longer T-units are usually considered a characteristic of better writing, Martinez San Jose (1973), Stewart and Grobe (1979) and Jurgens and Griffin (1970) all found little or no relationship between the T-unit length and ratings of quality. These three studies cover writers from grade four to grade eleven.

On the one hand, then, we have growth in writing associated with maturity in syntactic complexity, while on the other we're told that syntactic complexity is not associated with improved quality.

Instructional implications

We'd like to suggest a resolution to this apparent anomaly. The young writer's initial task must be to gain control over the basic procedures, but then the nature of the task changes. Armed with a repertoire of basic skills, the writer has a new purpose: to become familiar with a wide variety of written forms, knowledge gained initially by listening and later by reading. Learning to compose within the constraints of a given form is a major accomplishment for the novice.

Perhaps an understanding of this developmental change in the nature of the task will help to resolve the dispute between Graves (1983) and Hillocks (1986). Graves advocates a free-writing approach; Hillocks presents research showing that approach is less effective than other kinds of intervention (see A Writing Curriculum, page 201). Graves' research was conducted with children in the early primary grades; Hillocks' research review deals with studies of upper primary children, secondary school students and adults. Since Graves' subjects are in the process of mastering basic writing skills it matters little what topic or form the writing assumes. During this phase the children's two major preoccupations are the creative act of composition (which is not accessible) and rules governing surface structure (which are learned for the most part tacitly). Since there's little left for the teacher to do but encourage them in their exploration, the reactive role Graves advocates is appropriate at that level. A more active leadership role may be more appropriate when the writer begins to use a variety of written forms. As Hillocks demonstrates, active interventions with older students appear to have highly beneficial effects on the development of writing ability.

Donaldson (1978) reviews studies indicating that young children are capable of producing more complex language when functioning within the meaningful flow of everyday events than when "disembedded" language demands are placed on them. One two-year-old child was unable to repeat to an investigator sentences he himself had produced the day before. Donaldson argues that children's capacity for language is supported by their understanding of the situations in which particular speech acts occur. When this support is withdrawn, their linguistic competence is reduced. Any situation that requires children to deal with decontextualized language, therefore, ensures that they are practicing at a level below their capacity.

If this line of reasoning applies to older children as well, and to written forms of language, then the implications for instruction in the classroom are enormous. It suggests that any activity or exercise that requires children to examine and manipulate decontextualized language actually decreases opportunities for linguistic growth. It seems that children rise to the demands placed on them by real communicative situations and that their language grows at those times. If such situations are replaced by disembedded language activities, then potential learning opportunities are lost.

In practical terms the argument suggests that having children write real letters to real people for real reasons is better than having them learn the form of a contrived letter to an imaginary person for no good reason. Writing a story for someone who genuinely wants to read it is better than writing one for a teacher who will regard the task of "marking" it as onerous!

Our extension of Donaldson's argument to writing suggests why the teaching of grammar is an ineffective means of developing writing and why an environmental approach has such positive effects (Hillocks, 1986). The teaching of grammar necessarily involves the decontextualization of language; an environmental approach creates situations where genuine written communication is required.

CHAPTER 1

EARLY LITERACY

READING READINESS

We thought the reading readiness issue had been settled, that Holdaway's brilliant phrase *emergent reading* (or *writing* or *literacy*) had rendered the seemingly endless debate irrelevant. But the continued demand for reading-readiness tests and programs suggests it's still with us.

Some people still feel there's a period in children's lives, roughly the first five or six years, when they are free from significant literacy events. Natural maturing and experience combine to make them ready to read, and reading-readiness tests are available to measure that maturing process and determine when it's time for formal instruction. Readiness programs are designed to provide them with non-literate experiences for the development of those essentials that are presumed to underlie reading ability — like distinguishing geometric shapes and determining figure-ground relationships. (It's interesting to note that no one has ever devised *writing*-readiness tests and activities.)

But Clay (1975), Ferreiro and Teberosky (1979), Harste, Woodward and Burke (1984), Applebee (1973) and many others have demonstrated that the lives of many preschool children are filled with literacy events. Daily routines in many homes include reading and writing in numerous highly functional and meaningful ways: shopping lists, letters from distant relatives, messages on the refrigerator door, bills, newspapers, religious rituals, television schedules, bedtime stories, greeting cards, etc. Not all children will have had the same quantity and quality of interaction with print, of course; indeed, the discrepancies are very wide. As a result, some children with more limited literacy experience may appear to be "slow" on school entry. The truth is simply that they have farther to go than others with richer preschool experiences.

The idea that it's possible to say when a child should and shouldn't be taught literacy is an illusion. Children do *not* wait to learn to read until they enter school. They do *not* begin learning to read when the lesson labeled "reading" begins. Nor do they stop learning to read when the reading period ends. Children learn something about reading every time they are required to interact meaningfully with print, when they need to find the right bathroom, distinguish the principal's office from the nurse's room, or find which locker in the gym contains the soccer balls.

Thus the singleminded focus on "formal" reading instruction becomes irrelevant; it can't be maintained unless we believe that significant learning derives only from the pages of the reader and the workbook. Those of us who reject the notion of formal reading programs and perceive literacy as gradually emerging through the immersion in, and meaningful interaction with, written language will never choose a day to begin "formal" instruction. We have no need for reading-readiness tests.

Nor is there any need for reading-readiness programs. There's no evidence to support the idea that a body of non-literate instructional activities exists that will promote children's readiness for reading. Leinhart, Zigmund and Cooley (1981) found that time allocated to indirect reading tasks — any activity assumed to be related to reading but not actually requiring a direct engagement with print; for example, circling pictures with a particular sound in common — was unrelated to reading performance. Reading performance was found instead to be directly related to the amount of time spent doing silent reading.

Children need relevant, interesting and achievable experiences with literacy in warm, tolerant, supportive and forgiving environments. For us, these kinds of experiences and learnings are summed up in Holdaway's phrase. Children learn to deal with any meaningful aspects of their lives: parents, television, siblings, weather, dogs, traffic, trees or texts. If literacy events are a meaningful, normal, regular and reasonably frequent part of their lives, literacy behavior will develop.

Harste, Woodward and Burke (1984) have even questioned Holdaway's concept of emergent reading and writing on the grounds that very young children are already language users in their own right, employing the same kinds of language processing strategies as adults, and for the same ends. We agree with their respect for learners, but we don't feel that the concept of emergent readers should be abandoned. Over broad periods of time children's language does change systematically in the direction of the language of the adult community, and their means of representing meaning become increasingly conventional. Their language increases in breadth and power as they learn to deal adequately with a wider range of vocabulary and to embrace increasingly abstract concepts across a wider variety of situations. To debate whether such changes can legitimately be regarded as "better," "more mature" or "developmental" is to engage in sophistry. Most teachers would become increasingly alarmed if children's use of language did not sooner or later begin to move towards the adult conception of adult language.

But Harste, Woodward and Burke do offer a convincing argument against invasive intervention. They demonstrate repeatedly that children have all the strategies necessary for a continuing development of language. They don't need us to sequence a set of skills which we believe will cause language development to occur — or without which it will fail to occur. What children need are environments that encourage them to deploy their existing language learning strategies. The suggestions in this book help build such environments. Teachers who use them will provide children with careful and extensive guidance at a strategic level without presuming to know precisely what each individual requires on a specific day at a tactical level.

GENERAL GOALS OF LITERACY INSTRUCTION

We've had at least 80 years of seemingly endless debates over what approaches should be taken towards initial instruction in reading. The debates are always polemical: "this" *vs.* "that" — phonics *vs.* look-say *vs.* whole language *vs.* ITA *vs.* programmed instruction *vs.* words in color, and so on and so forth. Which feature of written language should be brought first to children's attention? (Programmed Instruction) How does spelling relate to pronunciation? (Phonics) How do spoken and written words relate? (Look-Say) What is the relationship between written texts and their meaning? (Whole Language).

Theorists offer competing models: bottom up (learn phonics first), top down (learn meanings first), interactive (start in the middle and go up and down). Some say reading is compensatory (we use strengths to make up for weaknesses). Some say we look at spelling patterns; others argue syllables. Some say we use syntax; others schemata.

Like a blind man describing an elephant, each theorist seems to get hold of a single piece of a multi-faceted phenomenon and cry, "Eureka!" And teachers, consciously or unconsciously, pick up the theory they like and select the "appropriate" feature of written language to bring to the attention of the children. But reading is complex and varied. Children have to learn the whole well-proportioned elephant.

No instruction can change the final goal, although it can make learning to read either easy or difficult. Fortunately children are amazingly resilient. Even if we offer programs that tell them reading is the tedious business of synthesizing the sounds of letters, many still manage to learn that it's a joy that involves prediction, pattern, inference, character, morality, mood, theme and point of view. If we offer programs that tell them reading is the naming of words, many still manage to learn that there exist tangled but systematic relationships between the ways words are pronounced and the ways they are spelled. Even when we offer passages that present vapid characters performing purposeless antics, they still manage to learn that real stories include ambition, passion, love, endurance and courage.

Any debate in reading that argues for X *vs.* Y is probably ill-founded. Children need phonics and sight vocabulary and meaning and prediction and a sense of structure and cohesion and a multitude of additional characteristics of language that have not (yet) found their way into instructional programs. They need all these things correctly balanced and integrated into a single skill. Reading programs should reflect the harmonious richness of real language.

A second reason for giving literacy programs a broad and comprehensive base is the varied nature of the school clientele. Children arriving at school are at various points along Holdaway's emergent reading continuum. Even if we did have tests that could tell us precisely where each child is and exactly what each one needs next, the resources available to a single teacher of 25 children who vary in so many ways wouldn't be sufficient to address the specific needs of all.

The only way we know of providing language instruction that carries learning opportunities for a wide variety of children is to offer a program that requires the children to hear, speak, read and write meaningful language.

WHOLE LANGUAGE: AN INTEGRATED LITERACY PROGRAM

We would like to stress the wholesomeness of whole language. Whole language programs offer texts which, although they may be conceptually simple, are at least as linguistically complex as the oral language of the children. They encourage children to make the language of the text their own through a series of meaningful, open-ended activities. The richness of the language and the open-ended nature of the activities permit individuals to learn those aspects of written language they are "ready" to learn. During a shared reading session the rank beginner, who is still working out that text runs top-to-bottom, left-to-right, receives many demonstrations of this organization. Meanwhile independent readers sort their way through some of the vagaries of our sound/spelling system, receiving many opportunities to see and hear the visual and oral forms of several regularly and irregularly spelled words.

A whole language philosophy suggests that all components of language must be harmoniously integrated into the instructional program. Some proponents of a whole language approach have declared themselves to be "opposed" to skills or "against" phonics. We categorically reject such a polemic stance. Skills must be learned, but they must be embedded in meaningful activities. Phonics must be learned, but they must be incorporated smoothly into the seamless process of making meaning from print.

We often describe the major goals of a school's literacy program through the use of a web, since we believe they are all facets of literacy and all in a dynamic relationship with each other.

The purpose of writing

Children learn that writing is a way of recording experience, information or imagination that can be used to inform, instruct, direct or entertain.

Organization of texts

Format. Children learn that information is organized from top-to-bottom, left-to-right on the page and front-to-back in longer texts. Written words are bounded by spaces.

Concept. Children learn the organizational patterns of stories, poems, expository and functional texts.

Comprehension

Children learn to respond to printed information in the same ways they respond to information presented pictorially or orally. Comprehension activities include relating the ideas in the text to their personal lives, making judgments, predicting, drawing inferences, summarizing and providing evidence to justify a position. Children also learn to express these processes in written form.

Vocabulary

Sight vocabulary. Children learn the visual form of words that are in their speaking and listening vocabularies.

Meaning vocabulary. Children learn the meaning, sound and visual form of words that are new to them.

Decoding and encoding

Children learn the major correspondences between the ways words are pronounced and the ways they are spelled. In decoding they learn to predict pronunciation from the spelling that appears in the text. In encoding they learn the conventional way to represent the written form of a particular word. They understand that, while regularities exist, the spelling of many commonly used words is not readily predicted from their pronunciation.

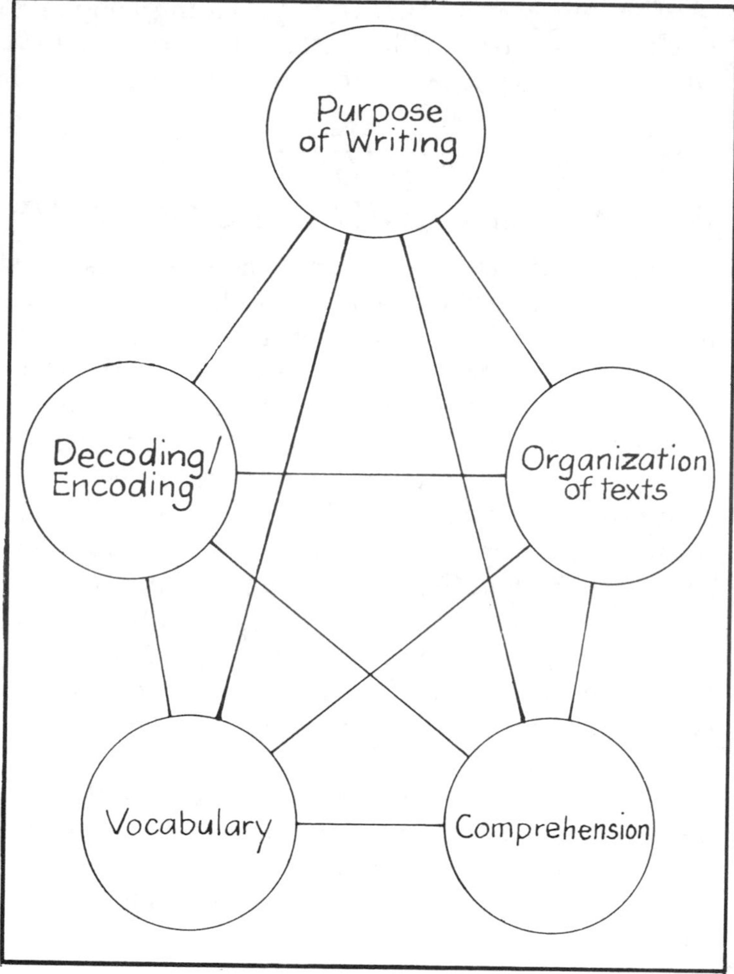

Figure 1.1 The major goals of a literacy program

Decoding and encoding are complementary phases of an understanding of the relationship between written and spoken language.

GENERAL LITERACY ACTIVITIES

Each of the following activities contributes valuable insights into the nature of literacy and is worthy of its place in the early primary curriculum.

Reading Aloud

Reading aloud to children accomplishes at least four things: it makes books attractive to children, teaches them what print is for, shows them how texts are organized and introduces them to literary language.

Appeal

Human beings like stories. Narrative has the power to hold our attention. The need for closure on problems and tensions aroused early on in a story provides a powerful drive to get to the end. Stories heard at home are often experienced in a precious and private space with a loved and trusted adult. As a consequence, books become strongly associated with warmth, pleasure and security. Stories in school are heard at times of relaxation and shared community experience.

The purpose of print

Reading to children teaches them that books can be a source of enjoyment, excitement and interest — which provides an impetus for the children to get at books for themselves.

The organization of texts

Children learn that narratives have a characteristic form and sequence. Tacitly they learn that stories involve a chronological narrative concerning characters who strive to solve the problems that beset them. Poetry is associated with rhythm, repetition and image. Exposition is presented by a more sober voice that relates factual aspects of the world.

Literary language

While writing and speaking share some features, it isn't true that writing is simply speech written down. Written sentences are structured differently from oral ones. Written vocabulary is different from oral vocabulary, and it tends to be more formal. Gestures, intonations and the shared concrete reality that are present in a conversation are neither available to, nor shared by, authors and readers. So authors are often more elaborate in their language, to make up for these missing elements. The oral language of the home or street won't provide an adequate preparation for the language of books. Being read to is the only way for beginning readers to get access to literary language.

Limitations

Reading aloud doesn't ensure that listeners will pay close attention to the print. Some children learn to read by repeatedly listening to texts they can see at the same time, but not all do. Children listening to a story read in school may not even be able to see the print.

Conclusion

Reading aloud to children teaches them many valuable fundamental truths about written language. For some children it creates the conditions for a start to be made on learning to read, but not for all.

Language-Experience

There are perhaps as many variations of the language-experience approach as there are practitioners. The procedure involves three phases, either for individuals or for groups:

- Having or recalling an experience.
- Talking about the experience, followed by (dictated) writing.
- Reading and rereading what was written.

Individual stories have a very personal meaning for the author, but it's difficult to get around to each child quickly or often enough. Group-dictated stories are easier to manage, but their impact on each individual is somewhat diluted.

A language-experience approach is valuable in teaching children the purpose of writing, the organization of texts and the foundation for decoding. It may also encourage vocabulary growth.

The purpose of writing

Language-experience activities teach children that writing can be a way of symbolizing and recording experience and that reading is a means of vicariously reliving that experience.

The organization of texts

One of the most powerful kinds of teaching occurs when children witness their talk being transformed into sequentially organized written symbols. As the writer's hand moves across and down the page it leaves a trail of marks that can be used to reconstruct what the children said.

The foundation for decoding

Language-experience stories show children that there's a connection between what is said and what is written. They also provide opportunities for detailed attention to the correspondences between spelling and pronunciation, although they don't ensure it.

Vocabulary

The language-experience approach offers many opportunities for children to become familiar with the visual form of words. Many children avail themselves of these opportunities, but for others the quantity and complexity of information is too great (see Refining Attention to Text, page 18).

Language-experience is a language generating activity (see Language Generation and Language Enrichment, pages 159-168) and thus is not primarily focused on increasing the child's meaning vocabulary. However, where experiences are arranged around new and broadening situations (a visit to a museum or the hatching of a chick) they may cast up new words which are encountered orally and then used in writing during the dictation and rereading periods.

Limitations

In the first place, the reading back of our own words is a highly unusual reading act: we usually spend most of our time reading the words of others. So the reading of language-experience stories doesn't prepare children for what we actually want them to do. Secondly, the language of language-experience stories is rarely memorable. It lacks the rhythms and cadences of good literature and the informational value of expository texts. Language-experience texts are unlike the texts we expect children to read.

Conclusion

Language-experience stories provide young children with an excellent *introduction* to literacy. However, the act of reading language-experience stories and the nature of such stories is at variance with what we require of children. The writing of others should be introduced as early as possible and language-experience activities should evolve into a writing program in which authors read their work to a receptive audience.

Environmental Language

A wide variety of reading and writing activities are embedded in the flow of daily life and used for the sole purpose of getting things done. We read signs, notes, prohibitions, warnings and labels and write many similarly varied instrumental forms.

Focusing on environmental language is useful for indicating the purpose of writing.

Purpose of writing

Functional reading and writing demonstrate to young children that literacy is useful. Taking the children on a tour of the neighborhood and drawing their attention to street signs, billboards, store-front ads and other environmental language will show them that reading can help them function more independently.

Limitations

Environmental language is quite different from literary or expository writing. It's often short, terse and elliptical: STOP, NO STANDING or KEEP OFF depend heavily on the concrete context in which they occur for their meaning. A painted STOP on a red hexagonal sign applies to motorists and not pedestrians. A lighted red STOP sign on a crosswalk applies to pedestrians and not to motorists. The reading and writing of signs, notes and labels is a minor part of the literacy behavior required in schools. Much of the children's time will be occupied with literary and expository texts.

Conclusion

Environmental language is valuable in that it teaches children that reading and writing are useful. However, the language of environmental print is distinctly different from school texts. Learning to read signs and labels is not an adequate prerequisite for reading literature and exposition (see "Functional literacy in the classroom," page 25).

Talking Books

A talking book is a electronic recording of a competent reader reading a book aloud. Children follow along in their own books. The endless patience of children, along with the fact that they can see the words they hear, makes a talking book an excellent substitute for a live performance from a caring adult.

Talking books help children to learn the purpose of writing and the organization of texts and provide opportunities for them to develop vocabulary.

Purpose of writing

The unfolding of a well-told tale will teach children that books can be a source of pleasure.

Organization of texts

Format. The provision of bells or beeps may help to keep young children on the right page. The match between the sequence of words on the recordings and the words on the page will help them appreciate how written information is organized.

Concept. All the structural patterns learned through listening to a live reading (see Reading Aloud, page 11) can be learned by listening to an electronic recording as well.

Vocabulary

Sight vocabulary. The matching of spoken and written words makes it possible for some children to learn the visual form of words. We came across one girl of four and a half who could read with excellent expression and good comprehension any simple text that was placed before her. As far as we could tell she had learned from being read to by the babysitter, listening to talking books, watching *Sesame Street* on television and having her questions about words answered by her mother. We've also met concerned parents who have read to their children since birth, and provided talking books, but whose offspring have shown no particular interest nor any progress in learning to read. A persistent interest in words and letters and questions that are answered by caring adults seem to be crucial to early reading. Learning to read seems to require interaction with text, not merely exposure to it.

Meaning vocabulary. The exposure to and interaction with literary language may increase children's meaning vocabulary.

Limitations

As excellent as they are, talking books are only substitutes. The well-modulated tones of the recorded actor will never stop and ask children what they think about the story, or answer their questions.

General Literacy Activities: an Overview

General literacy activities provide an excellent *introduction* to reading and writing. Being read to is a source of learning and pleasure enjoyed throughout a lifetime. Language-experience should evolve into a writing program sometime during grade one. Environmental language surrounds us everywhere. Talking books can be phased out as the children become independent readers.

But valuable though they are, these activities don't demand the behavior we actually require of children. Ultimately we would like children, independently, to select books that are within their conceptual frame of reference and to read them silently, with pleasure and a reasonable degree of comprehension — all with no adult intervention, preparation or guidance necessary. The general literacy activities described above are not designed to achieve this level of performance. For some children these kinds of exposure to and interaction with texts are sufficient to trigger their natural learning proclivities and they develop independence with remarkably little direction from adults. However, others need continued guidance and support.

GETTING INTO BOOKS: SHARED READING

One activity that forms a bridge for the transition from emerging to developing reader is shared reading. Because shared reading experiences usually use text with letters large enough to be read hallway across an average classroom, we hear them referred to as "doing big books." We prefer the term shared reading, since it's the sharing of the text and not the size of the book that's crucial.

Reading is a very complex activity, and because it occurs inside the head it's next to impossible to explain to children what it is we do when we read. It's certainly impossible to tell them what they should do when *they* read. All we can do is model and describe the process and get the children to join in. Big books make it possible for them to see the print as we're processing it; print projected on a screen with slides or an overhead projector works just as well. An aide, parent or older child sharing a normal-sized book with one or two children will also serve.

Modeling

To model, you or another competent reader should read the text slowly but expressively; that is, adding phrasing, pauses and the melodic rise and fall of your voice to render the text meaningful. None of these added features is represented by the marks on the page. There are no printed symbols that tell you how to raise the pitch of your voice to form a question. Competent readers know from their experience with oral language that questions have a particular melodic contour and they add it to the words of the text as they read aloud. You can also add melodies for statements, emphasis and moods and encourage the children to emulate the expressive reading you model.

The text need not be new to them. Indeed, it helps if they can recite a text "by heart" before they encounter the written form.

Tracing and Tracking

Trace with a finger or a pointer below each bit of text as you read, asking the children to track the relevant text with their eyes as they read along aloud. The hope is that they will recognize a match between what they say, hear and see so that when they encounter the same piece of text another time the visual image will prompt them to remember, and say aloud, what the text says.

Repetition

Read the text several times — three or four times at a single sitting if it's short. Or you might read the same text at intervals throughout the day and/or over a period of several days. Add new texts constantly and reread old ones intermittently.

Fading

As the group grows in confidence, your voice can progressively fade out, beginning at points where the text is highly predictable; for example, "Old King *Cole* was a merry old *soul*" where you stress *Cole* but say *soul* faintly or not at all. Gradually withdraw support until the children are reading on their own. Then call on sub-groups to read all or part of the text — from this beginning a variety of choral speaking activities may develop.

Framing

Once the children are thoroughly familiar with the text you can frame a portion of it with cupped hands and ask them what the framed portion says. Complete lines, phrases, content words, structure words, syllables, spelling patterns and individual letters can all be framed. We recommend that you introduce framed text in a sequence that reflects progress from the general to the specific. More random framing can be done once the children are comfortable with various segments of the text.

You could also reverse the procedure: name/read a portion of text and call on volunteers to frame it. The same general-to-specific sequence should be observed.

Framing can be done for comprehension as well. You might ask, "Who can frame what it was that Little Miss Muffet sat on?" or "Who can frame who it was the spider sat beside?" You might cover highly predictable words and ask the children to say the hidden word or spell it, dictating for you to write on the chalkboard. The children can then compare their suggestion with the original. Removable gummed stickers can be used to cover and uncover words easily.

Materials for Shared Reading

All the equipment and materials used in shared reading should be made available to the children during free choice periods. Groups will frequently organize themselves and go through some of the procedures you've modeled.

Materials for shared reading should be meaningful, memorable, good quality literature which is highly structured, short, energetic, robust and rhythmically repetitive. The text should stand meaningfully on its own and not be dependent on illustrations.

Materials that meet these criteria include:

Nursery Rhymes. Nursery rhymes meet all of the criteria listed above. They are short, don't take long to prepare and don't present the children with an overwhelming amount of text. In addition they don't require illustration, although pictorial representation may be added if you wish.

A great deal of time, energy and money has been misspent on lavishly illustrating nursery rhymes as big books. Full-color commercially prepared big books are expensive. Some teachers also expend a great deal of time and energy illustrating their own big books. The central purpose of a big book is to have children attend to the print. Pictures may make books appealing to the eye, but where the text is meaningful on its own, the illustrations contribute little to the task at hand. Furthermore, the provision of pictures robs the children of an excellent comprehension-developing opportunity for creating their own illustrations. If the rhyme says, "Little Miss Muffet sat on a tuffet," you might ask the children what they think a tuffet looks like. Or how old they think Miss Muffet is. How do they suppose she's dressed? Various artistic interpretations produced by the children can be appended temporarily to the relevant portions of text and referred to whenever the text is read.

Playground rhymes. All children have rhymes for skipping or deciding who's "it" in chase games. Such chants, some faintly scatological, have the same driving energy that is characteristic of nursery rhymes. Ask your children to tell you some.

Selected poems. Poems with the same features as nursery rhymes and playground rhymes will also serve.

Pattern stories. Folktales and modern derivatives with ritualistic repetition, refrains and cumulative chants work very well. Once a particular pattern has become familiar you can call on the children to write a parallel version which will then be included in the class repertoire.

Shared reading activities like those described above are sufficient for some children to work out the regularities and irregularities of English spelling for themselves as they independently transfer what they know to new, self-selected, unrehearsed texts. But other children won't be able to do that. They'll continue to need the structured guidance provided by an instructional program.

REFINING ATTENTION TO TEXT

The suggestions described in this section are designed to help children pay increasingly close attention to the details of text. We particularly recommend them if you are concerned about teaching phonics. We fully appreciate that children must learn the sound value of letters and letter groupings, and the activities we describe are designed to teach exactly that. What we don't endorse is the idea that children need to know that *car* has an *r*-controlled vowel or that *e* and *i* (usually) make the preceding *c* "soft." Children need to know how *car, far, war, cell, call* and *cull* are pronounced, but they don't need unnecessary detours into lessons about spelling.

Sight Vocabulary

Text matching

Reproduce a familiar text and cut it into lines, phrases or words. Have the children match the pieces with the original. If you write the words on individual cards of equal size you can clip them together to form lines and phrases as well as single words. This means you have to produce only one additional copy of the text rather than three.

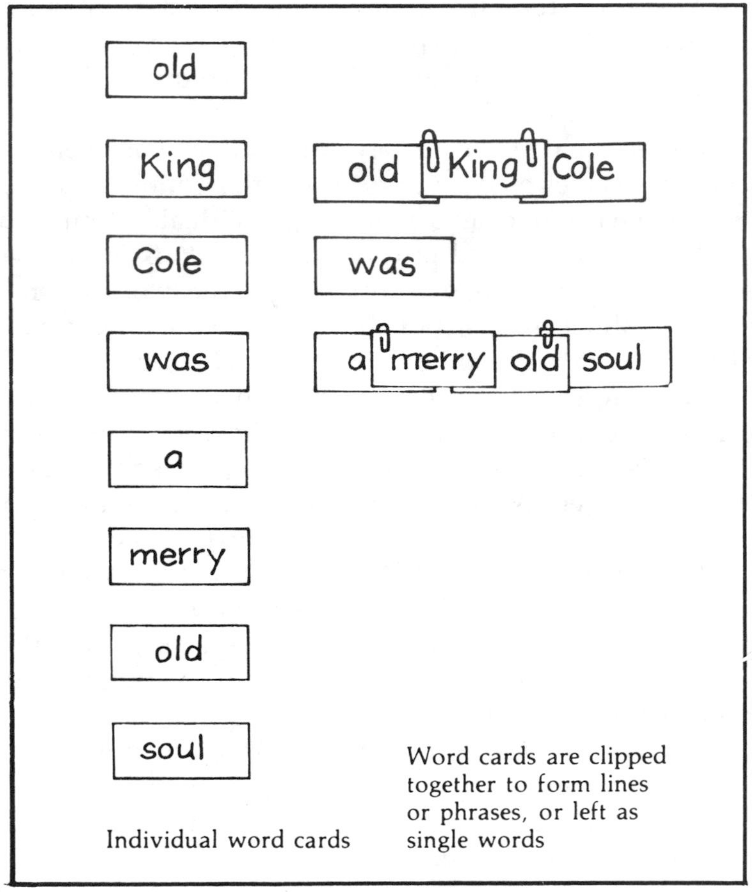
old
King
Cole
was
a
merry
old
soul
old King Cole
was
a merry old soul
Individual word cards
Word cards are clipped together to form lines or phrases, or left as single words

Figure 1.2 Words of equal length are clipped together to form phrases, lines or sentences

Word substitution

Insert other familiar words for selected words in the text. The children must detect, denounce and correct the substitution.

- Old King Cole was a merry old bowl.
- He called for his curds and whey.

Word transpositions

Present familiar texts with certain words transposed. The children must detect, denounce and correct the transpositions.

- Old King Soul was a merry old cole
  He called for his bowl and he called for his pipe
  And he called for his three fiddlers.

Text reconstruction

Put the words of a familiar text on cards of equal size and present them to the children in random order. Working individually or in pairs, they must reconstruct the text. You may or may not make the original text available to them.

Phonics

Letter substitutions

Present familiar texts after substituting incorrect letters or letter groups. The children must detect, denounce and correct the substitution.

- Old King Cole was a berry old soul
  And a berry old soul was she.
- He called for his fiddlers fee.

Letter transpositions

Present familiar texts with certain letters transposed for the children to detect, denounce and correct.

- Little Miss Muffet tat on a suffet.

Systematic letter substitutions

Present familiar texts with systematic letter substitutions for the children to detect, denounce and correct.

- *i/a:* Lattle Mass Muffet
- *i/a switched:* Miry hid i lattle limb.

Word chains

Provide the children with a familiar word, such as *peg*, and with a sequence of oral clues that change the meaning and spelling of the word:

peg	Take something away and add an *n* to make it write.
pen	Take something away and add an *a* for cooking.
pan	Take something away and add an *i* to make it sharp.
pin	Take something away and add a *t* to make a hole.
pit	Take something away and add an *f* to make it the right size.
fit	*etc.*

Competent writers can print for themselves. If you provide less able children with a set of letter cards, the composition of each new word is much more rapid.

The routines described in this section help children with sight vocabulary and phonics. However, they've been applied to familiar texts only. We still haven't reached our goal of having children read unrehearsed texts.

Present behavior	**Desired behavior**
• familiar	• unfamiliar
• rehearsed texts	• unrehearsed texts
• read under your guidance	• read independently
• involving the manipulation of familiar language	• involving the identification of visually unfamiliar words.

We still need some activities that will help the children move away from the security of familiar texts and apply what they've learned to the reading of unfamiliar material. Some children will make this transfer with little or no help; others will require careful support and guidance.

TEACHING FOR TRANSFER

It's important to distinguish between instructional activities and the behavior those instructional activities are designed to teach. Take, for instance, the presence or absence of your guidance: children can perform at much higher levels when following your directions. They can readily get back on track if you're there to point out that they're off.

But their performance will likely deteriorate when you withdraw your support. Classroom performance is a function not only of the children's ability but also of your wise guidance. Nevertheless, it's important to avoid maintaining artificial supports that keep the children dependent; for example, preteaching vocabulary in reading and providing spellings in writing.

Preteaching Vocabulary

It's a common practice for teachers to identify "new" words in a passage and teach them before the passage is encountered. But that practice is ill-advised. In the first place it robs the children of an opportunity to use context in combination with their decoding ability to identify the word. Outside your reading program they'll encounter numerous texts that contain new words and there'll be no one around to preteach them. Classroom instruction should give children general strategies to cope with commonly occurring challenges.

Secondly, the practice presumes that all the children are unfamiliar with all the "new" words. In fact "new" simply means they are just now being introduced into the reading program; the children may already have encountered them elsewhere. Ironically, another common practice is to list "new" words on the chalkboard and invite

identification. Every time the children identify a word, instruction is shown to be unnecessary.

Thirdly, preteaching vocabulary erroneously presumes that all the children know all the "old" words and no special attention need be paid to them. But some children will continue to need help with words introduced earlier.

It's much simpler to ask the children to read the new passage, guessing or skipping over any words they don't know, perhaps faintly underlining them. After they've finished reading they can indicate which words presented problems — new or old. If possible, those words should be identified by other children who know them; if not, you can help the class use context and decoding to identify them (see figure 1.3). Everyone benefits: even those children who already know the words have additional demonstrations of how to use context and decoding to identify unfamiliar words.

Assume the children have read a story that contains the sentence: *Pam sat on the sofa* and that one or more children indicate, by gesture or verbally, that they don't know the word *sofa*.

Teacher talk	**Children's response**
Read the sentence up to the new word.	*Pam sat on the . . .*
What did Pam do?	Sat on it.
So it must be something to sit on.	
Where is Pam?	At home.
What kinds of things do we sit on at home?	Chairs, benches, couch, stool, sofa . . .
Now let's look at the word. What letter does it begin with?	S.
What sound does *s* tell us to make?	/S/.
So which word might it be? Could it be *chair*?	No.
Why not?	*Chair* doesn't begin with /s/.

[Other possibilities are eliminated, with sound/symbol justifications, until only words beginning with *s* are left.]

Could it be *stool*? What other sound do you hear in *stool*?	T, /t/.
Is there a *t* in our new word?	No.
What about *sofa*? What sound do you hear in *sofa*?	[Sounds out.]
Does our new word have an *o* in it?	Yes.
Does it have an *f* in it?	Yes.
Could it be *sofa*?	Yes.
Does *sofa* make sense in the story?	Yes.

Figure 1.3 Identifying words through context and decoding

Providing Spellings

In two ways many teachers keep children dependent on them for spelling: by providing the conventional spellings of words when the children ask for help during the writing process and by "marking" first drafts, substituting conventional spellings for the invented spellings of the children. These practices may improve the spelling of the teachers, but most teachers can already spell quite well. It's the children who are in the process of learning and they don't need that kind of help. Stress can be reduced and learning increased if the responsibility for conventional spelling is returned to the children.

Asking for spellings. Children should be taught to ask for confirmation or disconfirmation of *attempted* spellings. "Is this how you spell . . . ?" rather than, "How do you spell . . . ?"

Correcting spellings. During the revision process young authors should routinely be expected to check their own spellings. Words whose spelling they are unsure of should be underlined. All work should be read by a classmate who, among other things, checks and offers assistance with spelling. When you receive the piece you might indicate which words warrant another look, but not what the spellings should be; the children should consult a dictionary or the class word bank for those. In compositions with numerous unconventional spellings you may choose to limit your indications to a few of the more frequently used words only (see Written Comments on Children's Written Work," page 181).

Figure 1.4 Four stages in creating bits and pieces

Routines

Using familiar language in changed circumstances

Find It. The children prepare clue cards based on a familiar text and play the game of Find It. The procedure is described in detail in

Find It: a Forty-five Minute Writing Project, page 112.

Reconstruct text. Prepare word cards that each carry one word of a familiar text (see the illustration on page 18). Alone or in pairs the children reconstruct the text, with or without the complete text available as they work. If the text is accessible, the task becomes a relatively simple matching exercise.

Bits and pieces. Characters, places or objects from a familiar text are named, labeled, captioned or commented upon (figure 1.4). Drawings and written additions are collated to form "My Book of [*name of the original text*]."

The four procedures — naming, labeling, captioning and commenting — are listed in a rough developmental sequence. You can teach the children all four activities and then encourage them to use any routine they feel comfortable with. These suggestions encourage the reuse of the language of the story, but the children shouldn't feel limited to the words in the text.

Or you might break the story down into various aspects and assign them to individuals, collating the products into "Our book of . . ." For example, each of the pursuers in *The Gingerbread Man* or each animal in Aardema's *Why Mosquitoes Buzz in People's Ears* could be assigned to an individual (or partners) responsible for drawing and providing written comments.

Trivia quiz. Create very simple questions that reuse the language of a familiar text to elicit a limited number of answers, also from the text (see Figure 1.5). Present the questions *in writing* and provide the children with a set of *written* answers. Each time you present one of the questions the children indicate which written answer is correct (see also The Little Miss Muffet Project, page 133).

It's important that the questions and answers be in writing since the purpose of the activity is to reinforce familiarity with the *written* form of the words. The questions aren't designed to develop comprehension.

Questions

Who kissed the girls?
Who came out?
Who ran away?
Who made the girls cry?
What did Georgie Porgie do when the boys came out?
Who cried when they were kissed?
What did the girls do when Georgie kissed them?
What did Georgie do to the girls to make them cry?
What did the boys do to make George run away?

Answer Sheet	
Georgie Porgie	ran away
kissed	the girls
made them cry	the boys
came out	

marker

Figure 1.5 The materials for a trivia quiz based on the nursery rhyme, "Georgie Porgie"

This activity works with either large or small groups. In a large group you can provide the children with answers on individual cards, or on a single sheet if you prefer, since that will be easier to prepare, store and reuse. The questions can be put on individual strips or on a chart. Individual question strips help the children focus on a restricted portion of text. Remain silent as you present the strip and have the children read the question (silently?) and place a button, ring or other marker on the chosen card or in the chosen rectangle. After every child has responded, read the question aloud and confirm the correct answer.

The answer sheet doesn't have to have the same number of answers as there are questions. Several questions in the example above have the same answer. Since the children have only one marker the same answer box can be used each appropriate time.

Children who are familiar with this routine can use the material independently in groups of two to four, or can create their own trivia quiz materials for other familiar texts.

Clues. Simple clues and sets of clues arranged to form a countdown are also excellent ways of encouraging the reuse of familiar language. Specific routines are described in detail in *Literacy Through Literature.*

Reading familiar language independently

Stories and poems you present to the class through big books can be read independently either by a small group with the big book or by individuals with small versions of the same title.

When you and the children make up big books of parallel or derived versions of stories or poems, you can make small books for each child as well, for use in class or at home for reading to parents.

Rehearsing new language without guidance

Display a new story or poem, announcing that you'll read the text aloud some time later that day. Invite the children to read it in the meantime, or to identify any words or phrases they know. When you later share the text, invite volunteers to indicate any parts they think they can read already.

A similar strategy works with small versions of big books: display copies and tell the children the story will be shared as a big book. Encourage them to examine the small version beforehand.

Reading unrehearsed texts

The books in the classroom library should reflect the interest range of the children rather than their reading ability. However, the library should include a number of books that are simple enough for the beginner to attempt. Natural texts are preferable, but controlled vocabulary texts from some basal reading programs may be suitable.

Encourage the children to browse. Regular reading periods should be a feature of every classroom from kindergarten up. Celebrate attempts to read the books but avoid pressure to produce accurate oral renditions. Allow the emergent processes described by Holdaway (1979) to develop naturally.

FUNCTIONAL LITERACY IN THE CLASSROOM

You need not stop another activity in order to engage in functional literacy activities. The following functional activities are graphic sinews that help get everyday activities done:

Taking attendance. Write the names of the absent children on the chalkboard. Spelling names may involve some dictation.

Morning messages. Write announcements of some of the day's events on the chalkboard for the children to read as they assemble in the morning. Read the messages aloud, in unison. At times you might introduce deliberate errors the children can denounce and amend.

Orders for snacks. Assign monitors in rotation to record and total the orders and deliver the goods.

Lost and found. Allow concerned individuals to post notices regarding items lost or found in the classroom.

Temporary absence from the room. Have the children sign out when given permission to absent themselves.

Letters of complaint. Insist that allegations of ill-treatment or wrongdoing by a peer be submitted in writing.

Notes and notices sent home. Encourage individuals or groups to compose all or part of a message to be sent home.

Displays. Ask the owners to compose and display explanatory labels for items from Show and Tell.

Note passing. Institutionalize note passing by providing a mailbox and deliveries twice daily.

Posters. Suggest that the children create posters announcing the staging of a play or the choral reading of a poem and display them.

Goodlad (1984) maintains that non-educational tasks take up to 20% of class time, causing significant stress in terms of time, divided attention and energy. You may want to review these tasks regularly to see what the children can do. The reduction in stress for you and the increase in self-esteem for the children can be considerable.

THEORETICAL REFLECTIONS

Reading and Rereading: a Transactional View of Literacy

In her transactional view of reading Rosenblatt (1968) distinguishes between *text* and *poem*. *Text* is the set of marks made on the page; *poem* is the transaction that occurs as readers bring their past experience to bear on the text. Thus a poem is not a thing but a process, not an object but an event. Moreover, it's a living, changing process. Any reader's prior knowledge at the time of the second reading includes what is remembered from the first reading. Thus the second reading is not merely a replay of the first but a new process that takes its form partly from the knowledge of the first reading.

(Note: When Rosenblatt uses the word *poem* she expects her readers to understand that she really means any piece of literature, including stories and plays. We use *story* in the same way to embrace chapters of novels, passages from expository texts, magazine articles, picture books, comic strips, movies, live oral readings, theater presentations, audio recordings and computer programs. Where it's important we specify the type of text we mean, but most of the time we expect you to understand that *story* embraces a wide range of presentations. When we use *text* we refer to the marks on a page — words, punctuation, illustrations, format — that readers use to create the "poem" or "story.") A similar kind of change occurs when children hear or read other people's ideas about a story. Because we bring our own set of world experiences to the text our reaction isn't likely to be

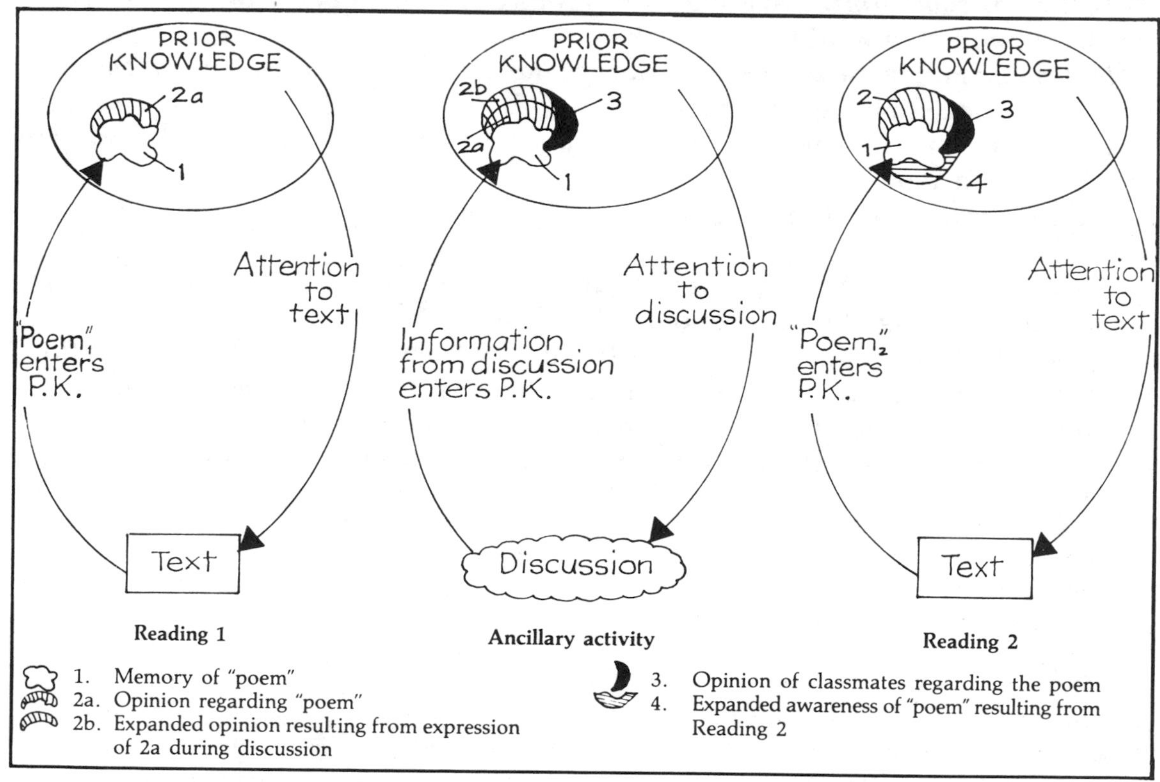

Figure 1.6 A model of the transaction involved in re-reading

identical to someone else's: we each create our own story as we read the text. But hearing a friend's view of that story will affect our next reading of it, whether or not we believe or appreciate our friend's view. Say a child reads Lewis's *The Lion, the Witch and the Wardrobe* as a simple adventure fantasy. If during class discussion someone compares the death of Aslan with the death of Christ, the child may reread the text with that idea in mind, and the second reading will be significantly affected not only by the first reading but also by the allegorical interpretation suggested during the class discussion.

Montgomery's *Anne of Green Gables* tells the story of a tempestuous but enchanting orphan girl who is raised by an elderly brother (Matthew) and sister (Marilla). College students who reread this story as part of their teacher preparation program frequently report how, as children, they identified with Anne. Now, as adults, they find themselves more in sympathy with and sensitive to the changes that occur in Marilla. Nothing in the text has changed. The words on the page are the same as those read 10 to 20 years earlier. The changes have occurred in the reader.

The process is represented in figure 1.6. The cycle is theoretically endless, but of course the law of diminishing returns applies. The 50th reading may not differ much from the 49th, but if the reader then has (or hears) a startling new insight, the next reading will again be affected more dramatically.

Unfortunately Rosenblatt doesn't address the impact of the reader's purpose, which also affects response. A child, a librarian responding to a parent's complaint about a book, a literary critic, a proofreader and the author's mother are all likely to read a text for quite different purposes — which will have a bearing on their responses, understandings and interpretations of it. Rosenblatt appears to assume that the text is always being studied in an educational institution for the purpose of critical evaluation.

Nevertheless, her transactional view of interpretation and understanding presents a serious challenge to traditional measurements of comprehension. In what sense can we meaningfully say that a given reader has understood a certain percentage of the text? Under specific circumstances that reader may have answered a certain proportion of questions correctly, but how much does this tell us about what the reader will understand of other texts read under different circumstances for different purposes? Can we make a general statement about the reader's comprehension ability that has any value?

Implications for instruction

Many traditional "comprehension" questions are little more than quizzes to see whether comprehension has occurred. We reject this inquisitorial role. Instead we believe it's our responsibility to create conditions that are likely to ensure increased comprehension. The transactional model of figure 1.6 suggests that comprehension develops through *reflection* and *rereading.* Consequently the vast majority of our suggestions involve four phases:

- Presentation: listening or reading.
- Reflection: sharing impressions (drawing, talking, writing, acting, moving).
- Representation: re-examination of the text through listening or reading.
- Conclusion: revised judgment or opinion.

The second and third phases interact. The activities pursued in phase three should encourage or require the learner to return to the text. Rosenblatt observes: "The teacher's task is to foster fruitful . . . transactions between individual readers and individual works." (pages 26-27)

We would like to believe that the routines we've described in this chapter, and throughout the book, achieve Rosenblatt's fruitful transactions, although we would broaden her use of fruitful to embrace enjoyment, social exchange and aesthetic elegance. The projects we recommend are designed to encourage children to reflect upon and reconsider the story in ways they likely never would without the benefit of your guidance. Each suggestion requires a second look at the text; many encourage or require a third, fourth or fifth.

During these return visits to the text the transactions occur. If it were possible to assess a learner's comprehension at each step in our model without affecting that comprehension, we believe the record would show improvement: the number and variety of associations the children make with the text would increase; the number of within-text connections would increase; patterns and progressions not noted on the first reading/listening would become evident. The possibility of alternative interpretations would have been raised.

Writing transactions

Rosenblatt confines herself to the role of the reader. However, the works of Graves (1983), Murray (1984) and Walshe (1981) clearly indicate that writing is also a transaction. The process of writing helps to form, clarify and fix the writer's perceptions. Everything Rosenblatt says about reading also applies to writing.

Participant and Spectator Roles

Pragmatic and aesthetic uses of language

Britton (1970) distinguishes between the *pragmatic* (he also uses *transaction* but in quite a different way; we've taken the liberty of substituting *pragmatic* to avoid confusion) and the *aesthetic* uses of language. During pragmatic language use the user is a participant. Attention is focused on the activity, not on the language being used. Pragmatic language is used in shopping, going to the park, catching a bus, obtaining a driver's license, meeting a friend or paying bills. In these situations the participants are expected to take an active role. Stop signs should be observed, bills paid or application forms filled in.

When language is used aesthetically, the role of the language user changes to that of spectator. No one expects a reader to do something as a result of reading a novel. The activity is not pragmatic but valued for itself. Analogies can be drawn with listening to music, looking at paintings or watching a dance troupe perform. During aesthetic reading the reader's attention is on the experience evoked by attending to the text.

Preschool experiences with language

All children learn language pragmatically: oral language is used for conducting the daily business of life. Much of the print in a preschool child's life is also pragmatic: TV schedules, road signs, shopping lists, letters and advertisements. Some children are also introduced to the aesthetic use of language through bedtime stories. The TV schedule is but a means to an end, but the experience of hearing a story carries its own justification.

For a long time most schools used aesthetic forms of language (stories and poems) to teach reading and writing. But this practice created two problems. On the one hand children who had learned only the pragmatic use of language were asked to deal with aesthetic language; on the other hand aesthetic language was being used pragmatically, selected for instructional reasons rather than for enjoyment. Both sets of children, those who were familiar only with the pragmatic use of language and those who were also familiar with language used aesthetically, had to make an adjustment on entering school.

School experiences with language

Children who came to school without several years' experience with bedtime stories had to make the biggest adjustment. They had to learn new skills with an unfamiliar form of language by means of unfamiliar language interactions. Their more fortunate friends had some understanding of how stories work and some familiarity with words that occur in stories but rarely in the real world, and were accustomed to answering questions about stories. All this was foreign to children who had dealt only with pragmatic language. TV schedules and shopping lists have structures and vocabularies quite different from poems and stories. Parents don't ask children to tell them which groceries were or weren't bought yesterday.

Children who came to school with a history of aesthetic experience in language faced a less severe challenge. At home, stories and poems were simply to be enjoyed. It's true that at school the written word became a vehicle for learning how to deal with written language and stories became objects to be studied for the purpose of acquiring new skills. But this additional burden carried by school literature didn't appear to disturb the children greatly. Most of them learned to read and write with relative ease.

The problem arose when educators permitted the instructional role of school-based literature to predominate. "Stories" lacking any literary merit were constructed simply to provide a specific vocabulary list. Even with good literature the attention of children was often drawn to aspects of language both meaningless and unappealing. We once came across a novel guide based on White's *Charlotte's Web* in which the first activity required children to mark the short vowels in certain isolated words lifted from the story. The second page dealt with long vowels.

Children learn through play. It may be reasonable for adults to identify the skills and knowledge children need to benefit from and contribute to our society. But we should be astute and creative enough to present those skills in *their* terms rather than in our analytic and abstract adult terms. We should be able to devise teaching sequences and activities that result in the learnings we deem necessary but that enable children to think and act as children.

Adult requirements and children's capabilities

This book records some of our attempts to bridge the gap between adult requirements and children's capabilities. We devised, sought out, borrowed and modified teaching procedures and activities that seemed to appeal to children as well as contribute to their experience with and control over oral and written language. We tried out the suggestions, then revised and modified them as a result of our successes and mistakes.

We also tried to assess our intuitive beliefs about skills development by consulting traditional skills lists in language arts curricula and attempting to identify which skills were exercised by any given activity. Such analyses overwhelmingly confirmed our intuition: an activity that requires children to interact meaningfully with meaningful language incorporates a wide range of skills in a totally integrated manner. Indeed, the results of these skills analyses were so predictable that we found ourselves increasingly reluctant to take the time to reach a foregone conclusion. We are now prepared to assert that *any* activity that requires children to respond meaningfully to language, written or oral, will incorporate a multiplicity of language skills. We are even prepared to claim that further skills analysis isn't necessary. The skills are embedded in the activity whether an analysis is conducted or not.

CHAPTER 2

REACHING OUT

A GENERAL TEACHING MODEL

We must continue to teach for transfer as our children develop their ability to read independently. Full independence goes beyond the ability to apply what we've taught them to new material; it includes taking responsibility for their own learning and coping with situations they haven't been completely prepared for.

Unfortunately, with the exceptions of kindergarten and graduate school, traditional schooling seems to demand, and thus create, *increasing* dependence of learners on instruction (Goodlad, 1984). The intervening period may show a few glimpses of self-directed learning, but for the most part each year is allotted a predetermined stretch of content that learners are expected to ingest.

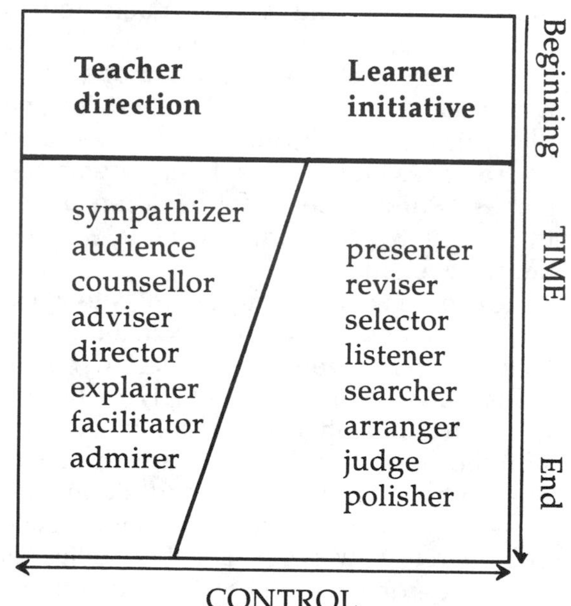

Figure 2.1 A generalized model for instructional progression

Instruction shouldn't be a continuous stream of further skills and more information. It should take place within a series of intertwined cycles: fresh input from the teacher followed by increasing autonomy for the learner and decreasing teacher direction.

At the outset a lesson, unit or project is characterized by a high proportion of teacher direction in the form of lectures, media presentation, reading aloud or giving directions. But as it proceeds, the proportion of teacher direction decreases and learner self-direction increases.

This pattern already exists, notably in social studies and science. Unfortunately it's less common in most language arts programs. Workbooks, skills sheets and study guides ensure that "sheep-dogging" action continues week in and week out. The children answer the teacher's questions and complete the teacher's exercises daily throughout primary and secondary school.

Learner initiatives should increase not only through the lesson, unit or project but also through the year and throughout the learner's school career. Teachers will dominate the general atmosphere at the beginning of a school year, but by the end of the year the class should be almost completely self-sustaining.

As the title of this chapter suggests, we think of the process as a *reaching out* on the part of children. The following routines are designed to facilitate that reaching out, that transition from *developing* to *independent* reader. Simple versions can be used by the middle of the second year (earlier for some children, later for others). Older children will be challenged if the routines are used with more demanding texts.

To teach a routine we usually choose texts we've already read to the children. Then they try it out on books they've chosen and read by themselves. The number of practice sessions under our guidance depends on the complexity of the routine and the competence of the children.

LAZY LETTERS

Modeling

Lazy letters, sold at some tourist resorts, use a multiple choice format with ridiculous options. We were attracted by that kind of playful use of language and tried to apply it to stories. We asked the group, a grade five class, to imagine that Snow White is writing to her father to tell him about the adventures she's had since she was abducted on the orders of the Wicked Queen.

Dear Father,

I have
- ❑ been eaten by a frog.
- ❑ become a truck driver.
- ❑ married a prince.

When the huntsman took me away I
- ❑ went scuba diving.
- ❑ become lost in the woods.
- ❑ set fire to your castle.

I finally found
- ❑ the cottage of the seven dwarfs.
- ❑ a motel.
- ❑ the home of the big bad wolf.

I lived with the
- ❑ big bad wolf
- ❑ dwarfs
- ❑ trucker

but the wicked queen
- ❑ tried to kill me.
- ❑ ran off with the seven dwarfs.
- ❑ made me marry a frog.

I bit into a
- ❑ frog
- ❑ poison apple
- ❑ medium-sized pizza

and fell into a
- ❑ deep sleep.
- ❑ pond.
- ❑ hole in the road.

The seven dwarfs thought I was
- ❑ dead.
- ❑ drunk.
- ❑ faking.

Fortunately a
- ❑ frog
- ❑ prince
- ❑ trucker

kissed me and I
- ❑ woke
- ❑ threw
- ❑ slipped

up.

Your loving daughter,
Snow White

Figure 2.2 A example of a lazy letter based on the story of Snow White

Implementation

We introduced the lesson by showing the children the letter illustrated in figure 2.2. They were amused by the silly options as we uncovered the letter line by line and read it aloud. At various points we left the next option covered and invited their suggestions before revealing ours.

We then read aloud Grimm's *The Spirit in the Bottle.*

> ***The Spirit in the Bottle:* a synopsis**
> A young boy finds an evil spirit in a bottle. When he releases it, it threatens to strangle him. The boy tricks the spirit back into the bottle but releases it again when promised riches. The boy is given a magic rag that heals wounds and turns things into silver. He turns an ax into silver and sells it for a princely sum, then uses the healing power of the rag to become a famous doctor.

We presented the children with a partially completed lazy letter (figure 2.3) and invited them to suggest choices, two per sentence. Their suggestions are in *italic.*

Finally, we asked them to continue the letter and add their own choices. One child's continuation is shown in figure 2.4.

Lazy Letter

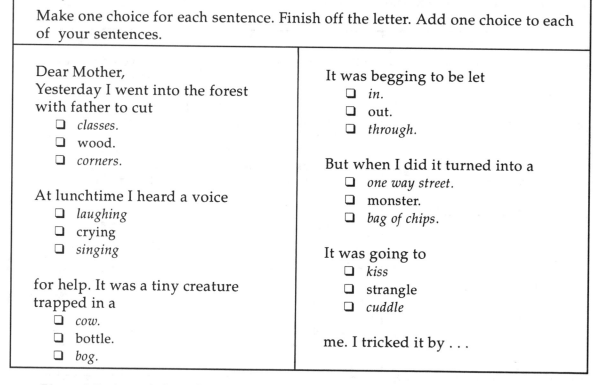

Make one choice for each sentence. Finish off the letter. Add one choice to each of your sentences.

Dear Mother,
Yesterday I went into the forest with father to cut

- ❑ *classes.*
- ❑ wood.
- ❑ *corners.*

At lunchtime I heard a voice

- ❑ *laughing*
- ❑ crying
- ❑ *singing*

for help. It was a tiny creature trapped in a

- ❑ *cow.*
- ❑ bottle.
- ❑ *bog.*

It was begging to be let

- ❑ *in.*
- ❑ out.
- ❑ *through.*

But when I did it turned into a

- ❑ *one way street.*
- ❑ monster.
- ❑ *bag of chips.*

It was going to

- ❑ *kiss*
- ❑ strangle
- ❑ *cuddle*

me. I tricked it by . . .

***Figure 2.3** A worksheet for a lazy letter based on* **The Spirit in the Bottle,** *with student suggestions in italic*

I tricked it by ❑ getting it to go back into the bottle. ❑ spitting on it. ❑ hitting it.	The spirit said, "I'll give you a ❑ reward. ❑ TV. ❑ popsicle.
I put him back where I found him and he ❑ kissed me. ❑ pleaded with me to let him out. ❑ pinched me.	So I let him out and he gave me a ❑ special rag. ❑ Hulk Hogan Wrestling Doll. ❑ bowl of tomato soup.

***Figure 2.4 One child's continuation of a lazy letter based on* The Spirit in the Bottle**

Extensions

You can modify this predicting routine by developing a lazy letter for a story unfamiliar to the children and providing somewhat more sensible options.

You might present the lazy letter below before reading the story it's based on: Arkhurst's *How Spider Got a Thin Waist* (see the synopsis on the next page). At any one point in the letter any option is plausible, although enough clues have been left in the passage as a whole for the children to work out a set of preferred answers.

Ghana, West Africa My Dear Wife, I am coming home for a long rest. Yesterday I was out ❑ sailing ❑ walking ❑ flying when I smelled ❑ food. ❑ fragrant flowers. ❑ a dead fish. It was time for ❑ bed. ❑ supper. ❑ harvest festival. But I was between two ❑ villages. ❑ elephants. ❑ lions.	I didn't know which one to ❑ go to. ❑ eat. ❑ hunt. I decided I would go to ❑ town. ❑ pieces. ❑ both. I had Kuma and Kwaka tie a ❑ snake ❑ rope ❑ creeping vine around me. When the food was ready in one ❑ elephant ❑ rope ❑ village Kuma would ❑ pull. ❑ push ❑ pump.	When it was ready in the other, Kwaku would ❑ do the same. ❑ call out. ❑ send a message. You will never ❑ remember ❑ hear ❑ believe what happened next. I will tell you all about it when I get ❑ even. ❑ home. ❑ out. Your loving husband, *Spider*

***Figure 2.5 An example of a lazy letter based on Arkhurst's* How Spider Got a Thin Waist**

***How Spider Got a Thin Waist:* a synopsis**
Greedy, fat-waisted Spider wants to beg food from two different villages during the harvest festival. He asks each of his two sons to tie a rope to him, then go to one of the villages and pull on that rope when the food is ready. Unfortunately the feasts are ready at the same time. Both sons pull and Spider's waist is squeezed as thin as we see it today.

Here is a possible teaching sequence:

1. Present the lazy letter.
2. Discuss the options. Have the children predict how the story will develop.
3. Read the story aloud.
4. Review and revise the letter.

After doing the routine two or three times with other stories, encourage the children to create their own lazy letters. They may need some help, however, since writing a lazy letter is much more demanding than responding to one; it requires a summarizing of the main events of the story, an intuitive grasp of syntax and grammar, and some facility with words.

Summarizing

We recommend that to teach the children how to write lazy letters you ask them, as a class, to help you create one. A teaching sequence might go as follows:

1. Read a new story to the class, such as *The Elves and the Shoemaker.*
2. Present part of a summary statement, perhaps in letter format, and collate the children's suggestions for the rest of it.

Dear Son,
You'll be pleased to hear that our shoe business is doing well. Our luck began one night when I was down to my last piece of leather. I left it out on the workbench and in the morning . . .

Teacher Talk	**Children's Response**	**Written Record**
What other things could we put as well as leather?	cheese frogs! cake	cheese cake
Where shall we make our next choice? The sentence reads, *I left it on the workbench.*	workbench	[Erase "workbench"]
What words could we use?	floor television bed	floor television bed
We must use *workbench.* Which two others shall we choose?	. . .	. . .

Dear Son, You will be pleased to hear our ❑ television show ❑ shoe business ❑ rabbit is doing very well. It began one ❑ night ❑ morning ❑ lunch break	when I was down to my last piece of ❑ leather ❑ ______? ❑ ______? I left it out on the workbench. In the morning . . .

Figure 2.6 The opening portion of a lazy letter based on **The Elves and the Shoemaker**

I tricked him by ______________________
He promised ______________________
So I ______________________
He gave me ______________________
The magic plaster could______________________
I tried it out on ______________________
The neighbor's axe was ______________________
I sold it ______________________
I gave father ______________________

Figure 2.7 A story ladder summarizing **The Spirit in the Bottle**

3. Revise the summary statement by deletion or abbreviation.
4. Present the initial part of the summary again, together with two or three options, as shown in figure 2.6.
5. Invite, accept and record suggestions for further options on the rest of the summary statement.
6. Review and revise all options.

Summarizing is a difficult task for children, especially young ones. They have difficulty judging what's important, and thus tend to report stories verbatim. However, with adequate guidance they can learn to do it. You should allocate sufficient time for guided practice and not be in too much of a hurry to assign individual work based on self-selected texts.

A story ladder (*Literacy Through Literature*, pages 34-37) can be useful for making summaries: the children complete each sentence fragment and then choose which word to use as a choice (see figure 2.7).

Or you can provide the summaries yourself, of course, if you have the time — although that will rob the children of the chance to develop their own ability.

Skills Development

Responding to a teacher-produced lazy letter requires simple recall; creating a lazy letter requires the ability to distinguish main ideas from supporting details and to order the main ideas to form a plot summary. Vocabulary development is promoted if you require that the options reflect the story vocabulary.

SPLIT IMAGES

This routine requires so little preparation time and is so easy to do that you may feel it can't have much value. We think otherwise.

We pair the children and allow each child of the pair to examine the pictures in one half of a picture book. Then we ask the partners to talk together and try to reconstruct the story, without the text. The physical arrangements may vary.

Hidden Faces

1. Have the children gather round you as you would for a storytelling session, with partners A and B sitting together.
2. Have the B's lower their heads and cover their faces with their hands.
3. Show the first picture in the story to the A's, making no comment about the picture and answering no questions.
4. With faces still covered, the B's listen to their A partners tell about the picture.
5. Then close the book and reverse the roles: the A's hide their faces while the Bs look up.
6. Show the next picture to the B's who report on it to their partners.
7. Continue alternating partners and pictures until the book is finished.
8. Call on individuals to share their interpretation of the story (be prepared for a wide diversity of hypotheses). Then have everyone re-examine the pictures to resolve disputes or establish points of fact.
9. Finally, read the story aloud, showing the pictures as you do so.

This arrangement is physically easy to manage. However, we know from our personal experience that the desire to look at a picture that's being described is very strong. Young children may just have to peek!

Facing Lines

You may prefer to use this alternate arrangement. Seat half the class with their backs to the book, the other half facing it (figure 2.8). Then move the book to the other side for the next picture. This can become cumbersome if the book has to be moved up and down the rows so everyone can see the details.

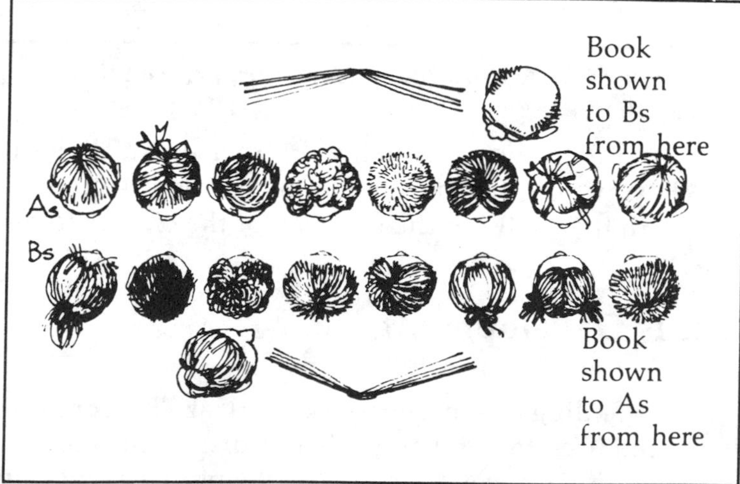

Figure 2.8 Seating arrangement for split images

We've also tried having partners change seats while the book remains stationary. This too is cumbersome and potentially disruptive.

The Children's Behavior

This routine provokes a great deal of productive talk as interpretation, inference and hypothesis formation occur spontaneously. Every child in the class is actively involved in speaking or listening, and each speaker has an attentive audience since the listener needs details to fill in the blanks in his or her own information.

It's fascinating to see the progress of the interaction between partners. Initial responses are usually descriptive commentaries:

There's some mice.
Six mice.
They're sitting on some rocks.

As more information is provided an appreciation of sequence appears:

Now they're taking the food away.
That one is still on his own.

Sometimes motives are proposed:

The others are talking to him.
I think they're cross with him.

And what variety of interpretation you will find once all the pictures have been shown! Some partners generate a "creative" interpretation near the beginning of the story and continue to misinterpret to remain consistent with their initial hypothesis. The meaning-constructing capacity of the human mind is very evident.

The limited amount of information available to each partner encourages productive communication between them. The limited amount of information available in the picture results in interpretation and tentative hypothesis formation. These hypotheses may be, and frequently are, revised in the light of subsequent information. The generation of hypotheses from the incomplete information provided by the pictures engenders highly motivated listening when the text is read aloud. The information in the text provides a sense of closure and resolves the cognitive dissonance produced by the demand to make interpretations based on incomplete data.

Materials

The books should be unfamiliar to the children. They should be short, boldly and simply illustrated, and have strong, progressive plots. The burden of carrying the story line should be shared between the pictures and the text: the children need sufficient information to form a hypothesis but not so much that there's little or no room left for interpretation. Textless books aren't particularly well suited since all the information is available in the pictures. (In saying this we aren't suggesting that textless books should never be used to stimulate talk. On the contrary, we feel textless books offer a rich stimulus for both oral and written storytelling.)

The stories need to be short because describing each picture can easily require up to 30 seconds. Thus 30 illustrated pages could take over 15 minutes to show. Further time is required for sharing interpretations and for the final reading. Such a regimen can overstress the attention span of some young children.

The illustrations need to be simple and bold because some of the children will be viewing them at a distance. Minute but significant details are easily lost. Moreover, you won't want to allow much time for each picture for fear of making the lesson too long.

In a progressive plot, most incidents are causally connected and lead to a logical outcome (see Story Grammars, page 74). This structure will help the children form a coherent interpretation. An episodic story, full of relatively unconnected events, is much harder to reconstruct.

Extensions

We've worked with several variations:

- Read or paraphrase the opening portion of the story so the central characters are named, the problem identified and the narrative style established.
- Have the children write their version of the story before hearing the author's original.
- Stop showing the pictures just before the climax and have the children complete the story, either orally or in writing.
- Teach pairs of older children how to do split images. Have each set of partners choose a suitable book and conduct the activity with a single pair of younger children.

Skills Development

The split images routine promotes careful observation, clarity of expression, and listening. Piecing together what is heard and what is seen develops skill in sequencing and a sense of story. Interpreting the partial information seen and heard requires numerous inferences.

STORY BOARDS

The Work of the Artist

When artists illustrate a manuscript for a book they don't take a bound set of blank pages and put pictures on both sides. Each illustration is created as a separate piece of art. Most artists will initially produce a complete series of detailed sketches, laid out in sequence, called a story board. As they create final art they constantly survey the proposed images to see if the intended sense of progression has been created, if the required parallelism has been maintained, or if a particular pattern has been fully worked out. Each picture must make a contribution to the whole. Together they are conceived and perceived as a single artistic statement.

The Reader's View

The reader-viewer receives a book with pages bound together and pictures fixed in their places, back to back. Only one or two pictures can be seen at a time.

This limited vantage point may result in the reader-viewer missing, or being only vaguely aware of, some of the effects the artist tried so hard to create. For example, we were faintly embarrassed that we hadn't noticed, until it was pointed out to us, that Sendak's *Where the Wild Things Are* begins with relatively small, framed pictures each accompanied by text. As the story proceeds the pictures spread, gradually pushing the text off the page. At the climax three gloriously mute unframed double spreads bleed off the edges of the page: the mute rage of the brain's right hemisphere. The reader's viewing point is initially distant and relatively uninvolved. As the story develops the viewpoint moves ever closer as the reader, with Max, meets the Wild Things almost eyeball to eyeball. As Max's anger subsides, the pictures and viewpoint retreat. Text, with its reassuring rationality, reappears. The left hemisphere regains control.

Only when Sendak's pictures are laid out in the form of a story board does his purpose become obvious. But we missed it from the bound form of the book, as did many others we've discussed the book with.

To Cut or Not To Cut?

We won't guarantee that every book will yield new appreciations when transformed into a story board. Only if the illustrator has planned sequences not readily evident in the bound form will the exercise be rewarding.

Lionni's Frederick will certainly repay the investment. From the bound version we already catch a progression in Frederick's position. First he sits centrally but low down on the page and we infer that he might be central to the story but not of high status. Succeeding pictures always show him as peripheral and isolated from the other mice who work as a group. As winter began and food becomes short, Frederick's status starts to rise and he moves towards the upper center of the page, looking down on his companions. In the final page he stands alone, high on the page, looking out at the reader. We and Frederick's companions have become one.

This progressive manipulation of Frederick's position on the page convinced us that it would be worth transforming this book into a story board, so we invested in two copies, cut them apart and mounted them on cards. Only then, to our delight, did we discover several other features:

- A repeated, parallel use of the Rule of Three. Three times Frederick's companions ask him what he's doing. When winter comes Frederick returns the three gifts he collected during the summer.

- The progression of the seasons — spring, summer, autumn and winter are all symbolized.
- The story is bisected into an "outdoors" and "indoors" sequence. The first half of the story shows the preparations for winter. The "indoors" sequence shows the struggle to survive the cold.

We now have a deeper appreciation of Lionni's work. Creating and viewing a story board can be a consciousness-raising experience for children as well.

Since creating storyboards is quite time consuming it would be a pity if they were used only for this activity. Here are some other uses for them:

- Present the boards in random order and have the children sequence them. A key to the correct sequence can be put on the backs of the cards.
- Present them in random order and have the children sequence them to tell their own story. Compare the class's version with the author's.
- Divide the class into small groups (two or three children per group) and give each group a card. As you read the text aloud, the group that believes it has the appropriate picture displays it to form the storyline.
- Display the pictures in random order. As you read the text aloud call on volunteers to place in sequence the pictures that go with the portion of the storyline heard so far, starting on the extreme left.
- Use the cards for Split Images (see page 36).

These suggestions will work more effectively if the text is removed so the children have to relate what they hear to the illustration they see.

WORD WEBS

Webbing is now being used in writing, science, social studies, the interpretation of literature, counseling and vocabulary development. It's been called webbing, networking, clustering, graphic overview, semantic mapping and literary sociograms. With minor differences, all these routines involve the creation of a diagram on which the relationships among selected words and phrases are arranged to reflect the child's or group's understanding of a text or situation. In *Literacy Through Literature* (pages 94-100) we've described our work with the use of a literary sociogram for the purpose of promoting comprehension and literary appreciation.

Word webbing has been advocated by Johnson and Pearson (1979) who suggest that children begin with a concept and connect words and phrases that, in their minds, relate to it. Children find this an engaging way to explore the inside of their own heads. This form of webbing makes an excellent prewriting activity (Rico, 1983).

We've also used webbing to enrich the children's vocabulary by having them examine how accomplished writers have used words, some familiar to them and some not (see Language Enrichment, page 159).

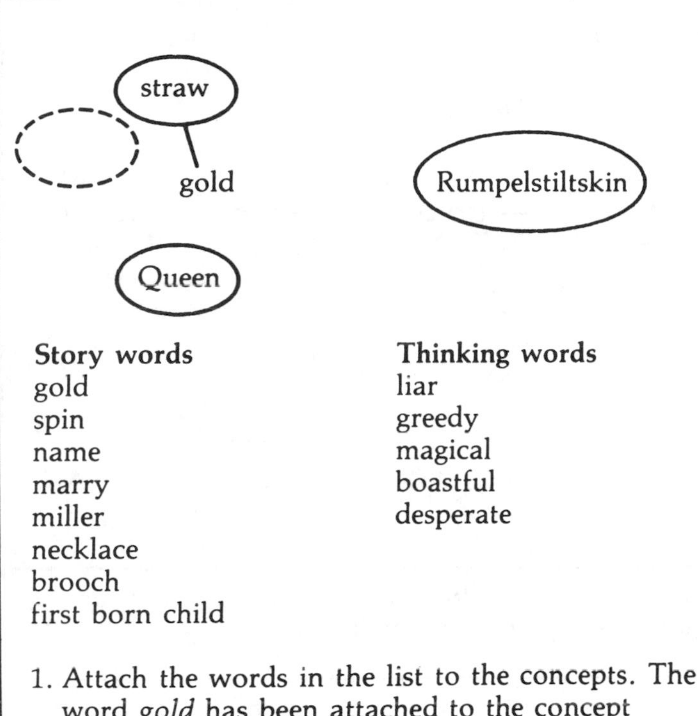

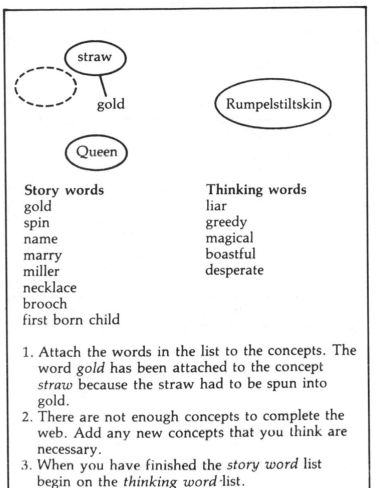

Story words
gold
spin
name
marry
miller
necklace
brooch
first born child

Thinking words
liar
greedy
magical
boastful
desperate

1. Attach the words in the list to the concepts. The word *gold* has been attached to the concept *straw* because the straw had to be spun into gold.
2. There are not enough concepts to complete the web. Add any new concepts that you think are necessary.
3. When you have finished the *story word* list begin on the *thinking word* list.
4. Be ready to explain why you connected the words together in the way that you did.

Figure 2.9 A worksheet for introductory word webbing using the story of Rumpelstiltskin

Modeling

We use a story the children already know well so they are free to attend to the routine. This particular worksheet (figure 2.9) is one we used for *Rumpelstiltskin.*

First we demonstrated what to do. We explained the reason for attaching gold to straw: because the straw was spun into gold. Then we attached necklace to Queen, explaining that the necklace belonged to the queen. We invited the children to suggest further connections and justify them. A few observed that some words could be attached to more than one other.

A number of the children then suggested that Rumpelstiltskin, the king, the queen and the miller could all be connected to gold. But the king wasn't listed, so he was added to the web inside the broken oval, which we then closed. The rest of the story words were left alone for the moment as we turned our attention to the first of the thinking words: liar. We asked the children where they would attach it. The answer we wanted was the miller, and we were rarely disappointed. We then asked them to justify why liar should connect with miller. Although the story doesn't actually say the miller was a liar, we trusted that someone would say he told lies to the king about his daughter's ability to spin straw into gold.

Along the way we made the necessary additions to the diagram which by then looked something like the one in figure 2.10 on the next page.

Next we distributed individual copies of the worksheet and asked the children to complete the diagram by attaching all the words from both lists. Children who could handle the responsibility were permitted to work in pairs.

The children worked independently while we circulated to offer individual assistance. When most had finished we called the class together to share their webs. We accepted any suggestions that were accompanied by an adequate rationale and collated them into our diagram.

We weren't trying to elicit the "right" answer nor produce the "correct" word web; differing interpretations were incorporated into the web where possible. For example, one child said magical should be attached to the queen, the king and the miller since the miller told the credulous king that his daughter could (magically) spin straw into gold. Others argued that only Rumpelstiltskin had magical powers. A diagram could accommodate both interpretations.

Some irreconcilable differences were left irreconciled if both parties could provide a rationale; whenever it seemed appropriate we stressed the idea that defensible differences are permissible. Our final diagram is shown in figure 2.11.

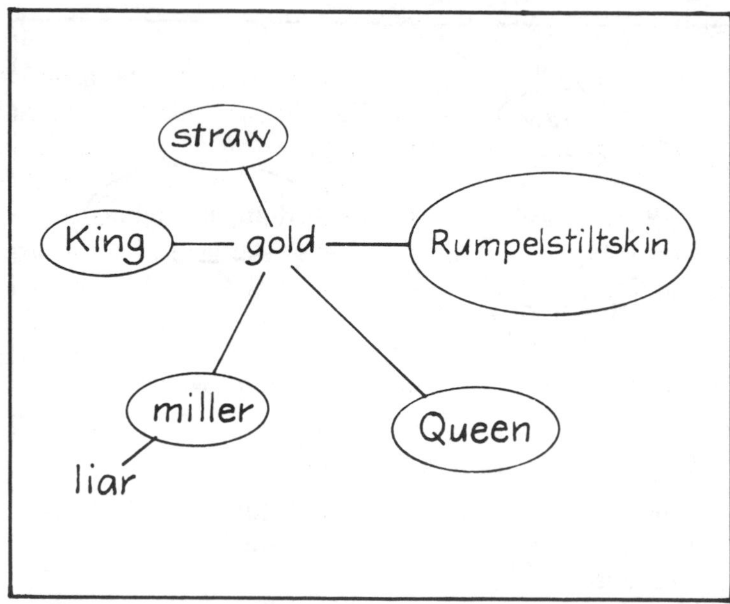

Figure 2.10 A partially completed word web based on the story of Rumpelstiltskin

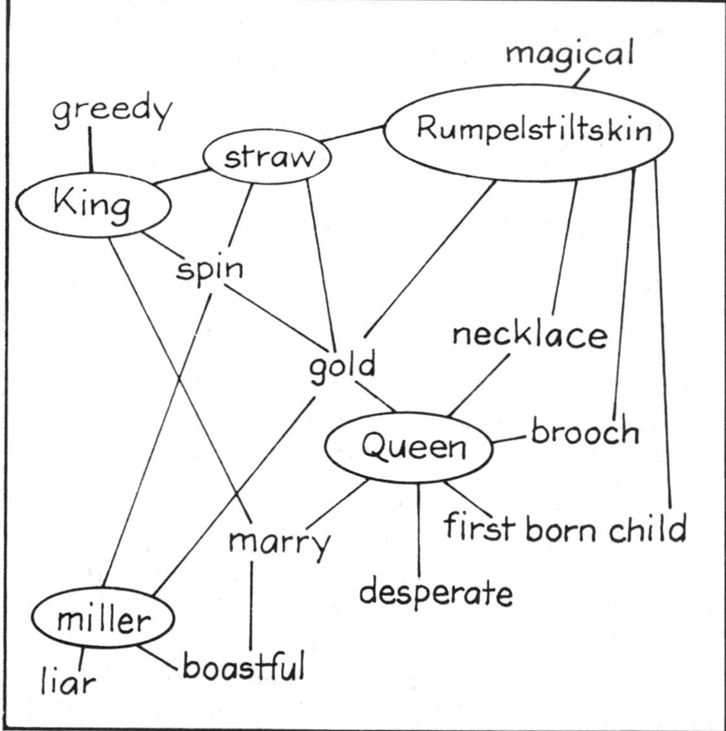

Figure 2.11 Completed word web based on the story of Rumpelstiltskin

Selecting Vocabulary

Webbing "story words" (those found in the story) to concepts requires a literal understanding of the story. "Thinking words" (not used by the author) require inference.

The purpose for webbing the former is to help the children trace out ways in which the author has developed relationships among the story words. We don't believe that words are isolated nuggets of meaning; they are intersections in a lattice. A child's vocabulary doesn't grow by examining and remembering words in isolation but by understanding how accomplished users weave words to form nets of meaning. Some growth will occur when children explore their own semantic nets, but more will result from close examination of the ways expert writers use words.

When we first introduce word webs we are primarily concerned with teaching the children how to create one from a piece of familiar literature. For that we use simple stories and unchallenging vocabulary. When we feel they are ready, we guide them in the development of word webs applied to more demanding stories with more challenging vocabulary.

For story words we choose those that are of central importance to the story — some we think may be demanding for the children and some we judge easy. We choose thinking words the same way, with the added proviso that they must be inferentially related to the story concepts. When selecting concepts we use people, places or objects that are central to the story. Since we eventually want to have the children create their own webs from their own private reading, we deliberately provide an incomplete set of concepts so they have the experience of developing the web for themselves.

Independent Application

You should work with the children on word webs as many times as seem necessary. Competent children may need only a single demonstration; then they should be encouraged to read a story of their own choice, pick out the key words and web them. Their webs can be shared with other members of the class.

You may want to offer the following advice as guidance for independent webbing: Choose and read your story, then pick out the key words. Things to consider are:

- The *characters*.
- The *actions* they perform.
- The *places* they go to.
- The *objects* they use.
- Words that describe the *qualities* of the characters and their actions.

At the beginning the children may want to form partnerships. If so, suggest that each child read a story and select a set number of key words (perhaps 10 or 15). Then have the partners exchange their stories and word lists. After reading the new story and webbing the words provided ask them to exchange papers again and examine each other's work.

Implementation

With simple texts you can use this routine with first grade children, or you can develop complex webs around texts that challenge university students. Intrinsically webbing is neither easy nor difficult; the degree of challenge lies in the text used.

***The Secret of NIMH:* a partial synopsis**
The home of Mrs. Frisby and her family is under threat of the farmer's plow. An old owl suggests that some "civilized" rats move the house to the "lee of the stone." The word *lee* baffles Mrs. Frisby. The rats examine a plan of the location of the house and realize what the owl means.

Webbing can be applied to any form of verbal communication: poems, plays, short stories, expository texts, television shows, lectures and portions of a novel. We tried it with a grade four class with whom we were reading Robert O'Brien's *The Secret of NIMH* (original title: *Mrs. Frisby and the Rats of NIMH*).

First we presented the children with the diagram shown in figure 2.12.

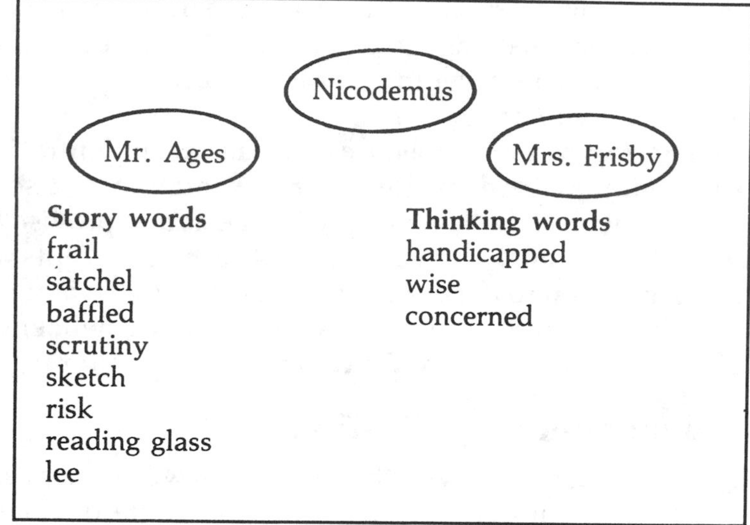

***Figure 2.12 A word webbing worksheet based on a chapter from* The Secret of NIMH**

The words *baffled, scrutiny, frail* and *lee* are of crucial importance to the story but we expected them to challenge the children. We presumed they would have little difficulty with *powder, satchel, sketch, risk* and *reading glass*. The only thinking word we felt would be a challenge was *concerned.*

We first showed them how to complete a word web by developing one around *Little Red Riding Hood.* Then we read the next chapter of *The Secret of NIMH* while projecting a master version of the worksheet on an overhead. We invited the children to suggest where the word lee might be attached. One child suggested Mrs. Frisby since she was the one who didn't understand what the word meant. To our delight a second child suggested Nicodemus also since he was the one who explained it to Mrs. Frisby. Once the class saw the possibilities, they developed complex connections they could fully justify. One child produced the diagram in figure 2.13 and the following commentary:

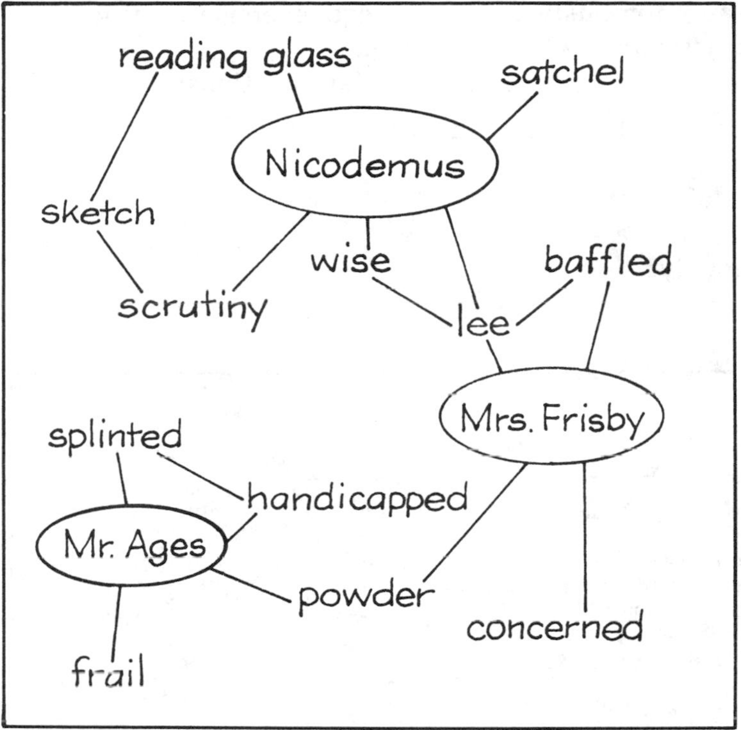

Figure 2.13 One child's word web based on a chapter from **The Secret of NIMH**

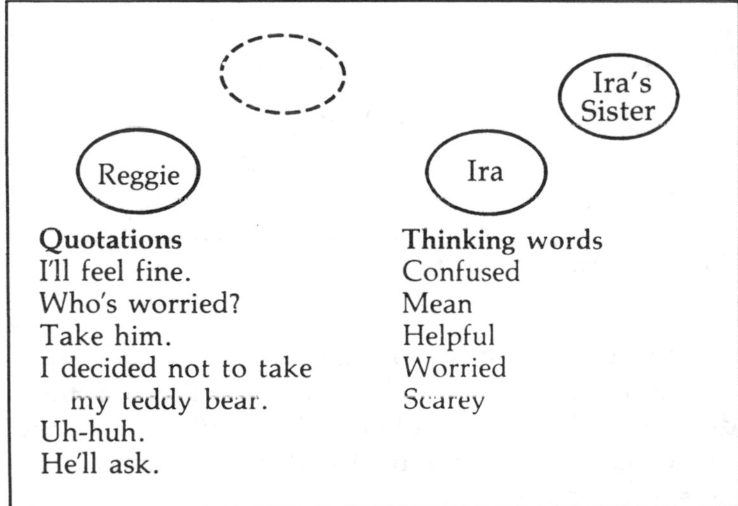

Figure 2.14 A worksheet for a word web using quotations based on **Ira Sleeps Over**

Mrs. Frisby was concerned about Timothy. She was baffled by the word lee. Nicodemus explained it to her. He was wise. He scrutinized the sketch with his reading glass which he kept in his satchel. Mrs. Frisby agreed to put a sleeping powder in Dragon's food because Mr. Ages had a splint on his leg and was feeling frail. He was handicapped.

What impressed us was the sense of autonomy with which the children spoke and the clear sense of ownership they displayed over their work. Clearly this was not an exercise to please us but an exploration of their understanding of the story.

Webbing With Quotations

Webbing can be done by lifting small stretches of text from a story and asking the children to link descriptive phrases and/or quotations, as in this sample worksheet based on Waber's *Ira Sleeps Over* (figure 2.14). When the children understand this variation they can choose their own story and select quotations from it, then give the resulting webbing exercise to a friend to be completed and returned for comment. At this stage the class begins to function semi-autonomously and you need exercise only general supervision, with guidance and assistance where required.

In sharing sessions children can address these and similar questions:

- Under what circumstances were the speeches made?
- How were the people feeling?
- What were they trying to do?
- What had just happened?
- What had been said previously?

Word Webbing of Poems

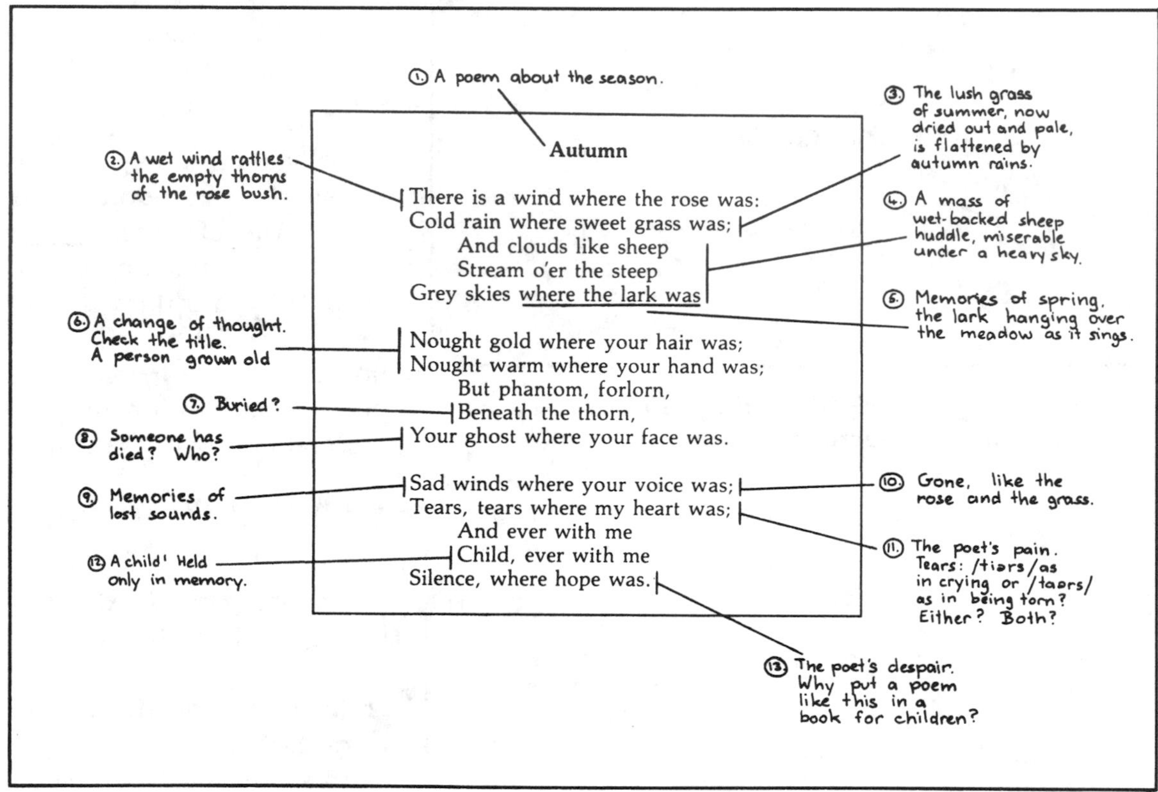

Figure 2.15 What the poem "Autumn" meant to one reader

This is a particularly valuable routine since poetic language is extremely dense. Poets frequently use ellipsis to create significant spaces for readers to fill from their own experience. They use words with deliberate double or triple ambiguity, some juxtaposed to resonate both phonologically and semantically. Poetic devices can be explored and represented by means of word webs.

Figure 2.15 is a reader's web based on Walter de la Mare's poem "Autumn," indicating some of the meanings the poem had for him. The intent, of course, is not to tell the children how they *should* interpret the poem, but to model for them a personal response by a more mature reader — to tempt them to emulate the procedure, not the content.

The webs of younger children will be much more literal and may have illustrations incorporated. Compare the poem below with its illustrated word webbing (figure 2.16). Figure 2.17 on the next page shows a representation of part of Taylor's *The Cay*.

Steam Shovel
The dinosaurs are not all dead
I saw one raise its iron head
To watch me walking down the road
Beyond our house today
Its jaws were dripping with a load
Of earth and grass that it had cropped
It must have heard me where I stopped
Snorted white steam my way
And stretched its long neck out for me to see
And chewed and grinned amiably.

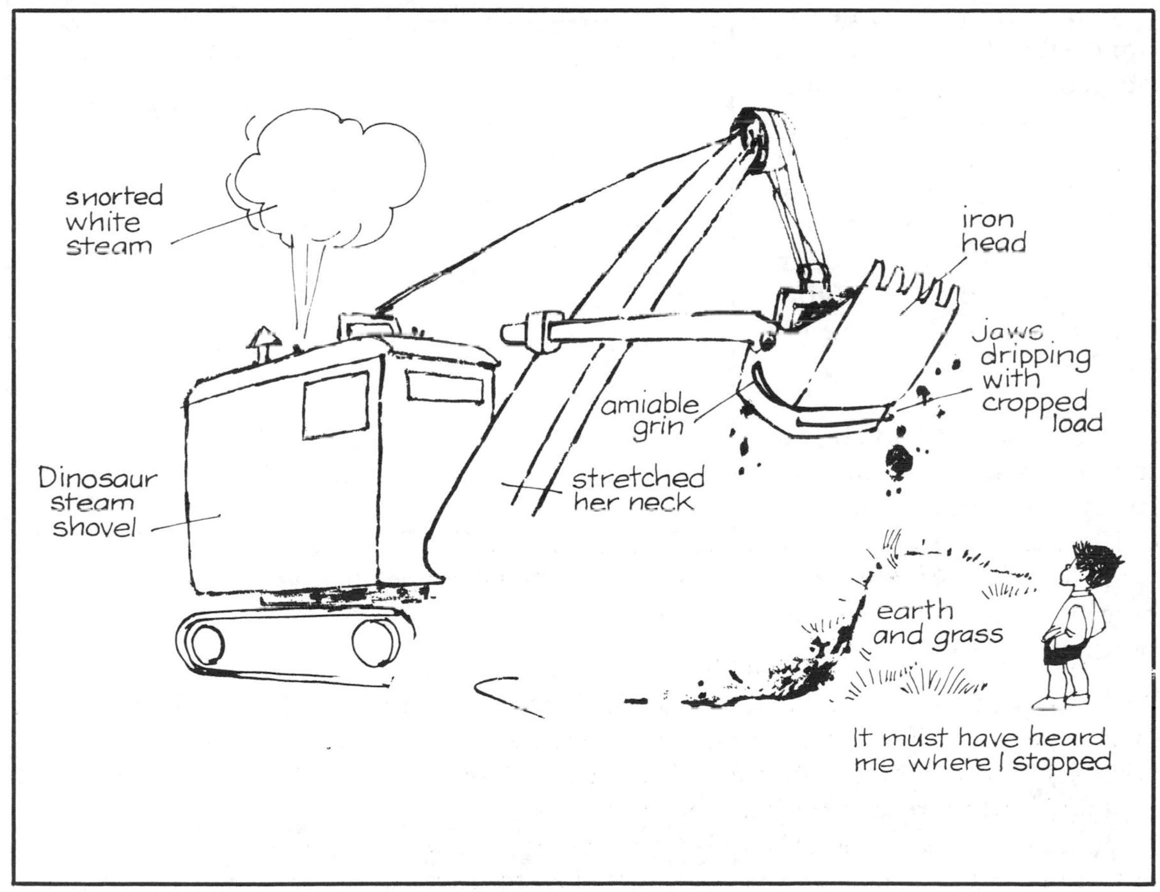

Figure 2.16 Combining a word web with illustration

Webbed Clues

A webbed clue is a statement in which two or more items in a clue are not fully specified, as in the example from Hoban's *A Baby Sister for Frances*, figure 2.18. The children must identify all the items marked in the clue.

The clues must contain a sufficient number of content words to enable the reader to solve them. If too many substantive words are removed the clue becomes insoluble; for example, "I put some in here" is nearly impossible to guess but "I put some into a coffee can" can be guessed.

With a grade four class we introduced the idea of webbed clues using *The Three Bears*. The children had no difficulty identifying I in the first clue (figure 2.19) as Goldilocks and *there* as the home of the three bears.

Note that we had circled the words to be identified. In the second clue the children had to identify which words needed webbing. They had little difficulty identifying *she*, *mine* and *my*.

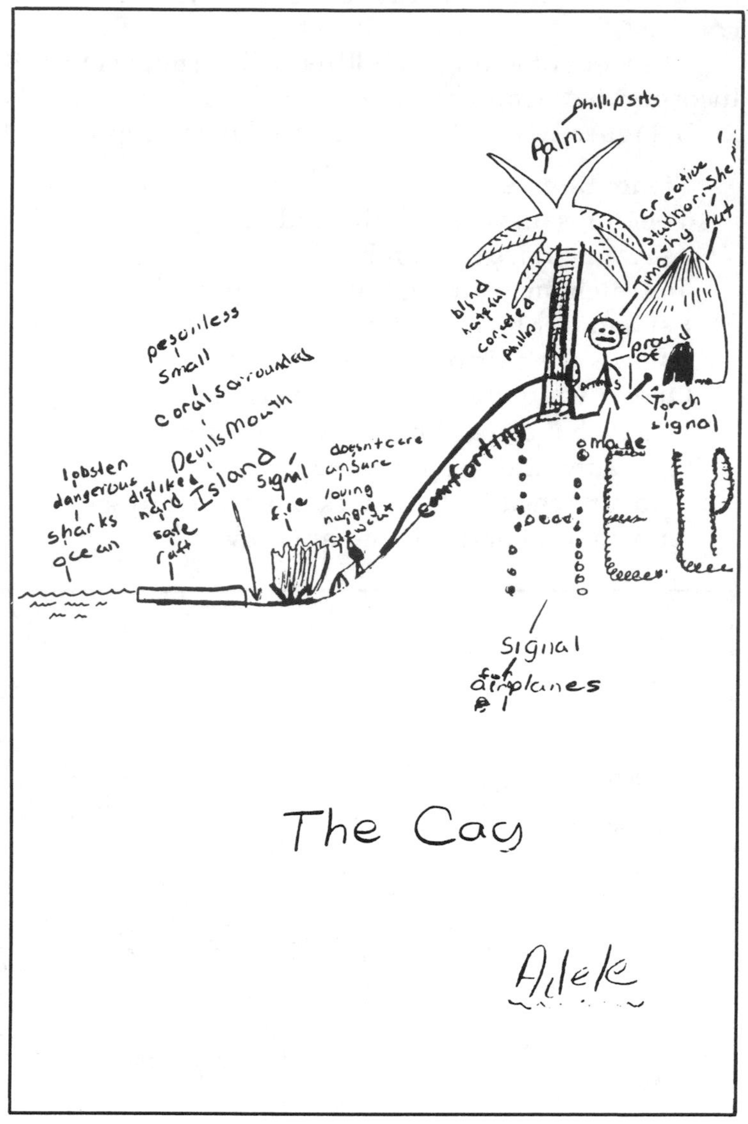

***Figure 2.17 The webbing of an illustration based on a part of Taylor's* The Cay**

***A Baby Sister for Frances:* a synopsis**
Frances has a new baby sister and things aren't going the way she would like. So she decides to run away under the dining room table. Mother and Father miss her. Frances misses them. Finally she returns home.

Clue 1	I ran away under here.
Solution	(I) ran away under (here.) → dining room table; I = Frances
Clue 2	I put some into a coffee can.
Solution	(I) put (some) into a coffee can.; I = Frances
Clue 3	She talked to me on the telephone and said she would be back soon.
Solution	(She) talked to (me) on the telephone and said (she) would be back soon.
Clue 4	I forgot to iron her blue one so she had to wear her yellow one.
Solution	(I) forgot to iron (her) blue (one) so she had to wear (her) yellow (one.) → dress; I = Mother, her = Frances, one = dress

Figure 2.18 ***Clues and webbed solutions based on Hoban's*** **A Baby Sister for Frances**

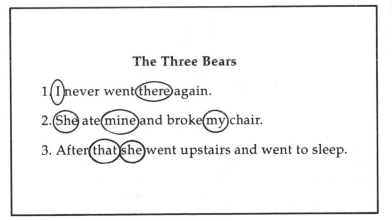

The Three Bears

1. (I) never went (there) again.
2. (She) ate (mine) and broke (my) chair.
3. After (that) (she) went upstairs and went to sleep.

Figure 2.19 ***Three webbed clues based on*** **The Three Bears**

The third clue was much more demanding. They found that they had to review the story to determine what occurred just before Goldilocks went to bed in order to identify what that referred to. The arrow is placed at a point of ellipsis. The children were to identify where Goldilocks went to sleep.

Next, the children followed along in individual copies as we read aloud *The Husband Who Had to Mind the House*. After that we gave them blank copies of the worksheet shown on the next page. The worksheet was developmentally sequenced as shown in figure 2.20. The children found it very easy to respond to the items we'd prepared, but much more difficult to create their own opaque statements to make suitable clues. Despite all the modeling and fading, some children were completely nonplussed by items 8-12. We employed successful early finishers as private coaches to get the non-starters going.

***The Husband Who Had to Mind the House*: a synopsis**
A husband complains that his wife doesn't do things right, so they switch jobs. He stays at home while she works in the fields. A series of domestic disasters culminates in the husband falling down the chimney and landing with his head in the porridge pot.

<table>
<tr><th>Item</th><th>Nature of the items</th><td rowspan="6">One or two items in each step were discussed orally prior to individual written work. When the written work was complete individual responses were shared orally.</td></tr>
<tr><td>A</td><td>A complete example</td></tr>
<tr><td>1-5</td><td>Clues with the words to be webbed identified</td></tr>
<tr><td>6-7</td><td>Clues without any words identified</td></tr>
<tr><td>8-9</td><td>Sections of the text to be transformed into clues suitable for webbing</td></tr>
<tr><td>10-12</td><td>An open invitation to create three clues suitable for webbing</td></tr>
</table>

Figure 2.20 Developmental sequence for the worksheet in Figure 2.21.

Janna exchanged papers with her friend Carrie, whose webbing of Janna's clues is shown in figure 2.22.

We've often noted that children respond much more readily to situations that have been structured for them; they are less confident in imposing their own structures on fluid or amorphous situations. However, the goal of education isn't merely to train children to respond to the structuring of others, but to have them become increasingly able to perceive and impose order on complex and seemingly orderless situations.

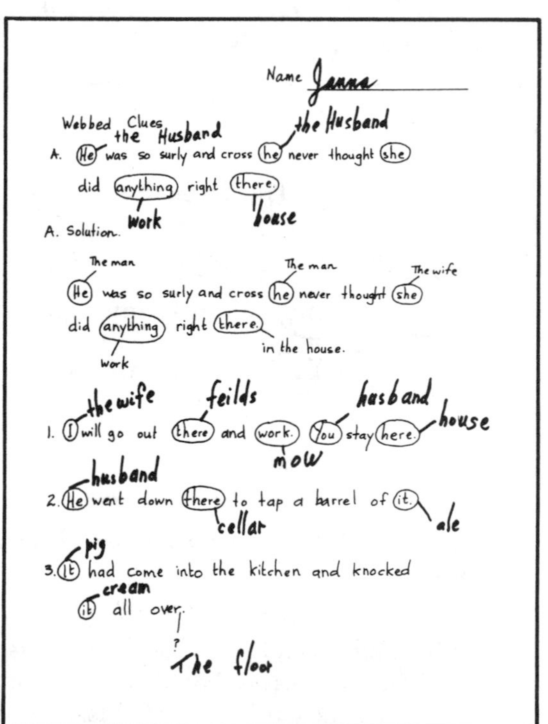
Name Janna

Webbed Clues the Husband the Husband
A. He was so surly and cross he never thought she did anything right there.
work house
A. Solution.
The man The man The wife
He was so surly and cross he never thought she did anything right there.
in the house.
work

the wife feilds husband house
1. I will go out there and work. You stay here.
mow
husband
2. He went down there to tap a barrel of it.
cellar ale
pig
3. It had come into the kitchen and knocked
cream
it all over.
?
The floor

***Figure 2.21 Janna's responses to an overhead based on* The Husband Who Had to Mind the House**

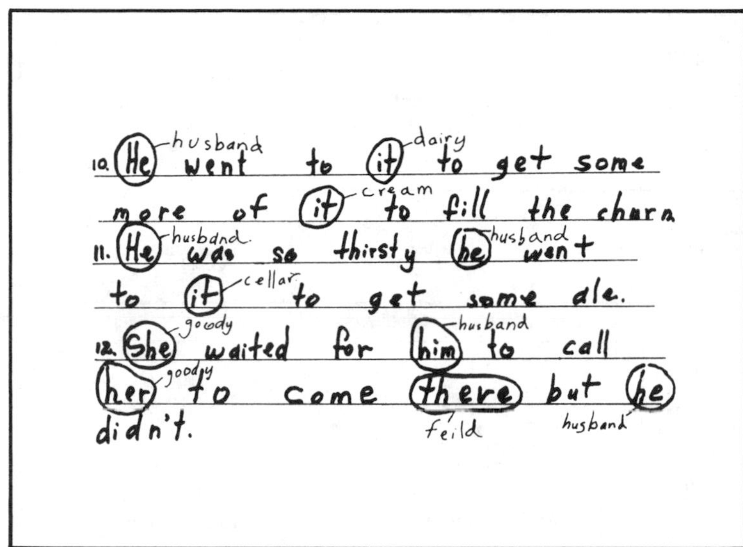

Figure 2.22 Clues created by Janna and webbed by Carrie

Webbing a Text

Webbing texts should be undertaken only by competent older students. This routine is best taught by modeling and Socratic questioning, as shown in figure 2.23 on the next page.

The complexity of semantic and syntactic ties in a text can make for serious visual cluttering if every connection is represented. Layers of connections should be built up gradually. If the children participate in and witness the development of the diagram, a much higher degree of complexity can be tolerated. It sometimes helps to use contrasting colors; for example, the wife in figure 2.24 might be shown in one color, the man in another, connections between

4. He gave it a kick and it lay for dead
5. It was shut up in there all that time and hadn't had a bit or a drop
6. He put her up there so she could eat what was there.
7. He filled it and hung it over the fire

Make up your own webbed clue.

8. One end of the rope he made fast to the cow's neck, and the other he slipped down the chimney and tied it around his own thigh.

He made it fast to her neck and the other he slipped it down there and tied it around his thigh.

9. While he was hard at it, down fell the cow off the house.

He was hard at it when she fell off it.

10.–12. Look through the story and make up three more webbed clues of your own. Try them out on a friend.

10. He went into it to get some more of it to fill the churn
11. He was so thirsty he went to it to get some.
12. She waited for him to call her to come there but he didn't.

objects and places in a third. If the text is on a transparency, the cohesive ties can be superimposed with a water-based felt pen. One set of connections can then be cleaned off and additional ties developed.

The example shows ties occurring in a natural text. Explanatory comments are included.

Skills Development

Word webs do more than just develop vocabulary. Repeated use of this routine helps children to realize that words are not entities but relationships — a great truth often distorted by word lists and dictionaries. Words don't have single meanings but carry arrays of potential meanings. Words give meaning to the contexts in which they occur and also derive meaning from them. The potential meaning of a word is realized only when it's used in a given context.

Teacher talk	**Student response**	**Written record**
Who is "she"?	The wife.	The wife.
How about the "she" in "she'd waited"?	The wife.	Connects first use of "she" to second use of "she".
Where is the wife referred to again? What word is used?	"She" – "when *she* got there."	Connects third use of "she".
The connections for the wife are traced throughout the text.		
What is meant by "there" in "But when she got there"?	The house.	
What word is used in the text?	"Home"	Connects "there" to "home"
Why did the wife cut the rope?	To set the cow free.	
Why would cutting the rope set the cow free?	It was hanging from the rope.	Connects "rope" and "hanging".

Figure 2.23 Teacher/children exchange in modeling the webbing of a text

This conception of vocabulary may appear abstract and subtle to many adults who prefer to regard words as finite units. But we have no doubt that children can begin to grasp our view of the inter-relatedness of words if they have numerous experiences in examining how they are actually used by accomplished writers. Word webbing is one way to help them do that.

The word *she* in "At last she thought" refers to the wife. This concept is linked to a chain of eight further references that take the form of *she, her* and *his old dame.* The word *there* in "when she got there" refers back to home. The word *hanging* is conceptually connected to the rope the wife cuts. The word *up* in "she ran up" connects to the ugly place, which earlier in the story we learn is hanging from the roof. The word *this* in "But as she did this" refers to the cutting of the rope. The phrases *her husband* and *his old dame* involve cross-references between the man and woman. The word *her* in "her husband" refers to the woman but the word *husband* refers to the man. Similarly the word *his* in "his old dame" refers to the man but *old dame* refers to the woman. The word *there* in "there she found him" refers to the kitchen.

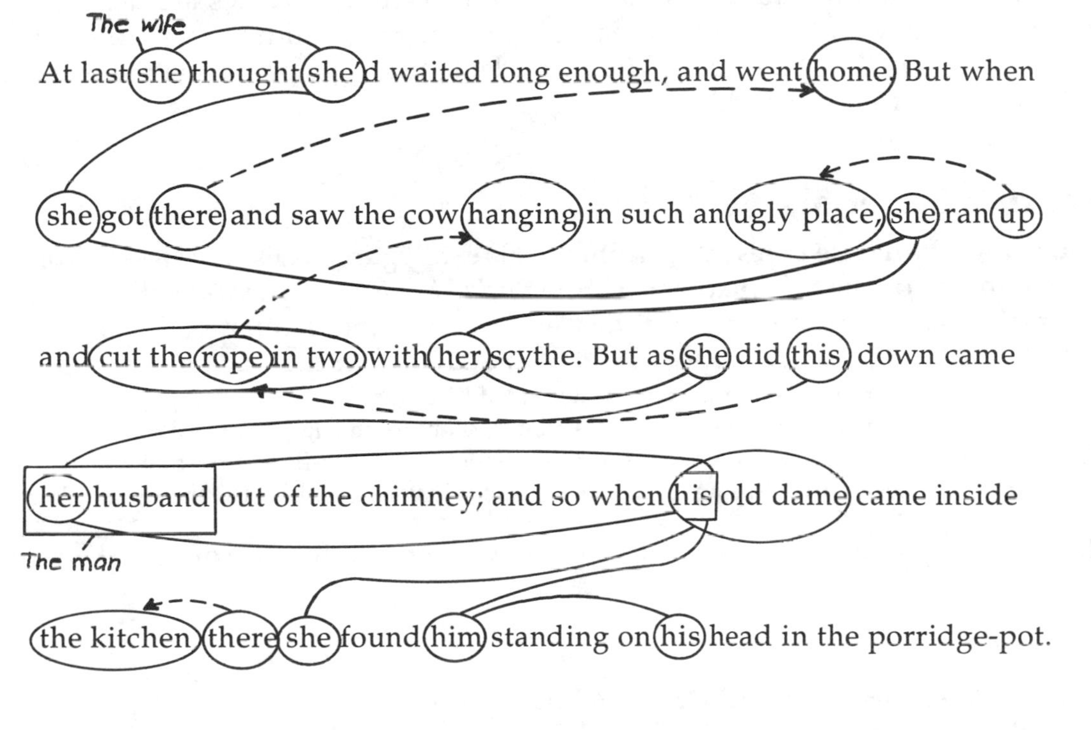

Figure 2.24 Syntactic and semantic ties in a natural text — **The Husband Who Had to Mind the House**

BOOK BINGO

Caveat

We've seen so many poorly conceived school uses of bingo that we were reluctant to include this idea. Most engage the children in the recreational and social aspects of the game without any useful educational side to them. For example, we don't think children should be given bingo cards with sight words they're supposed to cover when the teacher calls them out because:

- The words are presented in isolation.
- The activity is unrelated to any meaningful text.
- The children have to know the words already to play the game.
- It suggests that reading is the naming of words.
- Calling out a random sample of unrelated words is an undignified activity for a professional teacher.

That use of bingo violates our basic premise: children should be encouraged to make thoughtful, sensitive responses to the substance of a meaningful text.

We always base our routines on meaningful texts; our activities are designed to help children enjoy and understand real texts. Having the children react to artificial texts of instruction (like bingo cards) isn't an adequate way of preparing them to deal with language in the real world.

Preparing Materials

Our bingo cards use clues taken from a real text. Figure 2.25 shows a set of bingo card items based on the first chapter of C.S. Lewis's *The Lion, the Witch and the Wardrobe.* It lists major characters, objects, localities and events in the chapter.

***The Lion, the Witch and the Wardrobe:* a synopsis of Chapter 1**
Four children play in a large house. Lucy, the youngest, hides in a large wardrobe filled with fur coats. She pushes through the coats and finds herself in a snow-filled forest. She is astonished to meet a faun carrying an umbrella, who is just as astonished at the sight of her.

Below is a set of clues for Chapter 1, which we prepared for the concepts listed on the card.

Literal fact	*Inferential fact*
Four children were sent to his home.	She was curious.
It had a wardrobe in it.	This weather kept them indoors.
He had goat's hoofs.	It was bigger than it seemed.
Sometimes she talked like her mother.	He tried to prevent an argument.
The faun carried them.	He was rather ill-mannered.

Implementation

The first step

Provide each pair of children with a bingo card. Read out the clues and ask the children to cover the words or phrases of their choice with a marker.

Bingo lovers will realize that this is not (yet) a true bingo game since everyone has the same card and every accurate and attentive listener will likely "win" at the same

Lucy	nymph	winter
faun	tears	Christmas
daughter of Eve	kidnap	White Witch
Narnia	flute	handkerchief

Figure 2.25 A book bingo card for chapter one

Edmund	fur coats	Peter
Lucy	rain	parcels
Professor	faun	snow
spare room	wardrobe	Susan

Figure 2.26 A book bingo card for chapter two

time. The goal at this point isn't to play bingo but to show the children how to apply the game of bingo to a familiar text.

The second step

Develop a second bingo card based on chapter two of the same book. This time have the children generate clues for the character: each pair provides one clue for *each* of the concepts on the bingo card, perhaps (but not necessarily) on a worksheet like the one shown in figure 2.27 on the next page. Since the concepts are already listed on the card, a blank sheet of paper is sufficient for those children who can organize their own workspace.

When everyone has drafted a set of clues, volunteers select one of the concepts and read out a clue for it. The others decide which concept they think it alludes to, cover that concept on their bingo card *and* cancel out their own clue for that concept. For example, if team A reads out "Lucy fell asleep while this was played," the listening teams cover *flute* on the card and cancel out the clue they prepared for it, since it's useless now for this game. The same game can be played several times as long as different clues are used each time.

> ***The Lion, the Witch and the Wardrobe:*** **a synopsis of Chapter 2**
> Lucy foolishly agrees to accompany the faun to his home. There he gives her tea and tells her of the spell Narnia lies under: because of the evil power of the White Witch it is always winter, though never Christmas. The faun almost kidnaps Lucy, thinks better of it and returns her to the wardrobe.

The third step

Issue copies of blank bingo cards, together with a list of concepts (see figure 2.28) and ask the children to make up a clue for each concept. Then, the children write in the name of each concept on the bingo card in a space of their own choosing.

Since each card will be unique, the children can now play a true game of bingo, with winners for completed lines, columns, diagonals or cards.

The final step

To make their own bingo cards have the children work together to select concepts. Record their suggestions on the chalkboard. Accept more than the required number so the class can decide which are likely to produce the most interesting clues. Once a set of concepts has been determined, the procedure is the same as in step three.

The number of concepts from which selections are made should exceed the number of concepts that appear on any one card. This will mean that some clues read out will not apply to any of the concepts certain players have listed on their cards.

Make up one clue about each concept. The clue must be based on information from the story.

Used

☐ Lucy ______

☐ Faun ______

☐ daughter of Eve ______

☐ Narnia ______

☐ nymph ______

☐ tears ______

☐ kidnap ______

☐ flute ______

☐ winter ______

☐ Christmas ______

☐ White witch ______

☐ handkerchief ______

Be ready to read your clue aloud. Check off each clue as it is read aloud by someone else.

Figure 2.27 A clues worksheet

Levels of Difficulty

The level of difficulty can be controlled through the selection of concepts at both literal and inferential levels. In our example we included *fur mantle* and *dominions* because we felt these were challenging vocabulary items. The words *magic, trickery* and *greed* don't actually appear in the text although examples of each of these kinds of behavior do.

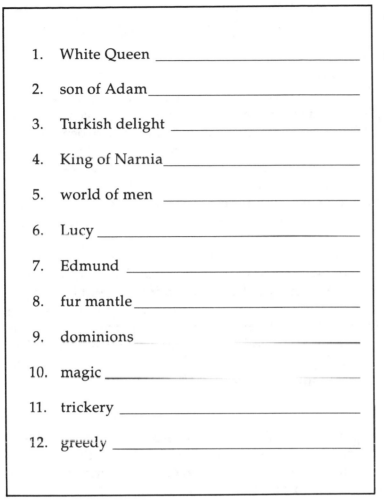

1. White Queen ____________
2. son of Adam ____________
3. Turkish delight ____________
4. King of Narnia ____________
5. world of men ____________
6. Lucy ____________
7. Edmund ____________
8. fur mantle ____________
9. dominions ____________
10. magic ____________
11. trickery ____________
12. greedy ____________

Figure 2.28 A list of concepts from Chapter 3 of **The Lion, the Witch and the Wardrobe**

An Overview

Here are the steps set out more succinctly:

- ***Step 1.*** You provide bingo cards with concepts and clues.
  The class plays bingo.
- ***Step 2.*** You provide bingo cards with concepts.
  The children provide clues.
  The class plays bingo.
  The children cover concepts and cancel clues.
- ***Step 3.*** You provide a list of concepts and empty bingo cards.
  The children provide clues and choose the placement of concepts on the bingo cards.
  The class plays bingo.
  The children cover concepts and cancel clues.
  "Winners" are identified for rows, columns and cards.
- ***Step 4.*** The children, as a group, determine which concepts will be used, decide on their placement and provide the clues.
  The class plays bingo.

Independent Practice

A group of children can create a book bingo game on their own based on a story they've all read. However, because bingo is basically a large group game it should be played with the whole class. Your supervision may still be needed when they play.

Skills Development

Book bingo contributes to comprehension at the critical, inferential and literal levels. It can be used to expand vocabulary. The selecting of concepts involves identifying main ideas and the provision of clues requires the identification of supporting details. A good deal of talk, listening, planning and cooperation is required, as is writing for an audience.

POETRY

Philosophical Ruminations

Knowing and learning about poetry is not dependent on knowing such terms as *alliteration, assonance,* and *metaphor*. These become useful only after the children have had numerous experiences of poems which use the devices. They must have numerous opportunities to enjoy the fun of "Peter Piper picked a peck of pickled peppers" or "bearded bears" and many, many others before the term *alliteration* is introduced. At no stage does the noting and naming of devices reach the heart of the poem, even though names may become handy lexical placeholders.

Poetry is a process of distilling language to touch on strongly held feelings and reflective thought in ambiguous, multilayered levels of meaning. Each reader tries a poem on for size. Does it speak to my life? Does the poet's experience impinge upon mine? Do these words resonate with thoughts and feelings I've had? Only after these kinds of concerns have been addressed may we wish to examine how the poet achieved various effects, and it's at this juncture that the examination and consideration of "devices" may be relevant. ("Devices" seems a singularly inappropriate term to apply to poetry — its metallic ring brings to mind unyielding machinery applied inconsiderately to the softness of the human body and mind.) The use of technical terms by people who have a clear idea of the concepts undergirding them assists in talking about the poet's choice of technique.

Meddling with Poetry

The teaching of poetry is fraught with pitfalls. Some procedures approach a poem as though it were an internal combustion engine. The teacher-technician disassembles the poem into "devices" and explains the form and function of each. Armed with a kit full of such devices as rhyme, meter and alliteration, the children are directed to assemble their own poems, with results that rarely please. The opposite approach presumes the poem to spring full blown of its own accord from the forehead of the hapless poet. The children are assigned rain poems on wet days, kite poems on windy days. Without guidance, the children use their notions of poetry absorbed from greeting cards or advertising jingles to produce heavy-footed doggerel.

We want to range between these extremes.

At the *inspirational* end of the continuum the poems we write that are most deeply meaningful to us tend to appear at times of intense emotion. But since we can't call up intense emotions in children according to a predetermined schedule, we're content to leave to chance the times when they feel impelled to write a poem. What we can do is provide numerous experiences, real and vicarious, and encourage them to write about those. One form response *may* take is poetry.

On the *mechanical* side we recognize that poetry is a craft that has techniques skilled practitioners use to express, amplify or intensify the impact of what they have to say. We see no reason why such techniques should be regarded as mysteries too arcane to be shared with children. Unfortunately it's all too easy to convey the idea that the poem is the sum of the techniques. Conversely, it's difficult to communicate the idea that the origin and heart of a poem is something the poet felt a need to express. Skilled writers are able to deploy, almost unconsciously, those poetic techniques that serve their purposes. Technique isn't allowed to dominate the poem. The danger is that when we bring poetic writing techniques to the attention of children this aspect is uppermost in their minds when they begin to write. To some extent we have to accept this situation and recognize that the attempts of beginners may be self-consciously clumsy.

Clozing Poems

The cloze procedure permits you to control which aspects of the poetry will be addressed but doesn't focus too intensely on the mechanics.

Examining the poem

We chose a poem we thought the children would enjoy, "Rules" by Karla Kuskin, and examined it to determine what Kuskin has done to achieve her effect:

- *Poetic intent*
  She is amusing.
  Her rules are silly, not to be taken seriously.
- *Semantic techniques*
  She puts wildly inappropriate things together, as in "wear a broom to breakfast."
- *Syntactic techniques*
  Each sentence is an admonition that uses the same grammatical structure.
- *Poetic devices*
  She uses an ABCB rhyme scheme in lines 1-8 but breaks the pattern in lines 9-12.
  She uses alliteration: "bearded bears"; "smoke cigars on sofas."
  She uses assonance: "ask a snake's advice."
  She uses repetition: lines 1-9 and 13 begin with "Do not."
  She uses a regular meter for all lines except the last two, which close the poem abruptly.

Rules

Do not jump on ancient uncles.
Do not yell at average mice.
Do not wear a broom to breakfast.
Do not ask a snake's advice.
Do not bathe in chocolate pudding.
Do not talk to bearded bears.
Do not smoke cigars on sofas.
Do not dance on velvet chairs.
Do not take a whale to visit
Russell's mother's cousin's yacht.
And whatever else you do
It is better you
Do not.

Karla Kuskin

Figure 2.29 "Rules" by Karla Kuskin

Determining objectives

From a list, as exhaustive as we could make it, we picked those aspects we felt confident we could convey to the children with whom we planned to work. We decided a third grade class would probably appreciate:

- the silly fun of the poem
- the use of repetition
- the creation of nonsense by putting inappropriate things together
- the use of rhyming words
- the use of regular meter
- the repeated use of the same sentence structure

Note that we didn't plan to talk to nine to 10-year-old children about these techniques as abstractions, but to get them to attend to these aspects in the poem itself.

Tattering the text

We wanted to leave intact two or more examples of a pattern or technique used by the poet and alter one or more subsequent examples for the children to predict. For example, the first two lines of the poem could be left untouched and "Do not" removed from line 3.

1. Do not jump on ancient uncles.
2. Do not yell at average mice.
3. ______ ______ wear a broom to breakfast.

We didn't expect children to appreciate that line four must end with a word that rhymes with *mice.* However, there's a strong semantic cue in the first five words of line four:

4. Do not ask a snake's ______

Address, name, age, license number are all possible, but the rhyming of *advice* with *mice* is confirming and closes the stanza very reassuringly. The "correct" completion of line four is necessary to establish the rhyming pattern.

The children's intuitive knowledge of grammar will tell them that the third word in line five is a verb:

5. Do not ______ in chocolate pudding.

Kuskin's four previous "rules" will suggest that it should be something inappropriately related to chocolate pudding. We've had *spit, swim, shower, wash* and *walk* suggested to us. This particular example highlights the peculiar power of using cloze with poetry. The constraints on the word that could appear in the blank are: syntactic (it must be a verb); semantic (it must be something that a human being could do with chocolate pudding); and poetic (it must be a one-syllable word that denotes something one is unlikely to do with chocolate pudding). These multiple constraints help the children to appreciate the incredible precision with which some poets use words.

Kuskin's use of alliteration appears in line three ("broom to breakfast") and line six ("bearded bears"). Thus we can expect the children to be sensitive to it in line seven:

7. Do not smoke cigars on ______.

We expected, and received, many non-alliterative completions (*purpose, Monday, holiday*, etc.). We also had *Sunday* suggested quite frequently although the children weren't able to explain the alliterative nature of the word when we asked why that suggestion: a nice example of a child's intuitive sensitivity to poetic expression.

The rhyme can't be predicted in line eight unless advice in line four has been correctly identified.

6. Do not talk to bearded bears.
7. Do not smoke cigars on ______.
8. Do not dance on velvet ______.

We recorded all suggestions for filling in the blank without comment: *pears, stairs, paws, rags, chairs, kittens*, etc. Then we looked at each one critically. We referred to the *mice/advice* rhyme in lines two/four:

pears: rhymes, is silly
stairs: rhymes, is somewhat silly, velvet stairs might be slippery and dangerous
paws: doesn't rhyme, is silly
rugs: doesn't rhyme, isn't silly
chairs: rhymes, is silly
kittens: doesn't rhyme, is silly, doesn't fit the rhythm.

To demonstrate the inadequacy of *kittens* we had the children beat out an exaggeration of the rhythm in lines five to eight, hoping they would realize it needs a word with a single syllable. The reader might note that this blank has two phonological constraints: rhyme and single syllable.

After this critical review the children collectively or individually chose which word they preferred. We tried not to impose our preferences, although we did indicate what should be considered in making a choice.

The blank in line nine had to be filled by a single-syllable noun that one would be unlikely to take on a yacht.

9. Do not take a ______ to visit
10. Russell's mother's cousin's yacht.

The prediction of *not* in line thirteen is easy:

12. It is better you
13. Do ______.

We included the final blank to make the children focus on the way Kuskin snaps her poem shut with the two words she begins with and uses so often.

Presenting the tattered text

It's important to convey to children that they aren't being asked to guess what word the poet used, but to suggest words that could reasonably fill the blank. So you should invite and celebrate multiple suggestions.

One third grade class offered numerous suggestions for each blank and had little difficulty appreciating how meaning, tone and rhythm must be satisfied. For example, when one child suggested "stick your finger" for line five: "Do not ______ in chocolate pudding," we reread the poem with an exaggerated beat and it was immediately clear the suggestion didn't maintain the pulse of Kuskin's words.

Rules

Do not jump on ancient uncles.
Do not yell at average mice.
____ ____ wear a broom to breakfast.
Do not ask a snake's ________.
Do not ________ in chocolate pudding.
Do not talk to bearded bears.
Do not smoke cigars on ________
Do not dance on velvet ________.
Do not take a ________ to visit
Russell's mother's cousin's yacht.
And whatever else you do
It is better you
Do ________.

Karla Kuskin

Figure 2.30 A tattered version of "Rules" by Karla Kuskin

They found the rhyme scheme a little complex. Several suggestions followed an AA pattern rather than the ABCB pattern Kuskin uses:

6. Do not talk to bearded bears.
7. Do not smoke cigars on *chairs*.

The children didn't appear to be sensitive to the use of alliteration. For line seven, "Do not smoke cigars on ______," *battleships, Mondays* and *bouncing balls* were all fine with them, although they did agree that *Sundays* and *sofas* were superior ways to complete the line.

We tried to have them choose, copy and leave words out of a poem, restricting them to five blanks. They were then to exchange poems with a friend. The more competent children responded adequately but the disorganized responses of the less able children indicated they had difficulty understanding the structure of the original.

Please remember that we don't give the technical explanations we've provided here to children. We simply present the cloze version of the poem and invite them to repair it. Multiple suggestions are recorded and critically evaluated. We may refer to other parts of the poem to draw rhythms and regularities to their attention but we try to avoid talking about poetic abstractions.

When we achieve consensus we read aloud the children's collective version. They always want to see the original and look very carefully at the words chosen by the poet, but they sometimes prefer their own choices!

Among other things, we hope the children will get the notion that the words of others are neither inevitable nor immutable. Poets choose words from alternatives and they always could have chosen others than the ones they did. Perhaps this realization will lay a foundation vital to all writing: that rules, regulations and laws are chosen by fallible human beings and equal or superior alternatives may well exist.

Deletion rates

The use of cloze in other areas often raises the question: "How frequently should words be deleted?" It's not really appropriate to talk about deletion rate in poetry since each deletion is made judiciously. A review of our work yielded about a 1:10 rate. However, it isn't the overall rate that's important; what matters is that the incomplete structures the children are asked to reconstruct have been modeled previously in the poem. Prediction is based on perceived regularities.

Developing independence

We know we can guide children successfully through a carefully structured cloze poem. We are less confident about our ability to show them how to structure self-selected poems for cloze, since that requires the ability to spot the poetic devices employed in any given poem. Some general guidelines they might observe include:

- Take out only a few words.
- Take out words in the second half or at the end of the line.
- Take out words from the second half of the poem.
- If you disturb a pattern be sure the same kind of pattern is used earlier in the poem.
- You should be able to point out the undisturbed parts of the poem that can be used to work out how to fill in your blanks.

If (older) children have already become familiar with some technical terms the rules can be made more specific:

- If you delete an alliterative word be sure that at least one or two examples of alliteration occur in the poem before the example you plan to tatter.

With these guidelines competent children could be allowed to select a poem, create a cloze version and give it to a friend for reconstruction. Afterwards both children can compare the reconstructions with the original.

Disturbed Poems

The value of substitution

You could also present a poem that has had words substituted. This routine has the advantage that the substitutions aren't marked, so the children have to weigh each word in the poem and consider its appropriateness. They then indicate which words they think have been substituted and offer what they consider superior alternatives. Inevitably they react critically not only to the substitutions but also to the poet's original words.

Implementation

We tried this routine with a sixth grade class. On an overhead projector we showed a disturbed version of Shel Silverstein's "Hug O' War" and asked them to detect and correct the errors it contained. We recorded each suggestion and asked the child making it to state the reason for it. The first claim would often be that a particular word "didn't sound right." When pressed for further explanations they were able to identify rhyme, rhythm, meaning and the number of syllables as sources of disruption, and offer further alternatives (see figures 2.31 and 2.32).

The amendment for line four is interesting in that it corrects the meaning and maintains the rhythm although it isn't the phrase used by Silverstein. In line seven the child who offered *kisses* said the poem was about hugging, which is nice, whereas

Hug O' War

I will not play at tug o' war
I'd rather play at hug o' war
Where everyone hugs
Instead of tugs
Where everyone giggles
And rolls on the rug
Where everyone kisses
And everyone grins
And everyone cuddles
And everyone wins

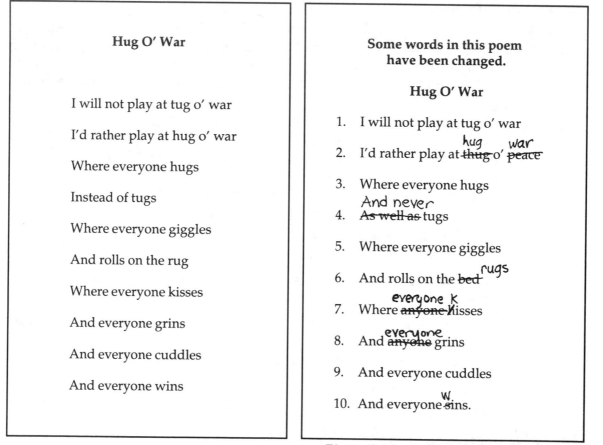

Figure 2.31 "Hug O' War" by Shel Silverstein

Some words in this poem have been changed.

Hug O' War

1. I will not play at tug o' war
2. I'd rather play at ~~thug~~ hug o' ~~peace~~ war
3. Where everyone hugs
4. ~~As well as~~ And never tugs
5. Where everyone giggles
6. And rolls on the ~~bed~~ rugs
7. Where ~~anyone~~ everyone ~~h~~kisses
8. And ~~anyone~~ everyone grins
9. And everyone cuddles
10. And everyone ~~s~~wins.

Figure 2.32 A disturbed version of "Hug O' War" with amendments offered by children

hissing is nasty — clearly a sensitive response to the mood of the poem. Another child, Ryan, suggested that line six should read "And roll on the rugs." When this was rejected on grammatical grounds he muttered that it had too many S's in it. It's interesting to note that Silverstein uses *rug* rather than *rugs* — perhaps he too disliked an overabundance of sibilants. Silverstein dared to disregard his own rhyme scheme.

After the exercise we presented Silverstein's original on an overhead projector without comment. We didn't ask them to read it, but every child in the room, except one extremely poor reader, did so. The routine carries its own motivation: the uncertainty created by the substitutions also generates a need for closure.

We handed out to each child a disturbed version of "The Bat" by Theodore Roethke The children worked individually or in pairs making changes to the poem. When everyone was finished, the modified version was displayed on an overhead projector. Oral suggestions for change were recorded (see figure 2.33).

The suggestion that *night* replace *day* in line one was eloquently rejected by Paul who pointed out that it was only during the day that the bat acted like a mouse. The insertion of *big dusty* in line two was defended on the basis of rhythm. *Beat* in line four was also removed for rhythm. The use of *clothes* in line five was clearly wrong but the children had difficulty offering an alternative. Rewriting the line as "He flies in crazy loops half the night" is an elegant solution. The *dead* from *still* change and *seen/missed* were defended on the basis of rhyme.

Some words in this poem have been changed.

The Bat

1. By night the bat is cousin to the mouse
2. He likes the attic of ~~an~~ [big dusty] old house.
3. His fingers make a hat on his head.
4. His pulse ~~beat~~ is so slow we think him ~~still~~ [dead].
5. ~~She~~ [He flies] ~~loops~~ in crazy ~~clothes~~ [loops] half the night.
6. Among the trees that face the corner light.
7. But when he brushes up against a screen
8. You are afraid of what our eyes have ~~missed~~ [seen]:
9. For something is amiss or out of place
10. When mice with wings can wear a human smile.

Figure 2.33 A disturbed version of "The Bat" by Theodore Roethke, with suggested amendments

Not every suggestion was productive, but they were all authentic attempts by the children to respond sensitively to the meaning and form of Roethke's poem.

When we showed the original, the children noted that the use of *aged* in line two was certainly an improvement over *old*. *About* in line three is better than *on*.

Next we gave half the class the poem "Mix a Pan-

Mix a Pancake

Mix a pancake
Stir a pancake
Pop it in the pan
Fry the pancake
Toss the pancake, —
Catch it if you can.

Christina Rossetti

Figure 2.34 The original version of "Mix a Pancake" by Christina Rossetti

Pancake

Mix a pancake
Stir a pancake
Pour it in the pan
Cook the pancake
Flip the pancake
Catch it if you can.

Figure 2.35 A child's disturbed version of "Mix a Pancake"

Sidewalk Racer or On the Skateboard

Skimming
an asphalt sea
I swerve, I curve, I
sway; I speed to a whirring
sound an inch above the
ground; I'm the sailor
and the sail, I'm the
driver and the wheel
I'm the one and only
single engine
human auto
mobile.

Lillian Morrison

Figure 2.36 The original version of "Sidewalk Racer" by Lillian Morrison

Sidewalk Racer or On the Skateboard

Skimming
an asphalt sea
I swerved, I curved, I
Sway; I speed to a whirring
sound an inch above the
ground; I'm the sailor
and the sail, I'm the
captain of the wheel
I am the one and only
signal engine
human auto
mobile

Figure 2.37 A child's disturbed version of "Sidewalk Racer"

My fingers are antennae whatever they touch bud rose apple cellophane crutch they race the feel into my brain plant it there and begin again this is how I knew hot from cold before I was even two years old this is how I can tell though years away that elephant hide feels leathery grey my brain never loses a touch I bring frail of an eggshell pull of a string beat of a pulse that tells me life thumps in a person but not in a knife signs that say please don't touch disappoint me very much

Figure 2.38 A destructured version of "My Fingers" by Mary O'Neill

My Fingers

My Fingers are antennae.
Whatever they touch:
Bud, rose, apple
Cellophane, crutch—
They race the feel
Into my brain,
Plant it there and
Begin again.
This is how I knew
Hot from cold
Before I was even
Two years old.
This is how I can tell,
Though years away,
That elephant hide
Feels leathery grey.
My brain never loses
A touch I bring:
Frail of an eggshell,
Pull of a string,
Beat of a pulse
That tells me life
Thumps in a person
But not in a knife
Signs that say:
"Please do not touch"
Disappoint me
Very much

Figure 2.39 The original and undisturbed version of "My Fingers"

cake" (figure 2.34) and the other half "Sidewalk Racer" (figure 2.36).

We asked the children to copy their poem, altering three words, and pass it to a friend for close observation. The three word limit was intended to prevent the destruction of the original fabric of the poem by too many substitutions, but it turned out to be too constraining. Many children made minor changes in personal pronouns. A review of our own samples showed we used seven or eight changes per poem and we realized we should have given the children the same latitude.

We were still delighted with some of the responses. The version shown in figure 2.35 retains both the sense and the single syllable in the three new verbs.

Lillian Morrison, in her poem "Sidewalk Racer or On the Skateboard" (figure 2.36) changes from a maritime to a motor metaphor. Jordie decided to sustain the maritime theme (figure 2.37) as he amended (but sustained) the internal rhyme in *swerved/curved*. Note the subtle change from *single* to *signal*.

Destructuring Poems

Presenting a poem in prose form is a much more subtle and demanding routine (figure 2.38).

No words are added or deleted. No attempt is made to render it as actual prose. The original words of the poem are simply set out in unbroken, unpunctuated lines and the children are asked to decide on the line arrangement and add any punctuation they feel is appropriate. Line arrangements can be shared with a partner, discussed and justified. Then the children look at the original arrangement (as in figure 2.39) and compare it with their own.

Skills Development

These routines ask children to attend to poetic intent, syntax, repetition, rhyming words, rhythm and alliteration, and encourage them to approach poetry critically and reflect on the poet's use of words. Some children may begin to appreciate the multiple constraints involved in poetic word choices. They are also asked to consider the significance of line arrangements.

The actual "skills" addressed are determined by the nature of the poems you select and the poetic techniques you choose to highlight.

SEMANTIC FEATURES

Pearson and Johnson (1979) suggest the use of semantic features as a means of promoting vocabulary development. Like all good vocabulary development activities, this involves a high degree of comprehension. They use the technique with expository material; we've also tried applying it to narratives.

semantic features / story concepts	boy	Velveteen Rabbit	Skin Horse	Nana	fairy	wild rabbits	model boat	nursery		
real	+1	+2	+2	+1	−1	+1	−1			
soft	+1	−	+1	+1	+1	+1	−1			
human	+1	−1	−1	+1	−1	+1	−1			
real life	+1	+2	+1	+1	−1	+1	+1			
inside	+2	+2	+1	+2	+1	−1	+1			
young	+1	+1	−1	−1	+1	0	2			
modern	0	−1	−1	0	0	0	+1			
important	+1	+2	+1	+1	+1	+1	+1			
magic	−1	−1	−1	−1	+1	−1	−1			
Total ∓										

Figure 2.40 A semantic feature list based on **The Velveteen Rabbit**

Creating Feature Lists

The example in figure 2.40 is based on Margery Williams' *The Velveteen Rabbit*. In choosing semantic features we selected ideas or values that were addressed in the story and made sure the concepts to be rated were characters, objects or localities that are significant to the story.

The heart of the activity lies in the selection of the features the story concepts will be rated against, to ensure that the children will review significant aspects of the story. We usually leave lists of features and concepts open ended and invite the children to add ideas of their own.

It's difficult to create a list of features that will apply to every story concept. For example, being modern or old-fashioned is discussed as it applies to the toys in *The Velveteen Rabbit.* Modernity is not mentioned in connection with the boy, Nana, the fairy or the wild rabbits. Consequently we have a four-point coding system (see figure 2.41)

Some clarification of the features may be necessary. For example, *real life* addresses whether the concept can or can't occur in real life. Thus the boy is not a fantasy figure but the fairy is. *Inside* refers to whether the character remained inside the house or outside it. We rated both the boy and Velveteen Rabbit as +/- since they functioned both inside and outside. Skin Horse was always in the nursery. The wild rabbits were always outside.

Some terms may be left deliberately open to varying interpretations; for example, we've rated Velveteen Rabbit as +/– on real life because both stuffed toy rabbits and real wild rabbits occur in the real world. However, we would acknowledge the idea that toy rabbits do not turn into live rabbits. Thus the item could be rated with a minus sign.

We aren't searching for correct or incorrect responses, but for those with reasonable justification. We *would* question matters of fact. If a child rated *The Velveteen Rabbit* as hard we would want to know why and be sure to have it noted that the author specifically said the toy was soft.

It's possible to ask for children's justification in writing, but we prefer oral rationales. Seventy-two statements would be required to complete figure 2.40; we prefer to use the rating sheets as the basis for oral sharing, comparing and discussing.

	Rating	Score
The concept does have that characteristic	+	+1
The concept does not have that characteristic	–	–1
The concept does have it at one point and does not at another	+/–	+2
The concept does not apply	0	0

Figure 2.41 The four-point coding system used for semantic features

You can give the activity some focus by asking "Which character or object is the most important in the story?" Each rating is converted into a score and the scores for each concept are totalled. If the characteristics have been well chosen, the most significant character will receive the highest score. With older children questions such as "Which character changes the most?" or "Which character is the most complex?" can be raised. Characters with the greatest number of

+/- ratings will be chosen. However, because of the variability of interpretation, we don't take the numbers very seriously. We'd be quite prepared to admit that character X came out with the highest score but that we still believe character Y is the best developed. And we'd review our list of features to see if we had overlooked any significant characteristic.

Introducing Feature Lists

We introduce the routine by means of a simple story the children are already familiar with, to show them how the procedure works. The example is based on *The Three Billy Goats Gruff* (see figure 2.42).

semantic features / story concepts	Big Billy Goat Gruff	Little Billy Goat Gruff	the troll	the bridge		
living	+					
animal		+				
real world			–			
large	+					
hungry	+/–					
dangerous				0		

***Figure 2.42 A semantic feature list based on* The Three Billy Goats Gruff**

Once the children are *thoroughly* familiar with the procedure we ask them to select a story, develop their own semantic feature list and choose the story concepts to be analyzed. This step is a valuable move towards independence, but its limitations should be acknowledged. We've already noted that the key to the rating activity lies in the selection of the features. Your mature appreciation of the story should enable you to perceive the more subtle or abstract elements, patterns or values being addressed and you should therefore be able to select those terms that will help the children think about the story in a reflective manner.

If the children select semantic features from a story only they have read, without your guidance, they can't go beyond their own current level of understanding; their selection of specific features will be a reflection of their present degree of comprehension and may not lead to a greater depth of appreciation. Consequently, working through challenging examples you've prepared before asking the children to try devising their own is crucial. Both are necessary. The former are designed to enrich and elevate the children's language capacity. The latter provide opportunity for them to practice independently and consolidate their newly acquired language skills.

Language growth will also occur when the children are required to prepare a semantic feature analysis activity for a friend. After a story is read to the whole class, partners independently prepare a worksheet complete with semantic features and concepts to be rated. Then they exchange papers, complete the exercise and return it to the originator. Together the two children discuss the expected and actual responses, and since each child will have a slightly different perception of the story, this sharing may lead both partners to an expanded appreciation of the text.

At a later date the routine might be repeated with each partner choosing a book, reading it, preparing a semantic feature chart and exchanging books and worksheets for completing and sharing. However, adults are better language models than children. While interaction with peers is a valuable and necessary part of the language program, interaction with adults is also vital.

Skills Development

Responding to semantic feature lists requires the making of inferences and judgments and the provision of substantiating material by reference to the text. It also contributes to vocabulary growth.

REACTING TO PROPOSITIONS

Developing Propositions

This routine is a minor variation on the old true/false test items, but we carefully include inferential and critical statements, not just statements of fact. We initiate the routine by generating a set of statements based on a text the children then become familiar with through listening or reading. We ask them to determine whether or not the statements are supported by the text, suggesting that through either quotation or paraphrase they cite that portion, or those portions, of the text that provide the support.

Propositions

1. Dete lives in Dorfli.
2. Dete is generous and unselfish.
3. Dete feels guilty about leaving Heidi with the Alm-Uncle.
4. Heidi is a cautious child.
5. The Alm-Uncle is a regular churchgoer.
6. Heidi will be happy with her grandfather.

***Figure 2.43 A set of propositions based on Chapter 1 of* Heidi**

For older children we include statements that are neither supported nor denied, or statements that receive both support and denial from the text (figure 2.43). For younger children it's probably better to use statements that are for the most part unambiguously supported or denied (figure 2.44).

Spyri's *Heidi*: a synopsis of Chapter 1
Dete, who has cared for Heidi since she was just one year old, now has a job in Frankfurt. She has brought Heidi to Dorfli to give her over to her grandfather, the fierce old hermit-like Alm-Uncle. While Dete gossips, Heidi plays with Peter. Heidi's grandfather accepts her less than graciously.

Variations

This routine may be modified in many ways.

- *Story presentation.* The children may listen to the story as you read it aloud, follow along in their own copies or read it silently for themselves.
- *Propositions.* Propositions may be presented orally or in writing.
- *Levels.* Propositions may require responses at critical, inferential or literal levels.
- *Sources.* Propositions may be supported or denied from one or more places in the text.
- *Responses.* Responses may be oral or written.
- *Sequence.* Propositions may be presented before the story to provide a purpose for listening or after to stimulate discussion.

With young or less able children we prefer a lot of oral work. You should note, however, that oral work of this sort means only a few children are called upon to share their ideas overtly. You won't know what degree of involvement non-participants have. A higher proportion of reading and writing can be demanded from older and more competent children, and written responses will increase the likelihood of active participation by all the children.

Creating propositions from a self-selected text is quite demanding. Many children will generate concrete, factual statements rather than statements calling for inference and judgment. You can give guidance by modeling: have them listen to (or read) yet another text, then ask them to generate propositions which you collate on the chalkboard. Examine each suggestion for the quality of thought required to react to it. You may also want to explain/model what determines a critical, inferential or literal proposition. There's a good deal of abstraction involved in this and perhaps only older and more competent language users should try.

Propositions
1. No one noticed Harry's new sweater.
2. Harry tried three times to lose the sweater.
3. The bird started to loosen the stitches in Harry's sweater.
4. Harry was given two sweaters.
5. Harry felt guilty when he heard Grandma was coming.
6. No one could find Harry's sweater.

***Figure 2.44 Propositions for* No Roses for Harry**

Implementation

We had intended to use the proposition around Zion's *No Roses for Harry* for a third grade class, but a scheduling error resulted in our teaching the lesson to a grade four group. We were afraid the children might find the story beneath them and the activity too easy but were wrong on both counts. They enjoyed the story and found some parts of the activity challenging.

> **Zion's *No Roses for Harry*: a synopsis**
> Harry, a small black and white dog, tries to lose a hated sweater sent by Grandma. A loose end is picked up by a bird and the sweater unravels. Grandma comes to visit and the missing sweater is found, now functioning as a bird's nest.

We discussed written answers to propositions one to four orally and got suggestions for possible wordings for the justifications. We stressed that every rationale had to be based on information from the story.

Name Irene

True or False?

Read each sentence. Say if it is true or false. Explain why.

✓ No one noticed Harry's new sweater.
It is false The people laughed and the dogs barked.

✓ Harry tried three times to lose the sweater.
Yes. He tried to losed it in the Pet dept. and Flower dept. Grocry dept.

✓ The bird started to loosen the stitches in Harry's sweater. No.
No he didn't losen it beacuse there was a string that was lose and Harry started to pull.

✓ Harry was given two sweaters.
True. Yes he was given two sweaters beacause Harry and the bird started to pull the string on the first sweater.

5. Harry felt guilty when he heard Grandma was coming.
True I think True beacause Harry felt guilty beacause he had pull the striging out of the sweater.

6. No one could find Harry's sweater.
True I think it is true beacause know one could find his sweater beacause he only Knows were it is.

Figure 2.45 Written responses by Irene to propositions based on No Roses for Harry

Figure 2.45 shows Irene's written responses. Like Irene, many of the children had difficulty with item five: "Harry felt guilty when he heard Grandma was coming." The text, when Grandma's imminent arrival is announced, says, "Harry thought of his sweater and his tail drooped."

All the children agreed that item five was true. The justifications provided included:

- Harry had lost his sweater.
- He knew that the sweater was gone. Grandma might get mad.
- He was scared that Grandma would get mad because he ruined the sweater.
- Harry felt guilty because Grandma was coming to see the sweater and him.

The children seemed to apply their knowledge of the world to the situation rather than citing the information actually provided by the text. We didn't criticize them (their responses were eminently sensible) but they needed to be helped to see the difference between what seems likely and the actual evidence in the text from which inferences can be made.

The children taught us that one challenge at a time is enough. A challenging activity based on a simple story is a good learning situation. When the activity has been mastered it can be applied to more demanding texts.

Skills Development

Reacting to propositions involves literal, inferential and critical comprehension. It requires listening, reading or rereading for a purpose and the substantiation of a judgment by reference to the text. Vocabulary development can be incorporated if the propositions include challenging vocabulary items from the story.

STORY GRAMMARS

Several types of story grammars have been described in the research literature. The form we've found most useful is based on a concept developed by Applebee (1978), based on the idea that a child moves through a series of developmental stages which include:

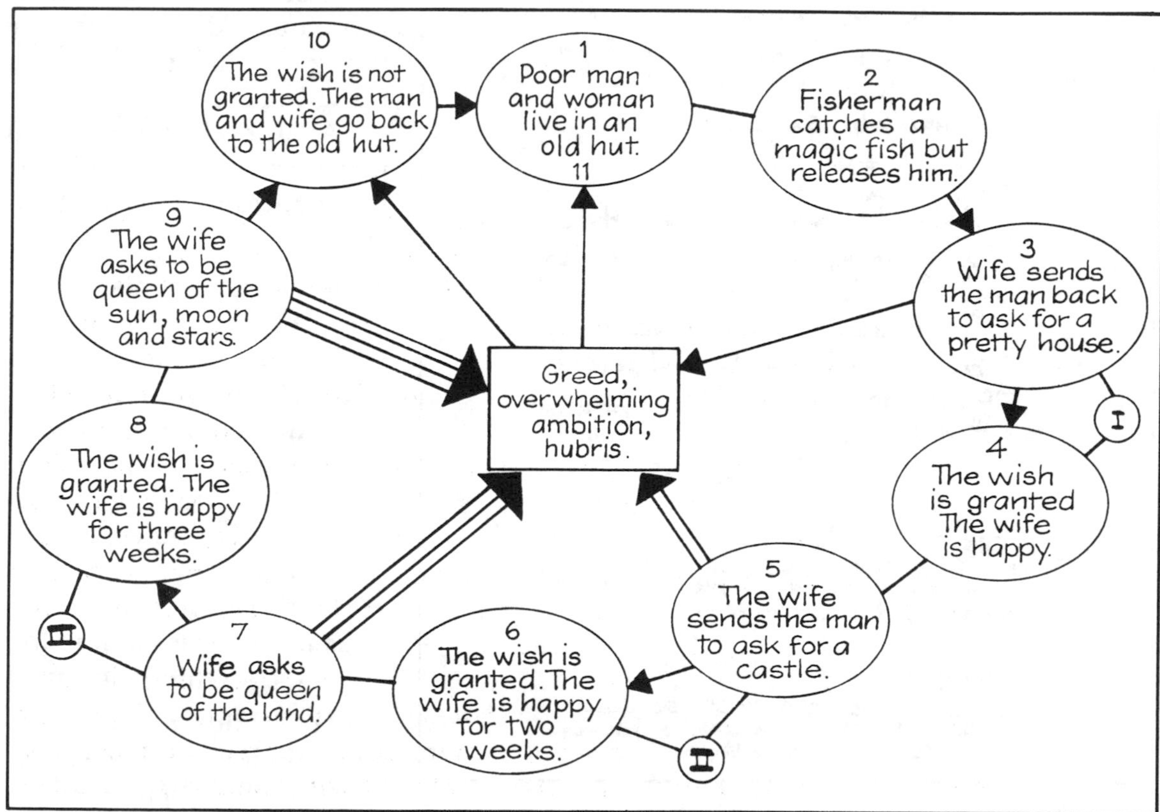

Figure 2.46 A story grammar based on **The Magic Fish**

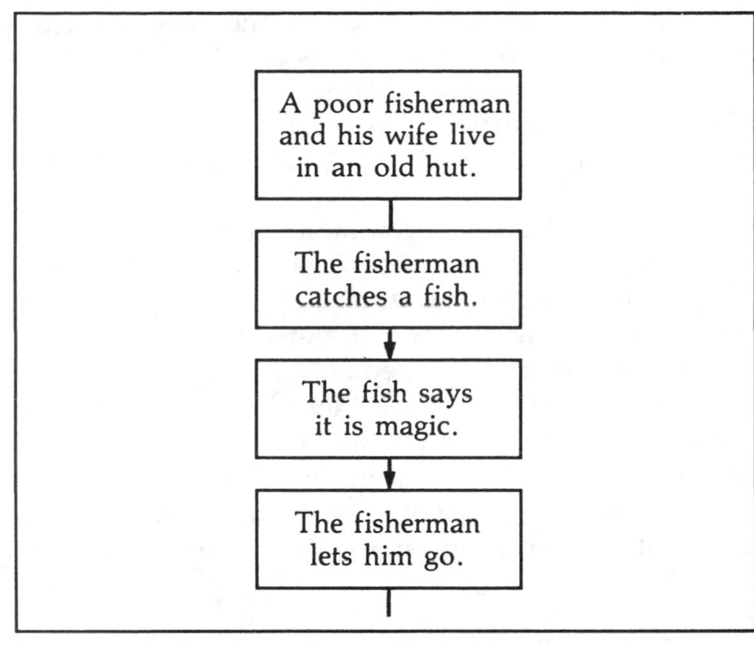

Figure 2.47 A listing of the opening events in **The Magic Fish**

- seeing stories as a series of discrete events
- seeing stories as a series of connected events
- finally perceiving stories as a series of connected events developed around a central idea.

This notion permits us to share the rhythms of narrative while still retaining the impact of each individual story.

A Simple Circular Tale

Figure 2.46 shows a story grammar based on *The Magic Fish* (Littledale's version). The events are arranged in a circle, reflecting the circle we perceive this tale to be (see also The Problems of Getting There: A Unit in Literary Map Making, pages 117-121). In this tale the fisherman and his wife begin in an old hut, rise in the world and return to where they started.

We chose to break the story up into ten events; it's possible to break it into much finer steps as shown in figure 2.47. Close analysis has the advantage of including the fine-grain detail by which young children recall the story. However, it results in an unwieldy number of events and a very complex diagram. Reducing the number of events encourages the children to summarize.

The form used in figure 2.46 indicates the relationships between events with a line or an arrow. A line indicates that one event is simply followed by another in time; an arrow indicates a causal connection. The wife sends her husband back to the fish in event three because he had caught the fish in event two. The level at which most children will respond to the story suggests that the connection between events four and five is merely temporal; event five is simply the next thing that happens. A more complex analysis might show that the wife's greed underlies all her actions, so her increasing demands are all causally connected.

The statements in the box at the center of the diagram represent different levels of thematic interpretation. Young children may simply agree that the woman's downfall was a punishment because she was greedy; a more sophisticated audience may appreciate that it's her fatally flawed character combined with the passive acquiescence of the fisherman that brings about their inevitable downfall.

The striped arrows indicate which events contribute (most) to the theme development. The increasing number of stripes on each arrow reflects the wife's mounting greed. Arrows that lead from events to the theme indicate the flow of the action. At steps 3, 5, 7 and 9 it's the wife who provides the driving force of the narrative. At steps 10 and 11 the situation is reversed. The magic fish says "No" and sets things as they were.

The Roman numerals indicate the Rule of Three, a common pattern in children's books. Three times the wife asks for more and three times her wish is granted. When wife and tale violate this rule, disaster falls upon the couple.

Everything in the diagram is variable: the number of steps, the shape of the diagram (linear, circular, other), the use of thematic statements, indication of causal relationships between events and links between theme and the events that develop it. The sophistication of the diagram depends on the complexity of the story you choose and the maturity of the children. You might begin with a simple listing of events that summarize the story, limiting the discussion to whether they should be laid out in a circle or in a straight line. You could introduce further aspects with additional stories.

Caveat

Our sophisticated analysis of this simple tale far exceeds anything we would attempt with the young children who would normally read it; we wanted you to focus on the routine itself, not how it might further understanding of the story — as a sort of model for upper primary and secondary students or student-teachers of how to develop story grammars. But the ultimate goal is to use a story grammar for the development of deeper insights into the workings of *complex* and *challenging* stories.

The Linear Tale

In many stories the central characters set out into the world to seek fame and fortune. They are soon beset by misfortune but, with effort, good luck and timely help, they win out. It seems reasonable to develop a linear diagram for those linear wish fulfillment stories.

Roland the Minstrel Pig (Steig) is an archetypal example of a linear journey of wish fulfillment (figure 2.48). The main events have been laid out in a smooth curve to represent the major rise and fall in tension. Things start out calmly (event 1), rise to a climax (10) and fall away to a satisfactory resolution (12 and 13).

The connections between events 2, 3, 4, 5 and 6 are ostensibly temporal. All these "inexplicable" dangers just seem to happen. However, the readers' knowledge of literary foxes and not so subtle verbal and pictorial hints alert them to the fox's true motive. So these events are also connected by the fox's base desire for a meal. Events 9 and 13 involve changes in point of view. In 9 we see things from the King's position; in 13 we learn of the fox's fate. These changes are represented by placing the events out of the main sequence of the story.

The Rule of Three shows up again in events 3, 4 and 5. As in *The Magic Fish*, violation (6) brings about the downfall of the fox.

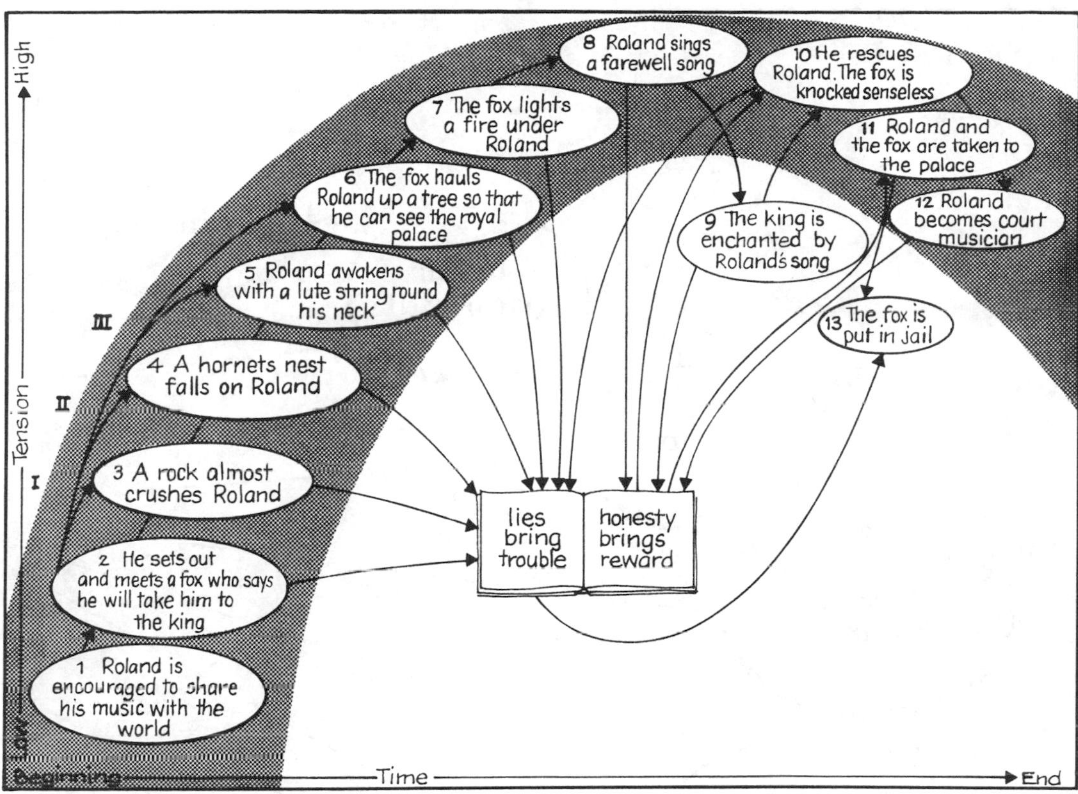
High
Tension
Low
I
II
III
1 Roland is encouraged to share his music with the world
2 He sets out and meets a fox who says he will take him to the king
3 A rock almost crushes Roland
4 A hornets nest falls on Roland
5 Roland awakens with a lute string round his neck
6 The fox hauls Roland up a tree so that he can see the royal palace
7 The fox lights a fire under Roland
8 Roland sings a farewell song
9 The king is enchanted by Roland's song
10 He rescues Roland. The fox is knocked senseless
11 Roland and the fox are taken to the palace
12 Roland becomes court musician
13 The fox is put in jail
lies bring trouble
honesty brings reward
Beginning
Time
End

Figure 2.48 A story grammar based on **Roland the Minstrel Pig**

The arrows going to "Lies bring trouble" represent the trouble that the fox's lies bring to Roland. The arrows leaving this statement and connecting with 10 and 13 represent the turning of the tables as the fox's lies bring about just retribution. Conversely Roland's artless desire to perform his art brings about his salvation (10) and reward (11 and 12).

This diagram reflects *our* interpretation, not a final or definitive one. Other readers may justifiably have other ways of depicting the story. Understanding and appreciation come from attempts to represent and share our own understanding and to hear the view of others, as well as from dispute, debate and defense.

A Circular Journey

Call It Courage (Sperry) is a modified circular story. The opening events, which provide the reason for Mafatu's problem, are sequenced in time rather than space and told in the form of a flashback. From then on the events are organized in both time and space as Mafatu faces his fears. It's difficult to represent accurately the proportions within stories involving physical journeys since outward journeys tend to be long and filled with arduous incidents while returns are usually swiftly told and incident-free. In figure 2.49 the circular pattern erroneously suggests that Mafatu makes his way home almost as painfully and as gradually as he sets out. In fact the

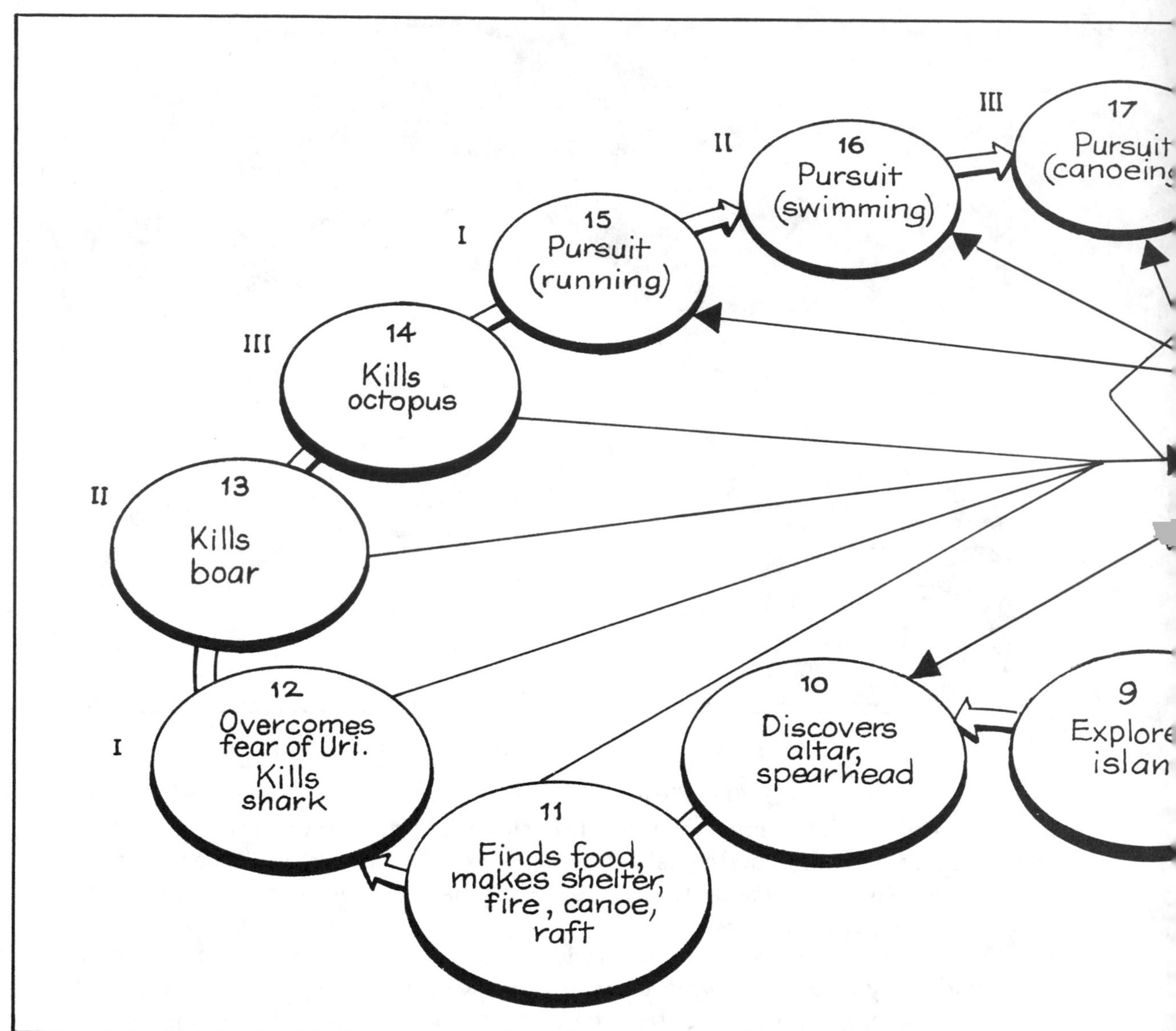

Figure 2.49 A story grammar based on **Call it Courage**

journey home is told in the fifth and final chapter. We've tried to overcome this distortion by having the artist present the circle as seen from above at a sharp angle so it appears as an ellipse. However some exaggeration of the return journey remains.

Whether events are causally or simply temporally connected isn't always a simple decision. The storm at sea (event 5) isn't caused by Mafatu's leaving (4); but Mafatu finds himself at sea in a storm because he left home. The point can be argued either way and the resolution is almost irrelevant. The dispute is what promotes understanding.

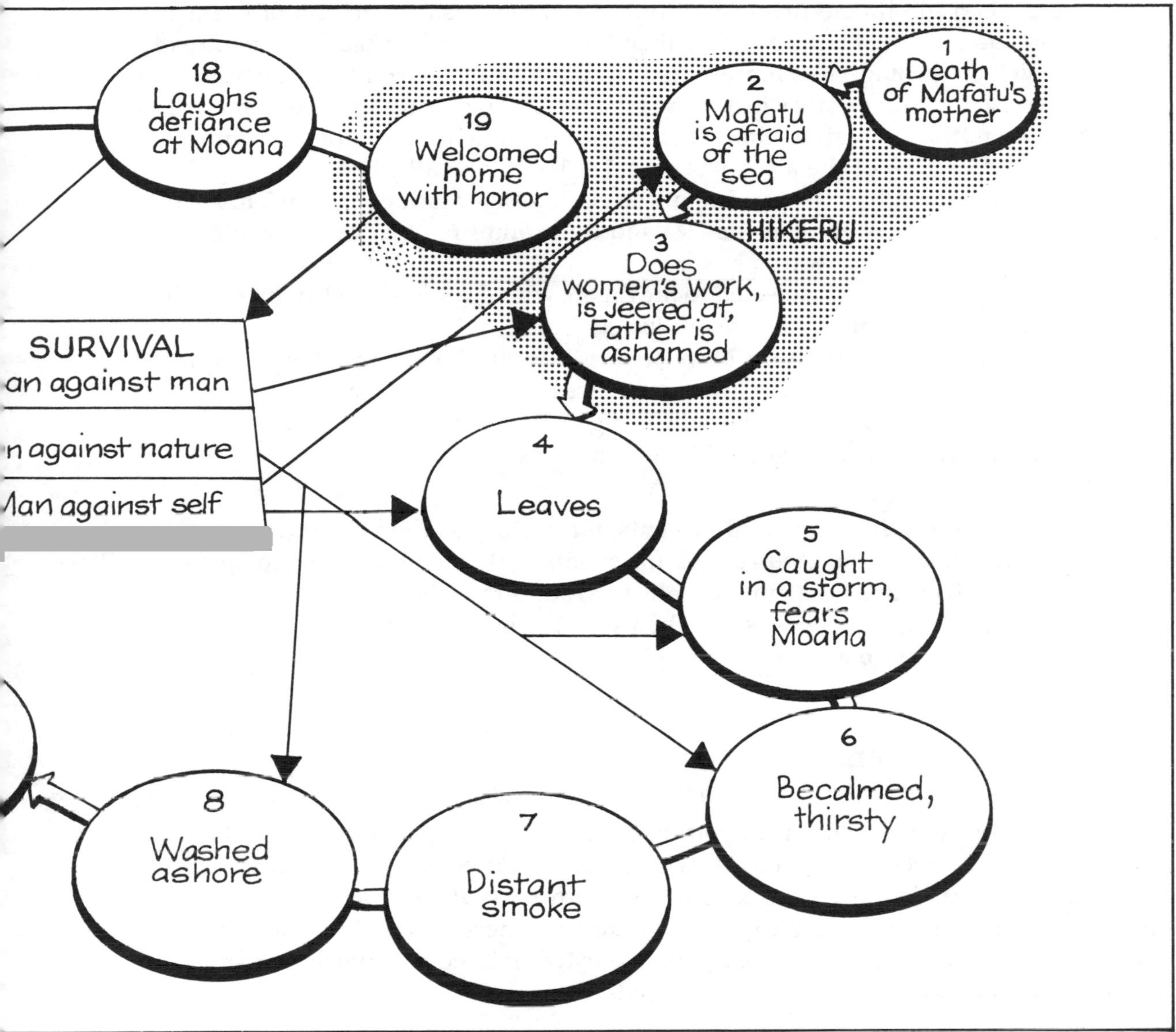

A more sophisticated analysis can go beyond the relationships between adjacent events and explore the connections between quite widely separated events. For example, the distant smoke (event 7) seems innocuous enough at first but turns out to foreshadow the discovery of the altar (10). Both events contribute to the climactic pursuit (15, 16, 17).

The Rule of Three shows in several ways: once in the killing of the beasts (12, 13 and 14) and again in the pursuit by the cannibals (15, 16 and 17). It is also evident in the three companions (Mafatu, Uri the dog and Kiri the albatross) and in the three settings: Hikeru, the sea and the cannibal island.

We've broken the theme of survival into the three classic conflicts of literature: man against man, against nature and against himself. In the first part events threaten to overwhelm the protagonist, represented by arrows going from the thematic statements to the events. As the story progresses the protagonist learns to overcome or live with the forces that threaten him. This is represented in the story grammar by reversing the direction of the arrows (11, 12, 13, 14, 18 and 19). The turning point in the story is represented by the turning of the circle. As Mafatu overcomes his fear of the altar (10), sees to his basic needs (11) and overcomes his fear of the sea (12), the circle begins to turn back towards Hikeru.

Events 15, 16 and 17 are connected to the theme with double-ended arrows because the cannibals menace Mafatu but are outwitted.

This is a relatively simple story. Nevertheless, for our diagram we have simplified and summarized considerably. Our experiences tell us that overly fine-grained analyses of novels produce an overwhelming mass of confusing visual data. We recommend that you use the Twenty Events Rule. It says:

- During the first draft set out the events of the story as they occur to you.
- Count them. If they exceed 20 look for events that can be omitted, collapsed or summarized until the number falls to around that number.
- If this turns out to be impossible, then select a portion of the novel and do a partial story grammar.

Statements Of Theme

We've had very little success in getting children to state the underlying theme of a story. Numerous secondary school teachers have reported the same, that it's next to impossible to get their students to construct something as abstract as a theme. Perhaps children, even adolescents, can't do it. The same teachers agreed that their students could recognize how a given theme, once suggested, related to a particular story.

We recommend that:

- any discussion of theme not be attempted before the upper levels of elementary schools, and
- children be provided with thematic statements rather than being asked to formulate such statements for themselves.

We try to devise phrases that result in the greatest number of connections to the events of the story. If we can't justify a connection between our thematic statement and a significant number of the events, we try to broaden our statement or introduce a second statement that connects with most of the remaining events. In the *Roland* example we were tempted by "virtue brings its reward" with its inverse understood:

"the wages of sin are death." But those phrases may not be self-evident to even our more sophisticated readers, so we offered our own two mirror-image statements. We invite you to substitute your own thematic statements for the book; you may have different observations to make.

Variations

Many other aspects of the story might be represented. To depict them all in one diagram would result in a hopeless visual clutter, but several interpretations can be recorded on the chalkboard in a series of diagrams. Simple diagrams can be elaborated. Competing interpretations set side by side can be compared. One set of relations can be erased and a new set presented. Diagrams can be developed, extended or revised as the story unfolds.

We suggested how events could be clustered by circling all those things that happened on Hikeru. Events at sea and on the cannibal island could be similarly clustered. Events that portray setting, problem, reaction, attempt, consequence, climax and denouement can be similarly marked, as can parallel plot constructions, points of view and flashbacks. The routine is generally flexible enough to summarize whatever writing stratagem has been used in the story if it is also within the ability of the children to appreciate.

We hope these three examples of story grammars demonstrate the flexible nature of the routine. Different aspects of the three stories have been presented. Similar aspects have been symbolized in different ways. The same approach has been used to show different aspects of the story. A story grammar isn't really a structure to be imposed on a story; it's a routine that can be used to:

- explore the various structures, patterns and rhythms used by the author, and
- share with other readers our attempt to interpret the story.

A story grammar almost always yields something new about a story. Our only caution is against the heavy analysis of simple stories; such analysis often fails to reveal any further insights anyway because the story was well understood on the first reading.

Skills Development

The type of story grammar we describe helps children to appreciate story structure. It involves all levels of comprehension, sequence and cause and effect relationships. Any writing strategies used by the author — foreshadowing, parallel plot construction, repetition — can be examined. However, story grammars rise above separate skills and encourage the children to represent their understanding of the story in an integrated and wholistic manner.

READERS' THEATER

Definition

Readers' theater is the dramatization of a story that involves using the text of a narrative as a play script. Performers face the audience and read directly from the script; lines need not be memorized. Photocopied material can be selectively underlined or highlighted to assist in reading a particular part, as an aid to interpretation. Minor changes in wording may occur but extensive rewriting to form a play script is neither necessary nor desirable.

Overview

We use nine steps to introduce readers' theater to children. Modeling can be reduced or eliminated once the children are familiar with the procedure.

1. Select two suitable stories: A and B.
2. Have a group of older children prepare story A as readers' theater.
3. Read story A to your class. (You may wish to delete the ending.)
4. Have the older children come in and present story A to your class as readers' theater.
5. Interview the older children regarding their preparation for the presentation.
6. Read story B to your class.
7. Plan story B as readers' theater.
8. Rehearse, offer constructive criticism, discuss, modify, experiment.
9. Present story B in the form of readers' theater to other classes in the school.

Procedures

Selecting suitable stories

Some stories lend themselves more readily to readers' theater than others. Use stories that have as many of the following characteristics as possible:

1. ***They should have literary merit.*** One of the injustices perpetrated upon generations of children is the selection or creation of poor or mediocre texts because they provide a convenient vehicle for a particular narrow instructional goal. It's important to note that while our focus may be on specific instructional objectives, the children's attention is much more diffuse. If you select a poor story the children may be learning not only about readers' theater but also that school, books and language are boring.

2. ***They should be short.*** Picture books, very short stories, fables and folk tales are usually appropriate. Incidents from novels — especially episodic novels such as *A Bear Called Paddington* (Bond) — work well if they are fairly self-contained.

3. ***They should have several characters.*** This requirement is more managerial than pedagogical. *Frog and Toad Are Friends* (Lobel) may make excellent readers' theater but it involves only two characters. If a single narrator is added, only three children are actively involved — and that makes eight to 10 groups requiring guidance and supervision. If you have aides available, then small groups are excellent since each child has the opportunity for a high level of active involvement.

Another major reason for selecting stories with numerous characters is that readers' theater truly enhances the presentation of the tale. Most readers can manage two or three "voices" for characters as they read but have difficulty maintaining six or more. Stories such as those in *The House at Pooh Corner* (Milne) or *Why Mosquitoes Buzz in People's Ears* (Aardema) have eight or nine characters.

You could also break up stories with fewer characters into scenes or events. Designate teams for each, have each team rehearse separately and then bring the whole class together to perform the entire story. When we used *Nothing to Be Afraid Of* (Mark) with a grade six class we broke the story into six sections, with four or five children assigned to each section.

4. ***They should feature dialogue more than action.*** The players remain seated and thus have limited room for action; facial expression and some gestures are possible, but little else.

Using older students as models

You're in luck if you have a colleague who teaches a more senior class and who has the expertise and willingness to prepare a demonstration for your group. Alternatively, you might coach a small group of older children after school. Perhaps you could invite "graduates" from last year's class to relive former glories. Performances could also be video- or audio-taped and played to subsequent classes.

Reading the demonstration story

Becoming familiar with the story first will free the children's attention so they can attend to the performance. If you are concerned about maintaining motivation, stop reading just before the climax and invite the children to speculate on the outcome. They'll discover the author's solution when the older class comes to present the story. Tell the children also that they will be able to ask the visitors how they prepared their presentation.

Watching the demonstration

The demonstrators should present the story in its entirety, simply enough for the young audience to emulate later what they've seen.

Interviewing the demonstrators

After the performance, lead the class in interviewing the visitors about the steps that led to their presentation. It will help if you've prepared both audience and visitors for this activity.

You should begin the interview to provide examples of the kinds of questions that might be asked, ranging from the general to very specific — for example, from "How did you get started?" to "When you read the part of Gollum you lisped. Why did you read his part like that?" Then the children should ask further questions.

Presenting story B

The manner of presentation will depend on the maturity and expertise of the children. For a first experience with a class of seven to eight-year-olds it would be best to read the story aloud while they follow along. Older and more experienced children could be asked to read the story silently. Motivation will be maintained if they know they are preparing for a performance.

Planning the presentation of story B

Before the class planning sessions you should decide on a tentative selection of parts and their interpretation. This advance work will give you a sense of direction and allow you to provide the necessary leadership. However, you should remain flexible and be willing to follow promising leads offered by the children.

Parts. At the simplest level this means identifying the characters and a narrator. However, some stories provide more complex arrangements. In *Nothing to be Afraid Of* some of the characters' voices can be used in the narration where thoughts or words are reported (figure 2.50).

Nothing to be Afraid Of

Section 1

Narrator 1 to read all narrative parts.

'Robin won't give you any trouble,' said Auntie Lynn. He's very quiet.'

Anthea knew how quiet Robin was. At present he was sitting under the table and, until Auntie Lynn mentioned his name, she had forgotten that he was there.

Auntie Lynn put a carrier bag on the armchair.

'There's plenty of clothes, so you won't need to do any washing, and there's a spare pair of pyjamas in case – well, you know. In case . . .'

'Yes,' said Mum, firmly. 'He'll be all right. I'll ring you tonight and let you know how he's getting along.' She looked at the clock. 'Now, hadn't you better be getting along?

She saw Auntie Lynn to the front door and Anthea heard them saying good-bye to each other. Mum almost told Auntie Lynn to stop worrying and have a good time, which would have been a mistake because Auntie Lynn was going up North to a funeral.

Narrators 2 and 3. Narrator 2 to read underlined parts.

Auntie Lynn was not really an Aunt, but she had once been at school with Anthea's mum, and she was the kind of person who couldn't manage without a handle to her name; so Robin was not Anthea's cousin. Robin was not anything much, except four years old, and he looked a lot younger; probably because nothing ever happened to him. Auntie Lynn kept no pets that might give Robin germs, and never bought him toys that had sharp corners to dent him or wheels that could be swallowed. He wore balaclava helmets and bobble hats in winter to protect his tender ears, and a knitted vest under his shirt in summer in case he overheated himself and caught a chill from his own sweat.

' Perspiration,' said Auntie Lynn.

His face was as pale and flat as a saucer of milk, and his eyes floated in it like drops of cod-liver oil. This was not so surprising as he was full to the back teeth with cod-liver oil; also with extract of malt, concentrated orange juice and calves-foot jelly. When you picked him up you expected him to squelch, like a hot-water bottle full of half-set custard.

Anthea lifted the tablecloth and looked at him.

'Hello, Robin.'

Robin stared at her with his flat eyes and went back to sucking his woolly doggy that had flat eyes also, of sewn-on felt, because glass ones might find their way into Robin's appendix and cause damage. Anthea wondered how long it would be before he noticed that his mother had gone. Probably he wouldn't, any more than he would notice when she came back.

Narrator 1 to read all narrative parts.

Mum closed the front door and joined Anthea in looking under the table at Robin. Robin's mouth turned down at the corners, and Anthea hoped he would cry so that they could cuddle him. It seemed impolite to cuddle him before he needed it. Anthea was afraid to go any closer.

'What a little troll,' said Mum, sadly, lowering the tablecloth. 'I suppose he'll come out when he's hungry.'

Anthea doubted it . . .

Figure 2.50 ***An assignment of narrator parts for the opening of* Nothing to be Afraid Of *by Jan Mark***

"Willie" narrator

When Willie awoke it was still very dark. The pain that had brought him sharply back to consciousnesss seared through his stomach. He held his breath and pushed his hand down the bed to touch his nightgown. It was soaking. It was then that he became aware that he was lying in between sheets. That's what they did to people after they had died, they laid them out in a bed. He sat up quickly and hit his head on the rafter. Crawling out of bed, doubled over with the pain in his gut, he hobbled over to the window and let out a frightened cry. He was in a graveyard. He was going to be buried alive! The pain grew in intensity. He gave a loud moan and vomited all over the floor.

"Tom" narrator

In the morning Tom found him huddled under the bed. The sheets were drenched in urine. He stripped them off the mattress and carried Willie down to the living room.

It was a hot, sultry day. The windows were wide open but no breeze entered the cottage. Willie stood in front of the stove. Through the side window he could see his gray garments and underwear hanging on a small washing line outside. Tom pulled the voluminous nightshirt over his head and threw it into a copper tub with the sheets. He sluiced Willie's body tenderly with cold water and soap. The weals stuck out mauve against his protruding ribs and swollen stomach. He could hardly stand.

***Figure 2.51 An example of narration divided between two narrators, from* Goodnight, Mr. Tom**

Sometimes a switch from one narrator to another is very effective, whether it is done simply for variety (as with some television news broadcasts), or for artistic reasons. If the story involves a change in point of view, a new narrator can signal that change. For example, the first paragraph of figure 2.51, from Magorian's *Goodnight, Mr. Tom,* depicts Willie; the second tells events from Tom's point of view; the third begins by focussing on Willie and then switches to Tom. A different reader could be assigned for each "narrator."

Interpretation of text. Without becoming too directive you should help the children explore and experiment with various readings. The discussion should focus on what effect the author is trying to achieve at this particular point in the story.

Dialogue. Trying to have the children decide how to read speeches is probably the easiest place to start, since this is where readers are likely to make the most noticeable voice modifications. Father Bear, wolves and trolls might be given gruff voices while children and princesses are given lighter expression. Discussion should focus on how the character is feeling and how this feeling can be expressed by voice, face, stance and gesture.

Narrator. The idea that a reader's voice can change during narration may be a novel one for some children. There are many reasons for doing so: varying speed can help distinguish action from description; tension, alarm, relief, surprise, fatigue, boredom, irony, etc. can be depicted.

Excellent and detailed advice is offered by Mallick (1984). Sam Sebesta, senior author of *Literature for Thursday's Child* (Sebesta and Ivenson, 1975), makes a superbly simple suggestion that achieves many goals without conscious application of technique: become what you read. If the narration describes alarming events, become alarmed. If the listener is to be surprised, then be surprised. If an angry character is described, then become angry. Appropriate voice modifications, facial expressions, posture and gestures will flow naturally.

All interpretation rests on understanding and readers will automatically reflect their understanding of a story. Any activity that promotes understanding will improve interpretation. Reciprocally, efforts to improve interpretation will contribute to increased understanding.

We suggest that identification of parts and the interpretation of text be done with the entire group, since both will involve a careful re-examination of the story as well as discussion of the author's intended effect and the ways that effect can be brought out in the reading.

Rehearsing

We suggest that when you first introduce readers' theater to children you direct rehearsals yourself, with the whole class working on the same story. Later the children can form small groups of three to five students and rehearse independently.

Before the first rehearsal, parts should have been allocated and readers asked to silently reread the *entire* story, since the way a particular speech or line is read may be significantly influenced by some other line quite removed from the one under examination.

Presenting story B to other classes

Real performances provide audience, purpose and motivation for planning and rehearsal. Children should know at step 6 that they too will become performers. Motivation in language learning doesn't rest on high-impact materials, bizarre content or cute, large-eyed, decorative and diverting bunnies, but on involvement in true communicative events.

Developing Independence

The steps described above show just one way readers' theater might be introduced. Since the immediate purpose is to teach the children how to "do" readers' theater, steps 6–9 should be repeated with new stories until they can proceed competently with a degree of independence. Some children will be able to work independently in groups before others. Older children will proceed more rapidly than younger ones. Your own classroom management and the ability of your children to work productively without direct supervision must also be taken into consideration.

Ideally the children will form mutually agreeable friendship groups that select, plan, rehearse and present stories in the form of readers' theater. In practice, younger and less able children will require your continued support, guidance and supervision.

The Value of Oral Reading

Having very young children read orally is vital. They need to experience the sounds and motor behaviors required for it and thus fix as real the thoughts that underlie and initiate oral reading. As they grow older they will become increasingly capable of thought without much outward manifestation. However, the need for some oral reading remains, even for upper primary and secondary students.

Assumptions Regarding Oral Reading

The benefits of oral reading will transfer to silent reading

Such an assumption isn't always justified. However, silent reading is impossible to model. Accomplished readers can talk about but can't demonstrate what they do when they read silently, while reading aloud is a public process that can be both modeled and discussed. Perhaps any increase in children's silent reading abilities accrues from the discussion and practice involved in arriving at an acceptable performance.

Children need to emulate expert models

Children need hundreds of experiences of having a text they can see brought to life by parents, grandparents, older siblings, accomplished peers and tape recordings. Given enough experiences, young readers will emulate these accomplished readers. At first the emulation will be overt and oral, but later it will be internalized to become covert and silent.

Oral reading is a dramatic performing art that requires practice prior to performance

Many traditional teaching practices would disappear if teachers experienced them the way children do. Imagine yourself in a group of peers whose good opinion you seek to maintain. Imagine the presence of a powerful authority figure whose displeasure you try to avoid. Imagine yourself with a rather limited ability to read music and play the violin. Without any advance warning you are handed a piece of music you've never seen before. Some of the notations are unfamiliar to you. You must stand before your peers and play. Discrepancies between the musical score and your rendition will be noted as errors. How well do you think you'd do?

That's what it's like for children who are asked to read an unfamiliar text without preparation. The voice is the instrument that transforms text into a living performance. The reader must view the symbolic markings on the page, decide on the author's intent and add the cadences of human speech implied but not represented in the text. It's little wonder that children stumble now and again. Oral reading must be practiced before it's performed. Reader's theater is offered as a superior substitute for round robin reading.

Round Robin Reading versus Readers' Theater

Worst versus best performance. Imagine now that you were first given an opportunity to hear your teacher play the violin, then a chance to practice privately before being called upon to go public. Professional performers practice for hours before performing.

Models. Round robin reading provides listeners with several examples of poor reading, the last thing they need. The models provided in readers' theater may not be perfect but they'll be close to the best the children are capable of.

Speed. In round robin reading in a grade five class a capable reader may have a

Round robin reading	**Readers' theater**
Readers give their worst performance.	Because practice precedes performance, the quality is improved.
Children provide poor models for each other.	Children provide their best performance for each other.
Good readers are reduced to the speed of the slowest reader.	Speed increases with practice.
Poor readers publicly demonstrate their inability.	Rehearsal enables poor readers to give their best.
Children dread doing it and are bored listening to it.	Children enjoy participating and listening.
No planning is involved. Designated readers deal with limited portions of the text.	Planning and rehearsal around the whole text promote sensitive and thoughtful responses and increased understanding and appreciation.
Neither procedure requires extensive preparation time.	

Figure 2.52 Round robin reading versus readers' theater

silent reading speed of over 200 words per minute — and may have to follow along with a poor oral reader who reads at less than 30 words per minute. Good readers are thus trained to read inappropriately. The amount of material covered is also artificially restricted.

Public humiliation and public glory. Teachers usually did reasonably well in school themselves and don't know what it's like to be the worst reader in the class. Readers' theater doesn't guarantee glory. But each child will have the opportunity to practice and receive guidance before being asked to perform.

Pain or pleasure. Teachers who share their childhood memories of round robin reading are nearly universal in their condemnation of the role of both performer (stress and fear) and audience (boredom). But most people report that they enjoy both the participation and the observance of reader's theater. Children who have reported that they didn't enjoy themselves complained that they didn't have big enough parts! It's important to ensure that the level of participation is distributed as evenly as possible.

Planning. Round robin reading takes the group from beginning to end of a story but there's nothing in the procedure to help children see implied connections or subtle patterns of thought — they will depend on your guidance. In readers' theater the group must deal with the complete text. In *Nothing to Be Afraid Of* Robin says very little but his final speech, "Let's go to the park," carries the crux of the entire story. An understanding of why Robin wants to return and of the way the words are expressed are inextricably linked to every major character, event and mood in the story.

Implementation and Assessment

We used *Nothing to Be Afraid Of* with a sixth grade class.

> ***Nothing to Be Afraid Of*: a synopsis**
> Four-year-old Robin is rendered passive by his domineering and overprotective mother. When he's left in the care of Anthea and her mother, Anthea takes him to the park and terrifies him with imaginary leopards, pythons, witches and Lavatory Demons. Three days later Robin's mother returns to complain about the terrors Anthea has let loose, but Robin sidles up to Anthea to ask if they can go back to the park.

We provided each child with a response sheet (figure 2.53) and reassured them that they wouldn't be marked down for not knowing what any particular word meant. We asked them to think about each word three times: before they read the story, before discussing it and after our discussion together. We also invited suggestions as to the

Indicate how well you know each of these words

✓ = Certain I know ? = Think so X = Sure that I don't

	Before Reading	After Reading	After Discussion		Before Reading	After Reading	After Discussion
1. perspiration				11. diverged			
2. squelch				12. celebration			
3. cod-liver oil				13. circuit			
4. extract of malt				14. doddering			
5. appendix				15. bough			
6. pining				16. bobble			
7. wall-eyed				17. investigate			
8. lamprey				18. lagged			
9. queue				19. Public Conveniences			
10. depending				20. cistern			

Figure 2.53 A self-report form on the learner's perceived level of familiarity with each of twenty words or phrases

meaning of the words, and we confirmed or rejected hypotheses. However, we were at pains to avoid providing definitions.

The children were also asked to indicate their level of acquaintance with each word at one of three levels of familiarity: certain that I know it [3], think that I know it [?], sure that I do not know it [X]. When we analyzed the results we weighted each response:

Certain	2 points
Think so	1 point
Don't know	0 points

	Before reading	After reading	After discussion
mean weighted score	16.25	20.1	29.2
total possible score	40.0	40.0	40.0

Figure 2.54 Mean weighted scores of children's self-report on their familiarity with twenty words and phrases

Figure 2.54 shows the mean-weighted scores. If you accept self-report data as a valid reflection of the children's true level of understanding it's evident that the activity contributed to growth in their understanding of the vocabulary. Mere reading contributes modestly, discussion appears to have a much larger effect. It's tempting to speculate on the results if the children had merely discussed the words without reading the story, as constant references were made to the story during discussions on the meanings of the words. Our intuition is that the discussion would not have been so fruitful had we not all recently experienced the story together.

Short Cuts or Short Circuits?

A number of books on readers' theater present certain stories as play scripts. There are benefits to be derived from regular play scripts, but such materials miss the point of readers' theater, which includes the gains derived when children attempt to transform an author's narrative into a dramatic presentation. Predigested scripts deny them half the challenge and half the learning opportunities by doing half the work.

Skills Development

Readers' theater contributes to the development of literal understanding, making inferences, identifying the author's purpose, character interpretation, identifying mood, reading for a purpose and fluent oral reading.

THEORETICAL REFLECTIONS

The Status of Skills and Strategies

Because "reading" appears in the curriculum and in the daily timetable, it has been regarded as a subject to be learned rather than a competence to be acquired. As a result, a body of knowledge about the nature of writing and the act of reading has developed which is passed on to learners in the belief that it will enhance their capacity to read. Thus children learn that some vowels are "long" and others "short"; that some letter clusters are digraphs, others blends; that paragraphs have topic sentences at the beginning, the middle or the end. Such fragments of knowledge are taught pragmatically; that is, the people who teach them believe that knowledge of such things will help the children decode written words and understand the message.

Much of what is taught is untrue. Almost all of it is irrelevant. Some "long" vowels are shorter than some "short" ones. The distinction between a blend and a digraph is irrelevant to learning to read. Many paragraphs, particularly in narration, don't have topic sentences. In any case, there are millions of competent readers who have never heard of long or short vowels or topic sentences. Such concepts don't describe what people do when they read. "There are a surprising number of long vowels on the front page of the newspaper today." "Yes, but did you notice the paucity of topic sentences in the editorial?" Nonsense! We read to find out what's going on in the world and to become acquainted with the opinions of others about these events. Skills are applied tacitly but aren't part of our conscious thoughts. If they become so, they interfere with and inhibit our central goal: the creation of meaning.

However, people may well grant that reading skills are *applied* tacitly without conceding that they are *acquired* tacitly. We disagree with the skills-based model of reading that presumes learners must be told and made to practice, separately and consciously, a multitude of skills; we maintain that much of the skill of reading *is* acquired tacitly. The details of how written and spoken forms of language are related do arise in the minds of beginning readers (a child in one of our groups wanted to know why cornflakes doesn't have an *x* in it) but beginners have exactly the same goal and orientation as the experts: to make sense of what is written.

Some evidence for the tacit nature of reading acquisition is found in the surprise adults and children exhibit when certain sound/symbol associations are brought to their attention. The past tense of *live* is given a /d/ sound but why is the past tense of *stop* spelled with an ed but pronounced with a /t/ sound? What is the past tense of *leap*? Is it spelled *leaped* or *leapt* and how is it pronounced? "Long e" with a /d/ or "short e" with a /t/? Readers have reported that they never noticed such apparent anomalies. Of course not! Such matters are of little concern to readers. The prime function of the ed in lived and stopped is not to mark a pronunciation but to signal a meaning.

The Nature of Reading Instruction

Linguists make a distinction between surface structure and deep structure. In speaking, surface structure is made up of noises that come from our mouths. In reading, surface structure consists of the marks on the paper. Deep structure, whether

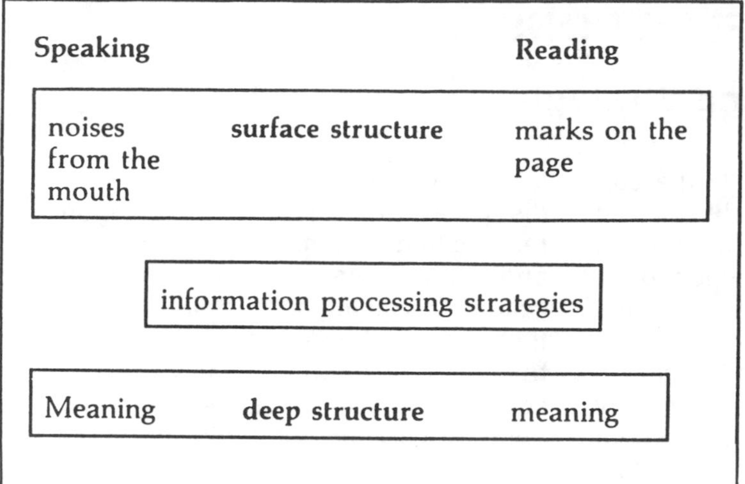

Figure 2.55 Surface and deep structure in speaking and reading

evoked by speech sounds or writing, is meaning.

Skill-based models of instruction address the surface structure in that they attempt to teach the many sound-symbol associations. Unfortunately, the relationship between writing and speech is so complex that the exceptions to rules often outnumber the rules themselves.

Some of the early psycholinguists suggested that meaning could be accessed directly (Smith, 1971). Information-processing models have modified the notion and have attempted to describe some of the general strategies readers use. It is this intermediate level of processing that offers the best entry point for instructional intervention.

Addressing surface structure directly is too superficial, too complex. Besides, it leads to a loss of meaning. But meaning (deep structure) can't be addressed directly since we can offer the learner no advice on how to proceed. Johnson and Louis (1985) and Estes and Vaughan (1986) concluded that instruction should provide the learner with mid-level information-processing strategies. These must be specific enough to be discussed and understood by the learners but general enough to apply to a broad range of reading situations. The application of such strategies leads to increased reading competence. Although the resulting competence can be broken down and described in terms of discrete skills, such skills are not acquired consciously or discretely. They are a by-product of meaningful interactions with print.

Work on metacognition also points to the value of teaching mid-level strategies. Competent readers appear to have the ability to monitor some aspects of their behavior (Baker and Brown, 1984), but only those aspects that have to do with their ability to make sense of the text. The same does not apply to syntactic or sound-symbol associations. Readers often report that they reread if they lose the thread of the author's argument; they don't report that they identified the main verb and subordinate clauses, nor that they noticed a certain blend, digraph or short vowel.

CHAPTER 3

BRINGING IT ALL TOGETHER

INTRODUCTION

While the suggestions in the preceding chapter will have some value if used on an *ad hoc* basis, their maximum benefit will be realized when they form part of a coherent curriculum made up of developmentally sequenced teaching units. In this chapter we describe some of the projects we've tried that incorporate those suggestions.

Our purpose is twofold: to convince you that such projects can be implemented and sustained without any extraordinary investment in time, energy, materials or effort, and to provide enough information for you to try something similar.

In selecting the units to include we kept in mind the usual needs of the elementary grades (K–7), as well as variety in length, topic and activity.

Limits to Integration

Few curricula are designed with integration in mind. Curriculum development is usually produced by subject area specialists whose rationale and structure don't necessarily coincide with the rationales and structures produced by specialists in other disciplines. This problem becomes acute when curricula designate content — when certain math concepts are required at a designated grade level, for instance, while other concepts, skills and specific content are required in language arts, social studies, music and physical education. As a result you might have to teach long division, business letters, European explorers, the migration of birds, harmony and soccer, each topic part of its own ongoing sequence. Yet there's no way you can sensibly incorporate all these topics into a single, unified curriculum.

We've found that we *can* sensibly and productively integrate *some* subject areas for *some* of the time. Language arts, social studies and science offer numerous opportunities for integration, with art and music frequently easy to incorporate into all three. But our art educator colleagues, for example, object when art is relegated to the role of handmaiden to other "more useful" subjects. They claim that art has a legitimacy of its own, with a characteristic developmental sequence, and deserves at times to be the central focus of the learners' attention. We make the same claim for literature, although we soundly reject the idea of language, reading, writing or spelling being regarded as *subjects*. These are "empty" processes that are best learned in the role of handmaiden to the content areas.

Keep in mind the clear difference between integration and correlation. In an *integrated* program, certain important aspects of two or more subjects are deployed to achieve goals centered around a substantial theme: a specific disaster, racial tension, the solar system, the water cycle, loneliness or survival, for instance. *Correlation* occurs when a trivial topic is used as a justification to tie together unrelated activities. "Eggs" is not a theme. The connections between doing egg science, egg social studies, egg literature and egg math are trivial and spurious. They don't achieve the goal of helping children to perceive their world as a dynamic set of interconnections. Successful integration is founded on a substantial conceptual base.

Conceptualizing Units of Literature

Our work usually springs from literature, but starting points can occur in any of the other subject areas. Devising a literature unit is relatively easy once the focus of the project has been determined. All you need to do is locate and sequence relevant material and devise appropriate activities. It may be harder to decide on the focus, since that demands a fairly broad familiarity with the world of children's literature and an understanding of the structure of the discipline. Units can be formulated around topic, form, structure or theme.

Topic

Topic is often used. You can identify four or five stories that deal with bears, for example. It's relatively easy to find suitable material and also easy for young children to see the connecting links between the stories. But we must confess to some reservations. Topic rarely provides a stable conceptual base to ground the unit on. Bear stories may include real talking bears (such as Bond's *Paddington*), talking toy bears (Milne's *Winnie the Pooh*), non-talking toy bears (Freeman's *Corduroy*) and non-talking real bears (Ward's *The Biggest Bear*). They may use a variety of structures and address a disparate range of themes. In short, they form a random collection inconsequentially dealing with bears.

We would tie topic to some motif, pattern, structure or theme that will contribute to the children's greater appreciation of literature. Thus we might devise a unit around *lost* bears, *questing* bears, or bears involved in the Rule of Three (see Story Grammars, pages 74-84).

Our unit on monsters (page 122) might be regarded as topic-centered except that the monster or beast is an archetype found in stories from all over the world. The unit is therefore more one of structure than of topic.

Form

Sometimes units are developed around haiku, short stories or fables. We have similar reservations about these: grouping by form can result in a group of texts that are otherwise quite disparate. And we adopt the same solution: we focus on some other characteristic also in the materials that permits interesting and useful comparison. Our unit on journeys (page 117) uses short, illustrated stories (form) that incorporate a significant journey (structure).

We are quite comfortable using form as the basis for various kinds of *poetic* language, including cumulative stories and some poetry. In both cases readers focus on the language. Part of the enjoyment each piece will offer resides in seeing how fresh expression occurs within a highly restricted form.

Theme

Theme provides an excellent focus. A body of books that address a similar theme will promote much valuable discussion and demonstrate both the endless variety and the limited number of vital issues in literature and the human condition. However, because there's a good deal of abstraction in themes we tend to reserve thematic units for older children (12 and up).

Theme shouldn't be confused with topic, though it often is. For example, in one list of books that were supposedly related in theme to Stevenson's *Treasure Island* were Ransome's *Swallows and Amazons* (Ransome) and Defoe's *Robinson Crusoe.* Ransome's book deals with young children pretending to be pirates in the English Lake District. *Robinson Crusoe* deals with surviving alone in an alien environment. We can see topical connections between these two books and *Treasure Island* but we can't see how they are *thematically* related to it.

Structure

It must be clear by now that structure is our first choice for the focus of a literature unit. We delight in sharing the thrill of discovering order in apparent chaos.

A STRUCTURAL APPROACH TO LITERATURE

The appeal of a structural approach to literature comes from a delight in rhythm and pattern — particularly when the underlying structures aren't immediately evident. Why do so many folk stories have handsome princes and fearsome forests? Why does the Rule of Three appear in folk tales and resurface again and again in modern stories? Why do so many stories involve quests? Why do so many protagonists experience exploration, oppression, struggle and victory?

The confusing mass of seemingly unrelated stories begins to exhibit a sense of order when you begin to recognize familiar themes, plots, characters, conflicts, goals, settings and moods.

The line between *archetype* and *stereotype* is hard to explain but easy to spot. Authors who arrange paper-thin characters in threadbare situations provide little for the mind. But writers who imbue stories with a sense of particular time and place may be surprised to find that they've re-enacted an ancient ritual in a new time and a new place, and that their stories speak with voices not entirely theirs. Young readers learn that forces which oppress and support the human spirit appear and reappear in many guises, times and places.

Stories tend to follow certain patterns and constantly reuse a limited number of elements. But it's also true that the human mind delights in variety. We take particular pleasure in creations that use familiar patterns but surprise us through creative interpretation of the "rules" or inspired expansions of familiar structures.

We describe here some archetypes, patterns and themes that frequently occur in stories.

Underdogs

Small, young and (physically) weak and inept characters are sympathetically presented. They are overwhelmed by some powerful force in the world. They attempt to cope but often make matters worse. Younger protagonists often succeed with limited help from a sympathetic and competent source (such as a Wise One). Older central characters succeed by their own unaided efforts.

Wise Ones

Wise Ones take on many forms. Wise men occur in folk tales more often than wise women. Older women in folk tales are, unfortunately, often witches. Parents, teachers, aunts, neighbors, etc. often take on the role of Wise Ones in modern stories, as do animals such as owls, ancient mice or aged horses. In all cases they offer the (impetuous? foolish?) protagonist limited help and limited guidance, often along the road of a quest.

Quests

The quest motif occurs so frequently it may not provide a sharp enough focus for a unit of work. We categorize quests into:

- Quest for material wealth
- Quest for security
- Quest for kin
- Quest for global good
- Quest for self

Quest for material wealth. Many stories are structured around a simple search for treasure which, when found, brings automatic and unquestioned happiness. In more mature examples, securing the treasure doesn't bring the expected happiness, or if it does, carries a high price (for example, Tolkien's *The Hobbit* and Stevenson's *Treasure Island*).

Quest for security. These stories portray individuals, families or groups searching for a secure and happy place to live. Unhappy with — or driven from — existing homes, they go out into a dangerous world. After near disaster, a secure place is found. Adams' *Watership Down* follows a group of rabbits, Peet's *The Caboose That Got Loose* tells of an unhappy caboose who finds a place to rest, and McCloskey's *Make Way for Ducklings* follows a family's search for a safe place.

Quest for kin. The central characters search for a family member or attempt to become reunited themselves. Unhappy or lonely children escape from unpleasant situations and seek out a long-lost father or mother. Lost children try to return home. In L'Engle's *A Wrinkle in Time* Meg and Charles Wallace attempt to find their father. In Holm's *I Am David* a young boy wanders across Europe in search of his family. Stories that follow what we call the Home Is Best pattern (page 98) involve quests for kin. They are most suitable for children in the early primary grades.

Quest for global good. The kingdom is threatened by titanic evil forces. A young, uncertain and ill-prepared protagonist is chosen to seek out and destroy the archdeacon of the dark forces. Lloyd Alexander uses this form of quest motif in his *Prydain Chronicles.*

Quest for self. Le Guin's *A Wizard of Earthsea* depicts this type of quest in complex and demanding ways. The quest for self-identity or self-assurance is often an underlying theme in stories dominated by other motifs. Eastman's *Are You My Mother?* and Lionni's *Pezzettino* are excellent examples of such stories suitable for very young children.

Shadows

The idea that human beings have a good and a bad side recurs in many religions, philosophies and mythologies. Folktales clearly separate the forces of good and evil, as do many examples of modern high fantasy. Authors often split the human psyche into two separate characters, one good and one evil, or one positive and one negative. The quest in *A Wizard of Earthsea* concludes with Ged finding that the evil he's released to the world is part of him. In Burnett's *The Secret Garden* the disagreeable death-oriented Colin is portrayed in sharp contrast to the Christ-like Dickon.

Other Motifs

Many more major and minor motifs recur, and each can become a major focus or an additional point of interest during the study of a text:

- *Plot:* journey, time slip, Rule of Three, leaving home
- *Character:* competent hero, incompetent hero, evil one, fool, trickster, monster
- *Setting:* underground, forest, mountains, "lost" worlds, valleys, gardens, islands.

Selecting Activities

With the focus of the unit clearly in mind we try to order the books into some sort of developmental sequence. We then devise activities that will bring out the significant literary qualities:

- plot profiles for books with strong or complex plots
- literary sociograms for stories involving complex human interactions
- maps for stories about a journey, etc.

We end the unit by comparing the stories on a grid (page 120), thus providing a sense of closure. Our more diffuse and long-term goal is to let the children discover that literature is not an inchoate conglomeration of isolated stories but that it has a structure that continually re-presents a limited number of patterns in an endless variety of ways.

HOME IS BEST: A WEEK-LONG PROJECT FOR GRADE TWO

Theoretical Foundations

This project had its genesis in an article by Jon Stott (1975) in which he noted that a number of books adhered rather closely to a fairly detailed plot structure he called Running Away to Home, represented, for instance, in Sendak's *Where the Wild Things Are* and Flack's *The Story About Ping*. We were familiar with both stories but had never noted the resemblance between them.

Running Away To Home

A small, weak character runs away from home. He goes out into the world and finds it to be dangerous. He is captured and is in danger of being eaten. He escapes and returns home where he is punished.

Home Is Best

A small defenceless character leaves home and enters a wider world which turns out to be dangerous. The character is trapped and a threat of being eaten arises. The character escapes and returns home, which is warm, loving and safe.

To see if the pattern would fit a significant number of stories for early primary children, we asked a class of undergraduates to help us examine a very large number of picture books. Numerous stories almost but not quite matched Stott's pattern. While central characters frequently left home, they didn't necessarily run away. For example, while Sylvester in Steig's *Sylvester and the Magic Pebble* leaves home searching for pebbles, he fully expects to return in time for supper. Hansel and Gretel (Grimm) and Ferdinand (Leaf) are *taken* from their homes. And the protagonists were rarely punished when they returned; they were warmly received instead.

So we modified the pattern to Home Is Best: the characters leave but return to a home that is warm, loving and safe.

Unit Overview

The question was, could we teach young children to identify the pattern for themselves and would they enjoy doing so? Would such a project contribute to the development of their language ability and their appreciation of literature?

To find the answers we devised a week-long unit of work. Each day we would help the children examine how well a given story fitted the HIB pattern. The Big Test would come on Friday when we planned to let them choose a book from a preselected collection. We wanted to see if, independently and relatively unaided, they could specify how well the stories they had chosen matched the Home Is Best pattern.

The Stories

- Monday: *The Story About Ping* (Flack)
- Tuesday: *Hansel and Gretel* (Grimm)
- Wednesday: *The Story of Ferdinand* (Leaf)
- Thursday: *Sylvester and the Magic Pebble* (Steig)

Teaching Materials

We prepared two charts, laminating them so we could wipe them off after use: figure 3.1 shows the wallchart used for checking individual stories against the HIB pattern; figure 3.2 shows the cumulative chart used for comparing stories. We also prepared worksheet versions of these charts for the children.

Two friendly librarians helped us obtain 28 titles (some in multiple copies, a total of 40 books) suitable in reading and interest level for seven to eight-year-old children. All had several characteristics of the HIB pattern.

The Site

Mrs. Diane Cowden "lent" us her grade two class for one hour each morning. This local teacher also kindly agreed to conduct follow-up activities such as completing associated art projects or providing time for independent reading.

The Children

The 23 children, from a middle-class suburban area, exhibited a normal range of ability.

Monday: Introducing the Unit and Getting Started

Introduction

We told the children some people up at the university felt that a lot of children's books followed a pattern and we would like their help to see if it was true. We showed the HIB wallchart to the children and expanded on the wording of each category, then read them *The Story About Ping*. We used the categories on the chart to formulate questions.

We recorded key words from the children's responses on the chart (figure 3.3, page 102) to see how well the story matched the pattern. Each element was then graded on a three-point scale:

1 fits perfectly
½ sort of fits, but not perfectly
0 doesn't fit

It's obvious the children felt *Ping* followed the HIB pattern exactly.

NAME OF STORY:		
PATTERN	**REALIZATION**	**SCORE**
1. A small defenseless character		
2. lives at home		
3. He/she leaves,		
4. goes out into the world		
5. which is dangerous,		
6. is captured		
7. and in danger of being eaten,		
8. grows lonely,		
9. escapes		
10. returns home		
11. which is warm, safe and loving.	Total	
Decision: **How well does it fit?**	Fits exactly	A
	Fits very closely	B
	Fits pretty closely	C
	Does not fit very well	D

Figure 3.1 Home Is Best wallchart

Pattern	Story 1		Story 2		Story 3		Story 4	
	Fit?	Score	Fit?	Score	Fit?	Score	Fit?	Score
1. small								
2. home								
3. leaves								
4. world								
5. danger								
6. captive								
7. eaten								
8. lonely								
9. escape								
10. return								
11. safe								
Total								
Name of story								

Figure 3.2 A cumulative chart used for comparing stories

Follow-up activity

To emphasize the *unity* of the story we prepared a story binding wallchart (figure 3.4), gave each child a worksheet (figure 3.5) and assigned the task of depicting one of the story elements.

At first we prepared individual assignment cards. A typical assignment card might read:

4. goes out into the world Draw Ping among the strange boats.

Later we learned to reduce preparation time by using the HIB chart to distribute these artistic responsibilities. We wiped the text from the laminated chart and wrote the names of the children responsible for depicting particular story elements in the adjacent space (figure 3.6 on page 104).

Name of story: *The Story about Ping*		
PATTERN	REALIZATION	SCORE
1. A small defenceless character	*Ping*	1
2. lives at home	*wise-eyed boat*	1
3. He/she leaves,	*hides in the grass*	1
4. goes out into the world	*Yangtze River*	1
5. which is dangerous,	*dark fishing birds*	1
6. is captured	*caught by the boy*	1
7. and in danger of being eaten,	*a duck dinner has come to us*	1
8. grows lonely,	*Ping is sad under the basket*	1
9. escapes,	*The boy lets Ping go.*	1
10. returns home	*He sees the wise-eyed boat.*	1
11. which is warm, safe and loving.	*He crosses the bridge and joins his family*	1
Decision: How well does it fit?	Exactly (A) (circled)	11
	Almost exactly B	
	Quite well C	
	Not very well D	
	Not at all E	

Figure 3.3 Home Is Best wallchart filled out for **The Story about Ping**

We had to do some logistical juggling. The HIB pattern had 11 elements: with the title-bearing picture at the center of the story binding chart, 12 jobs for 23 children. So we decided to produce two story bindings for each story. One early finisher took on a second responsibility.

A teacher colleague who tried the unit at a later date solved the logistical conundrum by clipping rather than pasting the pictures to the story binding chart. If the class size exceeded the number of jobs, two or more children illustrated the same element. All versions were clipped into place and rotated so that each had its turn on display.

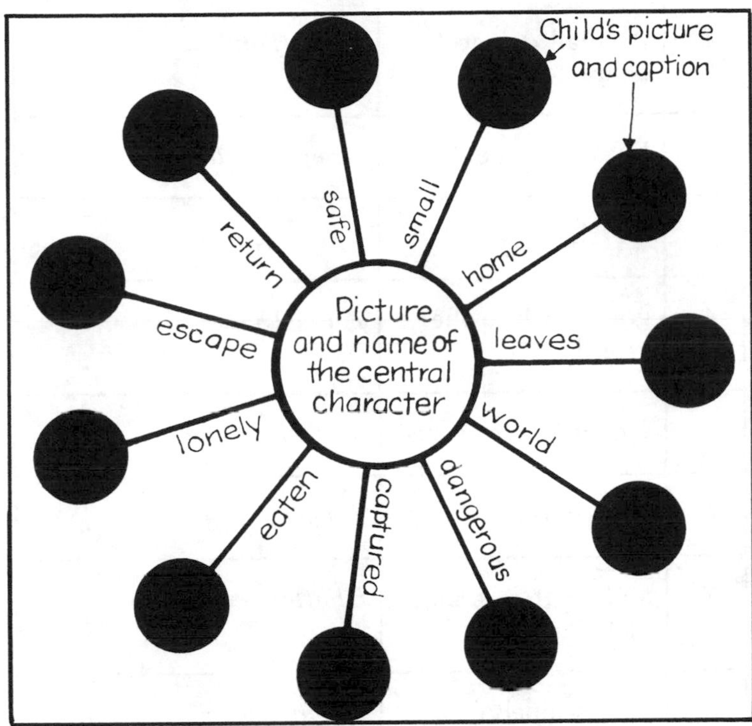

Figure 3.4 A story binding wallchart

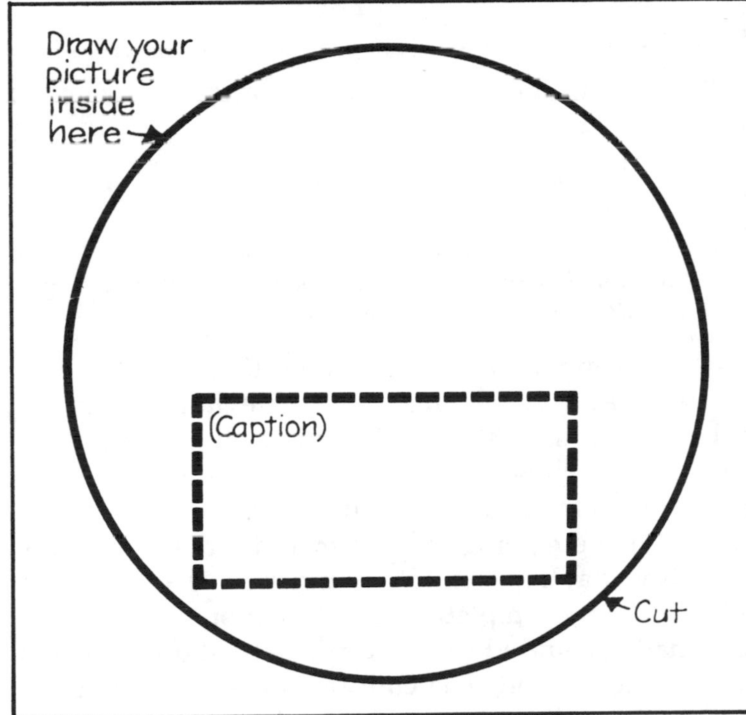

Figure 3.5 A worksheet for a story binding chart

Tuesday: Looking Back and Moving On

The next day we had the children review orally how *Ping* fit the pattern. We then read *Hansel and Gretel* and repeated the procedure. This time, although we reviewed all 11 elements orally, we recorded only the first seven.

We then gave an HIB worksheet to each child and asked them to copy the information from the chart and complete numbers eight to 11 independently. We circulated, giving individual assistance.

After everyone had finished we asked the children to read aloud their contributions. The children provided several acceptable alternatives, the gist of which we recorded on the chart. Since they were still illustrating *Ping,* we didn't attempt a story binding for *Hansel and Gretel* at that point.

When the children were finished their work they browsed through the display of HIB books and selected one for independent reading during the last 15–20 minutes of the lesson. No response was required for these books.

Wednesday: Accumulating Experience and Dealing with Developments

On Wednesday we reviewed both books by means of the cumulative chart. By laying out the bones of both stories in adjacent columns we hoped to reinforce in the children's minds the idea that stories which appear very different can follow a similar pattern.

The spaces on the cumulative chart are fairly small, but by this time the children were becoming familiar with the stories and the procedure and were able to suggest key words or short phrases to encapsulate each element.

Then we read *The Story of Ferdinand* and reviewed it. We used the same procedure except that we discussed only the first eight elements orally and recorded only four on the HIB chart. Our gradual withdrawal of support was building up to Friday's grand finale.

1.	A small defenceless character	*John, Tom*
2.	lives at home.	*Jessica, Andrea*
3.	He/she leaves,	*Karin, Jean*
4.	goes out into the world	*Alan, Derek*
5.	which is dangerous,	*Christine, Deborah*
6.	is captured	*Angela, Gwen*
7.	and in great danger of being eaten,	*Charles, Lee*
8.	grows lonely,	*Robin, Jeremy*
9.	escapes,	*Eric, David*
10.	returns home	*Jason, Justin*
11.	which is warm, safe and loving.	*Dallas, Don*

Figure 3.6 Home Is Best chart used to assign art responsibilities

We had saved *Ferdinand* for now because it contains a minor deviation from the pattern. Ferdinand is taken to the bull ring but the story makes no mention of his likely fate. We wondered what would happen when we reached number seven: "in danger of being eaten." The children responded to the item with a studied, uncertain silence. Then Jessica (bless her) said, "Well, they were going to kill him and that's almost the same thing." The general consensus was that that element should receive a half point.

The story binding chart for *Ping* was now complete so we started on two more for *Hansel and Gretel* and *Ferdinand*. We had become a little concerned about how some of the children approached the free reading period. The children were already accustomed to choosing their own books and a place to read them. The more competent readers tended to retire with their HIB books to the comparative privacy of their own desks. The less able ones, particularly boys, would engage in a variety of delay/avoidance tactics such as socializing, frequent changing of books, or taking an inordinate amount of time to choose.

We tried to give a little more focus to the free reading periods by introducing a reduced version of the cumulative chart. We told the children that when they had finished a particular story they could record how well it followed the pattern on their cumulative worksheets. Since the on-task behavior during free reading periods increased noticeably, this intervention appeared to work. Jeremy's work is shown in figure 3.7 below.

Name Jeremy H.

Pattern	Story		Story		Story		Story		Story		Story	
1. Small	✓	1	✓	1	✓	1	✓	1	½	?	½	?
2. Home	✓	1	✓	1	✓	1	✓	1	✓	1	✓	1
3. Leaves	✓	1	✓	1	✓	1	✓	1	✓	1	✓	1
4. World	✓	1	✓	1	✓	1	✓	1	✓	1	✓	1
5. Dangerous	½	?	✓	1	✓	1	✓	1	✓	1	X	0
6. Capture	X	0	½	?	½	?	✓	1	X	0	X	0
7. Eaten	X	0	½	?	✓	1	✓	1	X	0	X	0
8. Lonely	✓	1	✓	1	✓	1	✓	1	½	?	X	0
9. Escape	X	0	✓	1	✓	1	✓	1	X	0	X	0
10. Return	✓	1	✓	1	✓	1	✓	1	✓	1	✓	1
11. Safe	½	?	✓	1	✓	1	✓	1	✓	1	✓	1
Total		7		10		10½		11		7		5½
Name of Story	Arrow to the Sun		Petunia Beware		Henry the explorer		Hetty and Harriet		Angus lost		The Funny Man	
	Fit?	Score	Fit?	Score	Fit?	Score	Fit?	Score	Fit?	Score	Fit?	Score

✓ = Yes, it fits. Score 1 | ? = Well, maybe. Score ½ | X = Does not fit. Score 0

Figure 3.7 A child's Home Is Best cumulative worksheet

Thursday: Smooth Sailing

By now the children were used to the procedures and everything went very smoothly. We reviewed the three previous stories on the cumulative chart and read *Sylvester and the Magic Pebble* aloud. We reviewed the first eight story elements orally but wrote nothing on the HIB chart. The children filled out their HIB worksheets independently and shared their responses, which we then summarized on the HIB chart. The rest of the lesson was devoted to silent reading and the completion of cumulative worksheets.

Friday: The Moment of Truth

This was our moment of truth: had all our theorizing, planning and teaching enabled the children to see how the HIB pattern was realized in a book they had read independently?

We used the cumulative chart to review all four stories. Then we passed out worksheets and asked the children to choose a book from the HIB collection, read it and fill in the sheet.

They found it valuable to turn each HIB element into a question for the chart:

- Who in your story is small and defenseless?
- Where does he/she live?
- Why does he/she leave?
- What part of the world does he/she go out into?
- What danger does he/she meet?
- How is he/she captured?
- Who or what plans to eat him/her?
- How do you know he/she becomes lonely?
- How does he/she escape?
- How does he/she get home?
- How do you know that home is warm, loving and safe?

By this time several children had read almost all of our 28 titles. They simply selected a familiar story and began work on the analysis. An example is shown in figure 3.8. The less able children needed help in expressing their thoughts.

Name of Story: Where the wild things are Your Name: Dallas

PATTERN	REALIZATION	SCORE
1. small, defenceless	Max	1
2. lives at home	In the city	1
3. leaves	In a boat	1
4. goes out into the world	Where the wild things are	1
5. dangerous	The wild things!	1
6. capture	Does not fit	0
7. eaten, danger	The wild things roared!	½
8. lonely	Max said "I want to go home"	1
9. escape	the Island	1
10. returns	To his home	1
11. warm, loving, safe	His home	1
Decision: Circle your choice	Fits exactly	A
	Fits very closely	(B)
	Fits pretty closely	C
	Does not fit very well	D
	Does not fit at all	E

Figure 3.8 A Home Is Best worksheet filled out independently

We were generally delighted with the responses. Only the two weakest readers in the class didn't fill out the HIB worksheet in a coherent manner. It wasn't always evident why the children had selected particular words or phrases but everyone was able to provide well-supported clarification. We used the cumulative chart to share summaries. Volunteers read out their written comments and these we reduced to a single word to record on the cumulative chart. The full chart made obvious that all the stories seemed to follow the same pattern, despite wide differences in content.

Hindsight

We would do several things differently if we were to repeat the unit. First, we would keep quiet about the HIB pattern until after the children had recent experience with at least three stories that adhered to it. Children think inductively, not deductively. We knew very well (but forgot) that children don't work from principles to examples but from repeated examples to a principle.

Secondly, we would try to find more simple books for the less able readers. Authors of picture books tend to write for the interest level rather than the reading ability of their audience. Satisfactory literature seems to require a certain range of vocabulary and a certain complexity of expression. Only a very few authors such as Lobel, Seuss and Flack have been able to combine artistic excellence and simplicity of expression, but none of these has written much that follows the HIB pattern. We would display the simply written stories separately as well, since we found that the poor readers took a long time searching for books they could read.

Thirdly, we wouldn't use fractions with grade two children. Fortuitously, their own teacher had just introduced the concept of half to these children, so they could manage a single half score and even cope with adding two halves together. But three or more half scores threw their tenuous grasp of the concept into a dither.

Why Teach HIB Stories?

"Aren't you showing the children that these stories are written to a formula, and won't they get bored with them?" we've been asked. Our response is that neither we nor anyone else we knew was aware of such basic similarities among stories until it was pointed out. These stories are not *written* to a formula. They vary so widely in content, character, setting and style it seems impossible that they were merely reassembled from a sort of literary kit. Our response to Stott's insight was one of delight. Here was an unrecognized pattern in a familiar aspect of the world. The discovery that it applied even more broadly than Stott indicated was exciting and satisfying.

"What were you trying to do?" other skeptics have asked. Again our answer is simple: we hoped to share our delight in that discovery with children.

"Aren't you reducing stories to nothing but a pattern?" This is akin to the formula question. There *is* a reductionist tendency in the project but why the concern? We don't withhold patterns or regularities from learners in other areas. One of the goals in teaching mathematics, physics, chemistry, biology, psychology, anthropology or astronomy is to demonstrate that despite apparent diversity in variant structures, patterns or principles exist. Why should the sharing of recurring patterns in literature be undesirable?

Why Do Authors Write HIB Stories?

We base our explanation for the existence of a large body of HIB stories on a small group of books we've come to regard as pre-HIB stories: Ezra Jack Keats' *The Snowy Day* and Mark Taylor's *Henry the Explorer,* for instance.

In *The Snowy Day* a very small child explores the immediate neighborhood with no hint of capture or consumption. A mild suggestion of harm is provided by a group of snowball-throwing older children who are avoided by the young protagonist before he returns home to the nurture of mother, food, bath and bed. On the other hand, Henry, as the second title suggests, works on a slightly larger canvas. He sets off to explore but fails to return on time. His mother dispatches a search party but the resourceful Henry doesn't need it. Once again no capture or danger of being eaten is made explicit. However at one point Henry believes he is confronted by a bear — which the reader/viewer (but not Henry) discovers to be a bear-shaped pile of rocks.

In pre-HIB stories protagonists make a very small foray into a world where danger is only suggested. All the comforts of home await their return. In a full-blown HIB story the protagonist is actually confronted by destructive forces. The danger of annihilation is very real.

Pre-HIB stories are normally read to the very young (three to five years), HIB stories to the slightly older (five to seven years). Between three and five years of age children make their first independent excursions beyond the home; in the next two years they regularly spend significant periods of time outside the home without immediate supervision. Authors of pre-HIB stories are telling parents and children it's all right to explore, but with a hint that discretion is necessary. The authors of full-blown HIB stories are more direct. The story says, "Look, there are real dangers out there. Act with caution. You could be destroyed." Perhaps even from the authors themselves, the message is veiled in allegories of willful rabbits, fearful ducks, naive pigs or impetuous donkeys.

We don't make the "moral" of these tales explicit to the children; we are content to let the power of the stories work on their receptive minds.

Annotated Bibliography: Home Is Best

Intermittently during the unit we asked the children to write annotations that described the main character, his or her problem, and how it all turned out. Although we first produced, read aloud and analyzed two of our own examples, the children found the task very difficult. Their annotations were either too brief ("It's about a pig") or too long, as they attempted a verbatim recall.

Some of the following annotations were created by children. These are indicated by quotation marks. Some are terse, often downright elliptical. We suggest you follow the advice offered by the young reviewer of Steig's *Sylvester and the Magic Pebble.*

Alexander, Martha (1972). *And My Mean Old Mother Will Be Sorry.* Dial Press.
"Anthony could not stand his mother so he left. He went in a forest with a bear. He was sleeping in a cave with no pillow no blanket and he was VERY cold too. So in the morning he went home and was happy to see his teddy again."

Bright, Robert (1944). *Georgie.* Doubleday.
"Mr. and Mrs. Whittaker live in an antique house haunted by Georgie. Mr. Whittaker made it so the house will not be too squeeky but then they didn't know when to go to bed. Georgie leaves and spends a lonely winter in a barn."

Brookes, Leslie (undated). *The Story of the Three Little Pigs.* Frederick Warne.
"Three little pigs go off and build houses. One house is straw another sticks and the last one bricks. Along come the wolf. The wolf tries to eat the third little pig. The pig ate him!"

Brown, Marcia (1969). *How, Hippo!* Charles Scribner's Sons.
"A hippo was born in a clump of papyrus stalks at the edge of a cool river. His mother tried to teach him the how's. One day he swam up to surface to play with the palm fronds, he saw a crocodile, the croc got his tail. He yelled for help, his mother came, got croc in her jaws and baby hippo got away. After that his mother told him to mind his hows."

Burton, Virginia L. (1937). *Choo Choo.* Houghton Mifflin.
"Choo Choo is a little engine who runs away only to find the world a dangerous place. She is rescued from a dark and threatening forest and decides never to run away again."

Carrick, Carol and Donald Carrick (1982). *Sleep Out.* Houghton Mifflin.
"Christopher is a little boy who got a new sleeping bag for his birthday. They're going to the cottage that summer. He goes on a camping trip by himself. He gets scared because of the rain and the trees so he goes to a barn. He finally gets to sleep. The next morning he goes home."

Coombs, Patrica (1970). *Lisa and the Grompet.* Lathrop, Lee and Shepard.
"Lisa a little girl always is told what to do. So she runs away. In the process she sits on a grompet's front yard. The grompet starts yelling at her but then they make friends. Lisa puts the grompet on her shoulder and goes home. They eat supper (without Lisa spilling anything) then Lisa practises her piano without any mistakes."

dePaola, Tomie (1976). *When Everyone was Fast Asleep.* Holiday House.
"Two little children got woken up by a Token sent by the Fog Maiden. They met a elf horse and came to the troll house but they were not afraid. They were dressed for the ball. Then the Fog Maiden tucked them in to bed."

Duvoisin, Roger (1961). *Veronica.* Alfred A. Knopf.
"A hippopotamus named Veronica had such a big family her family did not notice her. She went to the city where she thought people would notice her but she almost got put in jail. A moving truck came to take her home."

Flack, Marjorie (1932). *Angus Lost*. Doubleday.

Angus explores beyond his own backyard and finds the world a dangerous and lonely place. A milkman aids in his safe return.

Flack, Marjorie (1933). *The Story About Ping*. Viking.

"Ping, a young duck, hides so that he won't be spanked." He is left alone on the Yangtze River and is captured by a family who plans to eat him.

Grimm, Jacob and Wilhelm K. (1971). *Hansel and Gretel*. Delacorte Press.

"Once there were two children. They had to get away from the witch. They got home with their father."

Grimm, Jacob and Wilhelm K. (1981). *The Seven Ravens*. Translated by Elizabeth D. Crawford. William Morrow.

"There were seven brothers who did not come home. So the dad said 'I wish my sons were seven ravens,' and his wish came true. When the little girl saw that they were lost she went to find them and she did."

Jeschke, Susan (1975). *Sidney*. Holt, Rinehart and Winston.

A young duck "dresses up as a fox but he can't get his mask off unless he proves that he's a duck!" He succeeds and he gets the mask off and he runs home.

Keats, Ezra Jack (1962). *The Snowy Day*. Viking.

Peter makes a tiny excursion into a snowy world. Big boys throwing snowballs are avoided. He returns home with a snowball in his pocket. "Before he got into bed he looked in his pocket. His pocket was empty. He called to his friend across the hall and they went together into the deep, deep snow."

Knight, Hilary (1964). *Where's Wallace*. Harper & Row.

"Wallace, an ape with middle-sized hair, reads and hears about places he would love to go. He escapes and goes all of the places he hears about. After a lot of looking they find him. Each time Mr. Frumbee (his owner) leaves Wallace he runs away. Wallace hides in Bumpus Brothers department store. Soon Wallace had his own chair."

Leaf, Munro (1936). *The Story of Ferdinand*. Viking.

"Ferdinand just liked to smell the flowers. Some people were looking for the fiercest bull. Ferdinand went to sit down. He sat on a bumble bee. It hurt! Five men took the bull to the bullring. But the bull wouldn't fight. So they took him back home."

Lobel, Anita (1983). *The Straw Maid*. Greenwillow Books.

"A little girl has gone out to sell their cow. She is captured by three robbers and the cow ran off. They take her to their house and she works for them. One day she maid a doll that looked like her and put straw on her. So, when they saw the doll they talked to it but it didn't answer and the little girl went out of the house and found the cow and went home."

Lobel, Arnold (1969). *Small Pig*. Harper & Row.
"Small Pig is a little pig that loves mud. One day the farmer's wife cleans her house so she wants to clean the farm. She cleans the mud puddle up. The next night the pig ran away. He tried to find a mud puddle. He thought the mud puddle was a puddle but it wasn't, it was cement. The farmer had to call the fireman who pulled him out."

Mosel, Arlene (1972). *The Funny Little Woman*. Dalton.
A little woman follows a runaway rice cake underground and ends up a cook for a group of demons. She escapes with the aid of magic.

McDermott, Gerald (1974). *Arrow to the Sun*. Viking.
A young Pueblo Indian boy searches for his father. He has to pass a series of tests to prove his worthiness.

Ness, Evaline (1967). *Mr Miacca*. Holt, Finehart and Winston.
Tommy Grimes was sometimes a good boy and sometimes a bad boy. His mother said to stay here and play and be a good boy, but Tommy didn't listen to his mother. So Mr. Miacca got him. He escaped once, but Mr. Miacca got him again. But he escaped again.

Oakley, Graham (1981). *Hetty and Harriet*. Atheneum.
"On a farm a chicken named Hetty was the youngest of all her brothers and sisters. Harriet was the next youngest chicken. They went to different places. They got into trouble and could have got hurt. They found a place where they could stay without being hurt and stayed there."

Peet, Bill (1965). *Chester the Worldly Pig*. Houghton Mifflin.
"Chester was a pig. But he didn't want to be a pig. He was no better than a cabbage or a carrot. He was just something to eat. One day he thought he would like to be in a circus. But where could he find one? So he started to look and look and look and look. He found one and he is very happy."

Potter, Beatrix (1903). *The Tale of Peter Rabbit*. Warne.
Peter goes to Mr McGregor's garden and nearly ends up in a pie.

Ross, Tony (1980). *Jack and the Beanstalk*. Delacorte.
"Jack gets a can thrown at him because he traded a magic bean for the cow. His mother turned white, then purple, then red. Then he planted the bean and it grew, and it grew, and it grew, and it grew. Jack climbed the beanstalk. 'Fee fie fo fum, I smell the blood of a little one,' he said."

Sendak, Maurice (1963). *Where the Wild Things Are*. Harper & Row.
"Max is a boy. He dresses up as a wolf. His mom says that he is a wild thing. So he says 'I'll eat you up.' So he goes to his room. He dreams about WILD THINGS and when he work up his supper was still hot."

Steig, William (1976). *The Amazing Bone*. Farrar, Straus and Giroux.
Pearl, a young pig, is captured by a fox who plans to eat her. She is rescued by a bone with a surprising range of abilities.

Steig, William (1969). *Sylvester and the Magic Pebble.* Simon and Schuster.
"One day Sylvester finds a magic pebble. On his way home he meets a lion. He wishes he was a rock. Read the book."

Taylor, Mark (1966). *Henry the Explorer.* Atheneum.
"Henry went exploring but he got lost. His mother got very worried. His next door neighbors started to look for him. Soon he found his trail of H's and he found his way home. So did his next door neighbors."

Whitaker, Muriel and Jetske Ironside (1979). *Pernilla in the Perilous Forest.* Oberon.
"Pernilla is a girl who sets out to find a horse who will eat sugar and lay his head on her lap. She finds a lion, serpent, wolf, goat, hog, bear, mole and finally, she finds a unicorn."

Zion, Gene (1956). *Harry the Dirty Dog.* Harper & Row.
"Harry is a dog who does not like baths! One day Harry heard the water going and Harry ran away with the scrubbing brush and hid it and ran off. He got very dirty but when he got home his family did not believe him that he was Harry but Harry got into the bath and they gave him a bath and they found out that he was Harry."

Running Away to Home: Books for Older Readers

George, Jean Craighead (1972). *Julie of the Wolves. Harper & Row.*
A young Eskimo girl struggles with her sense of cultural identity.

Richler, Mordecai (1978). *Jacob Two-Two Meets the Hooded Fang.* Random House.
A tongue-in-cheek cry for children's rights.

Sperry, Armstrong (1940). *Call it Courage.* Macmillan.
An epic tale of a young boy who grows to manhood as he survives alone in the Pacific.

FIND IT: A FORTY-FIVE MINUTE WRITING PROJECT

Introduction

We've included the description of this short project to show that it's possible to take young children through all stages of the writing process without extraordinary effort — and incidentally to show sound pedagogical use of games in the classroom.

Many teachers have made use of the fact that young children enjoy playing games in the classroom, though not always with maximum pedagogical benefit. The least productive use of games is as a recreational "break" — which implies that lessons are onerous. We believe that learning can be enjoyable.

Games are also used for drill and practice. That goal has some merit but we don't believe games have to be limited to that end. If they're well designed, preparing and playing games can result in increased learning.

The Writing Process

Donald Graves has convinced thousands of teachers of the value of a process approach to writing. He has provided detailed and elaborate descriptions (1983), based on the simple and common-sense notion that we show children how to write by taking them through the steps real authors go through. While we endorse Graves' approach, we feel that he doesn't put enough stress on audience. He grants that young writers need to identify an audience, but most children's writing precedes the identification of an audience. The vast majority of writing done by adults is initiated by a real need to communicate to an audience. We believe that children should also begin writing with an audience in mind.

Graves also places few restraints on the form of children's writing. While we recognize the beginners' need for free expression, the real world doesn't permit such latitude. When adults write they do so within the form predetermined appropriate to the situation. Writing a sonnet to your bank manager is unlikely to be a successful way of obtaining a mortgage at preferential rates of interest. In the real world, purpose, audience, motivation and form are all so tightly interconnected that they're best seen as a single construct rather than separate entities. We include many free-writing sessions in our program, but we also design situations where the form of the writing is clearly determined beforehand.

We've modified Graves' steps to form the following sequence:

- establish audience/purpose
- provide multiple examples
- examine examples
- provide experiences
- write first draft
- edit/proofread
- write second draft
- proofread
- present to the audience

With these steps in mind we made preparations for showing a grade three group how to construct and play the game of Find It.

Preparation

We prepared three clue cards based on the story of *The Three Little Pigs.* We wanted to show the children how to make clue cards around *People, Places* and *Things.*

Since we gave the lesson in early February we chose Marc Brown's *Arthur's Valentine,* which contains several items around which the children could make their own clue cards. To begin, we prepared the three clue cards for each story (figure 3.9).

Presenting the Lesson

1. We showed the children the *outside* of the three clue cards based on *The Three Little Pigs* and asked them to figure out who or what was being referred to. We were surprised by the amount of discussion they needed to determine that the

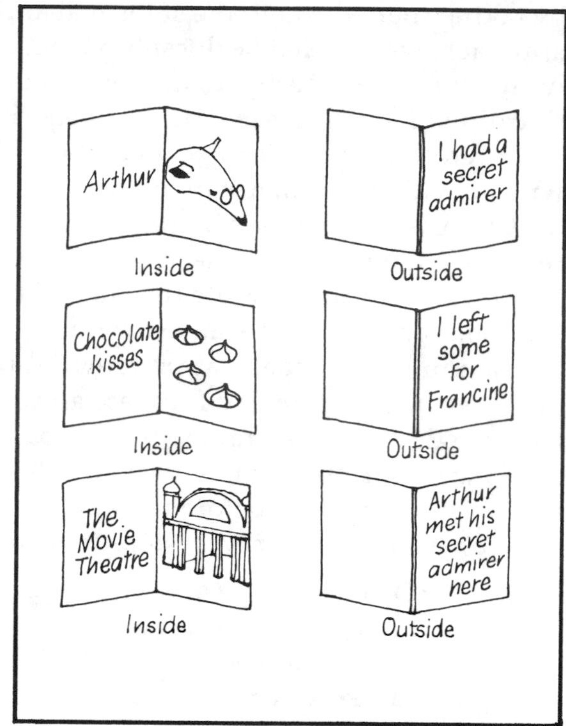

***Figure 3.9 Examples of three clue cards based on* The Three Little Pigs *and on* Arthur's Valentine**

clue "The wolf ate my two brothers" referred to the third little pig. Once they settled on the answer we showed them the inside of the card.

2. We asked the children to make their own set of clue cards for a new story and told them we would show them how to use the cards to play a game.
3. We showed them the outside of the three clue cards based on *Arthur's Valentine*. Fortunately none had read or heard the story, so no one could offer suggestions for answers.
4. We assembled the children on the story mat and read them the story, inviting them to listen to see if they could discover the answers.

> ***Arthur's Valentine:* a synopsis**
> Arthur is embarrassed because a secret admirer sends him valentines. A tryst at a local cinema is arranged. Luckily Arthur discovers the identity of the mysterious paramour and turns the tables on her.

5. When we showed them the three clue cards again, they readily identified the answers.
6. After the children resumed their seats we wrote three headings on the chalkboard: *People, Places* and *Things.* Their suggestions for items about which clues might be made rapidly filled up the space available.
7. We gave each child three pieces of scrap paper and showed them how to form a clue card.
8. We invited them to write three clues based on *Arthur's Valentine,* using the topics from the board if they wished. While they were writing we circulated, giving advice.
9. We showed the first two children who finished how to play the game of Find It.
10. As soon as the rest of the class had completed their clues the two Find It "experts" gave a demonstration.
11. Each child then chose a partner and played the game with the six clue cards they'd made. New partnerships were formed once a given pair had become familiar with each other's cards.

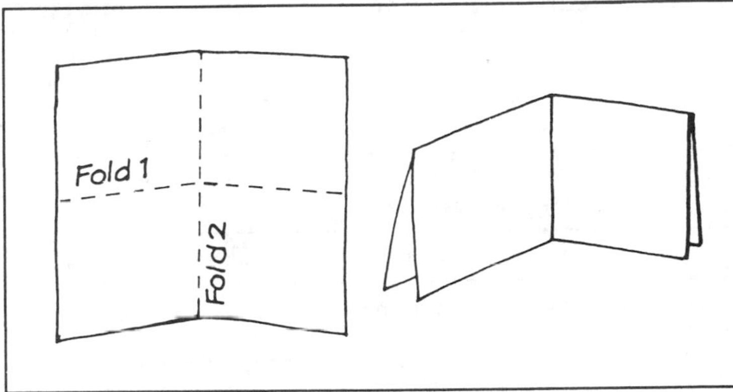

Figure 3.10 Folding a sheet of paper to form a clue card

12. We then gave the children actual cards, stressing that they'd be the only ones they received so they needed to be careful when writing on them. We asked them to choose the best clue from the first three they'd made and copy it on the card.

How to Play *Find It*

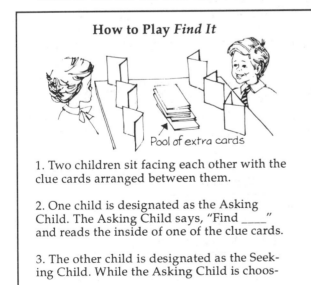

1. Two children sit facing each other with the clue cards arranged between them.

2. One child is designated as the Asking Child. The Asking Child says, "Find ____" and reads the inside of one of the clue cards.

3. The other child is designated as the Seeking Child. While the Asking Child is choosing the clue card the Seeking Child has his/her eyes closed.

4. Once the clue card has been named the Seeking Child opens his/her eyes and reads the backs of the opposing clue cards. He/she then chooses a clue card.

5. If the selection is correct the Seeking Child returns the card. If the choice is wrong the card is returned.

6. When a card is lost by the Asking Child it is replaced from the pool of clue cards.The object of the game is to win as many cards as possible.

7. When a turn is complete the roles reverse and the play resumes.

Figure 3.11 Instructions for playing the game of Find It

13. During the copying we circulated, giving individual assistance.
14. The cards they produced became part of our classroom resource materials, but we invited the children to take their first drafts home to show their parents and siblings how to play Find It.

We've described this lesson in close detail because we want to demonstrate that it didn't require large amounts of preparation time nor extraordinary teaching ability. The lesson was easy to manage. Because the responses elicited from the children were open-ended there was no need for ability grouping. Without much help, the more competent children wrote witty, subtle and clever clues in clear and concise language. And we had time to give the less competent children additional help, although even so they tended to produce simpler clues about the more superficial aspects of the story.

The lesson covered all the steps in our model of the writing process, as shown in figure 3.12.

Note also that although the context dictated the form of the writing, there was no sense of constraint. No child attempted to use any form other than the enigmatic sentence required by the situation. We believe it's possible to devise similar circumstances that call for other forms of writing just as painlessly: announce the presentation of a play with a poster, invite or thank a guest by means of a courteous letter, explain a process through an exposition. We think this approach to the teaching of writing is much more realistic than giving children "freedom" and hoping that control of writing in a variety of forms will emerge.

	Presentation of the lesson	The writing process
Step 1.	Provision of examples: *The Three Little Pigs*	Multiple examples
Step 2.	A game to be made	Audience/purpose
Step 3.	Provision of examples: *Arthur's Valentine*	Multiple examples
Step 4.	Reading the story	Experiential base
Step 5.	Examining the examples	Multiple examples
Step 6.	Collating suggestions	Pre-writing activity
Step 7.	Writing three clues	First draft
Step 8.	Assistance provided	"Conferencing": editing and proofreading
Step 9.	Game instruction	Audience/purpose
Step 10.	Game demonstration	
Step 11.	Game playing	
Step 12.	Copying out the best clue	Second draft
Step 13.	Assistance provided	Proofreading
Step 14.	Cards incorporated into class resource material	Presentation to the audience

Figure 3.12 A sequence of teaching procedures that cover the steps in the writing process

THE PROBLEMS OF GETTING THERE: A UNIT IN LITERARY MAP-MAKING

Introduction

In *Literacy Through Literature* we discussed the value and procedures of map-making as one way of responding to some stories (pp. 63-69). Here we want to describe a week-long unit of literary mapping with a grade three group.

The children involved in this activity lived in a racially mixed suburban area. All had an adequate command of English and the class covered a normal range of abilities. The regular teacher used a traditional basal reader but frequently incorporated literature into her program.

The stories we selected to introduce mapping were *Little Red Riding Hood*, Steig's *The Amazing Bone* and *Snow White*. In each story the central character makes a significant journey.

In 45-minute lessons, for four days we focused on three stories and on the final day had the children choose a book from a preselected group of stories, all of which detailed significant journeys.

Monday: Modeling

We introduced the unit by telling the children we would be looking at a group of stories in which someone takes a journey. First we would read *Little Red Riding Hood* and help them draw a map of her travels — which we did, without comment. We asked the children to suggest items that would have to be shown on a map of the story — for example, Little Red's house — and recorded oral suggestions on the chalkboard. If significant items went un-noted we asked the questions designed to help the children understand that items from the story must be shown in rational, logical relationships with one another.

Teacher talk	Children's response
Who rescued Little Red?	The woodcutter.
Where was he?	Working in the forest.
Near Little Red's house?	No – near Grandma's house.
How do you know?	He heard her screaming.

Figure 3.13 Teacher/children interaction designed to elicit items to be mapped

Using an overhead projector, we presented a partially completed map of Little Red's journey (figure 3.14 on the next page). Items already represented were identified and labeled; new suggestions were added. Characters were depicted where significant events occurred: Little Red was shown going into the forest, picking flowers, meeting the wolf and then entering Grandmother's house. The routes taken by the active parties (Red, Wolf, Woodcutter) were shown as trails through the wood.

Then we removed our example and asked the children to draw their own maps of the story on blank paper. We concluded the lesson by sharing their maps and indicating that the next day they would meet a pig that gets into a lot of trouble.

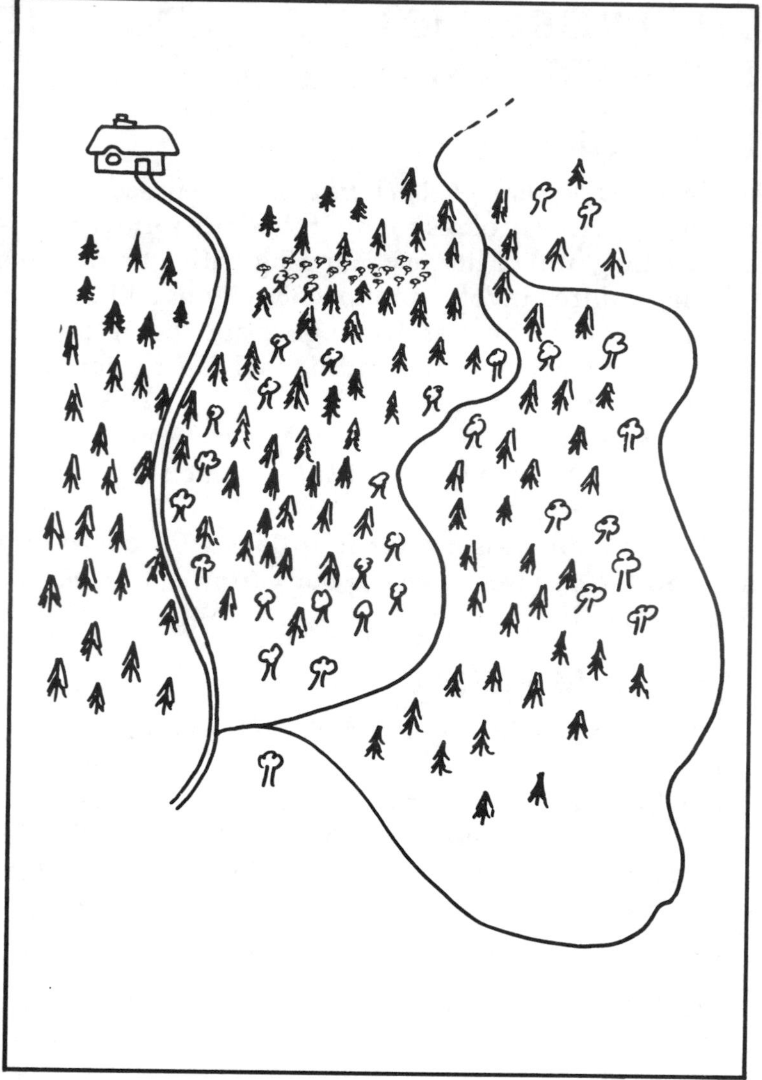

Figure 3.14 An incomplete map of the setting for **Little Red Riding Hood**

Tuesday: Guided Practice

First we reminded the children that we were learning how to draw a map of story characters making a journey and briefly reviewed the previous lesson. Then we asked them to listen carefully to *The Amazing Bone* because we wanted them to draw a map when it was finished. We read the story aloud, showing the pictures, and asked the children to suggest items that should be included on a story map. These we recorded on the chalkboard. Items not suggested voluntarily we elicited through judicious questioning. When the possibilities were nearly exhausted we provided the children with blank paper and asked them to create a map. A sharing session closed the lesson, after which we announced that the next day we would read about a young girl who got lost in a great forest.

***The Amazing Bone:* a synopsis**
Pearl, a hopeful young pig, is making her way home from school when she finds a bone with (limited) magical powers. She is accosted by three villains who are frightened away by the bone. A wily fox is not so readily intimidated and takes Pearl and the bone to his dismal den where he prepares Pearl for supper. At the last minute the bone unleashes unexpected magic and Pearl is returned safely to her loving family.

Wednesday and Thursday: Increasing the Challenge

On Wednesday we introduced *Snow White*, much longer and conceptually more demanding than the previous two stories. Since the spatial relationships among the Wicked Queen's castle, the spot where Snow White was abandoned, the home of the seven dwarfs, and the prince's castle aren't explicit in the story, their initial placement on a map is somewhat arbitrary. This lack of obvious structure gave some of the children problems and they had difficulty making initial decisions. However, once one location was (arbitrarily) determined, the logic of the story provided a framework for the rest of the settings. It was interesting to note that as the children encountered difficulties they tended to slip from a bird's eye view to a more familiar ground level view. Their representations tended to become less map-like and more like a series of connected scenes from the story.

Because of the length of the story and the complexity of the mapping activity it took two lessons to complete the *Snow White* map.

Friday: Independent Application

On Friday we introduced our story comparison grid (figure 3.15, next page). Each day we had begun with a review of the previous stories and closed with an "ad" for the next day's story. We were intent on conveying the continuity and cohesiveness of the project. Now the completion of the story comparison grid would act as a culminating summary of our shared stories.

We asked the children to choose a story from our library of journey stories and make a map for it. They had had access to these books all week and many of them selected a familiar story.

Some of the less able children had difficulty getting started. Rose chose *The Gingerbread Man* but simply sat staring at her blank paper. When we asked her what was wrong she said she didn't "get it." When we suggested that she place the house of the little old man and the little old woman at the top of the page and run the road down the page her expression brightened and she set to work. Less able children often have difficulty making the initial organizational decisions, but if you help them past the initial hurdle they know how to proceed to fill out the details.

Rose's problem exemplifies our point about the autonomy of the learner (see pages 160-161). If we'd provided a highly structured situation demanding simple responses, perhaps Rose would have experienced less difficulty. But a history of filling in other people's blanks wouldn't prepare Rose to deal with unstructured situations that require her to impose her own order.

We were pleased to note that in general the children selected stories suitable to their ability. The more able children chose longer, more demanding stories and produced logical, elegant, detailed maps. Relatively few able children chose unchallenging stories. The slower children were less able to make wise choices and some selected books that were beyond them. To them we offered judicious counseling to direct them to simpler stories. The "maps" of the less able children tended to be a series of illustrated scenes while the interpretations of the more competent children contained many true map-like features.

After everyone had finished, we invited individuals to share their maps and stories — a genuine sharing since not everyone was familiar with every book. Several children exchanged books as a result of this sharing session.

The problems of getting there				
Story	*Little Red Riding Hood*	*The Amazing Bone*	*Snow White*	your choice
central character	Little Red	Pearl	Snow White	
goal	get to Grand-mother's house	get home from school	escape Wicked Queen	
villain	wolf	robbers, Fox	Wicked Queen	
villain's goal	eat Little Red	eat Pearl	kill Snow White	
helper	Wood-cutter	the bone	seven dwarves	
outcome	Red rescued	Pearl got home safely	married the Prince	
ending	happy	happy	happy	

Figure 3.15 A comparison grid showing similarities among stories involving journeys

Skills Development

We were pleased to note the wide variety in the children's activities: listening to and discussing stories, jointly drawing and labeling maps, reading stories on their own, drawing maps of their own and explaining them to their friends. All these activities had incorporated the use and fostered the development of a multitude of language skills. We were particularly gratified that neither we nor the children had held skills development as the central purpose of any of the activities. Both we and they were happily engaged in making meaning through the exploration of stories we had enjoyed together.

Preparation Time

Most of our preparation time was spent identifying a sufficient number of stories appropriate for the grade level. Our pooled knowledge of children's literature gave us a start, but we also combed the shelves of the school and public library to compose our bibliography. We found librarians amazingly helpful. A list left with them usually resulted in a pile of suitable books two days later.

You may want to use our list as a starting point. That should reduce your preparation time to almost nothing since further time required to get ready for the project is negligible.

Postscript

Afterwards we asked the regular classroom teacher how she thought we had done. A woman with many years of teaching experience, she looked off into the middle distance and replied: "I thought you did very well — except you went at university speed instead of grade three speed." She was right and we were much chastened. We had gone into the classroom highly organized and had relentlessly unwound our unit according to our own timetable rather than at a rate comfortable for the children. We are learning to slow down.

Bibliography of Stories with Journeys

All the following books have journeys in them. The list may be supplemented by other titles available locally.

Burningham, John (1966). *Cannonball Simp.* Jonathan Cape.
Burningham, John (1967). *Harquin the Fox.* Jonathan Cape.
Burton, Virginia L. (1939). *Mike Mulligan and his Steam Shovel.* Scholastic.
Carrick, Carol (1977). *The Foundling.* Houghton Mifflin.
Dr. Seuss (1940) *Horton Hatches the Egg.* Random House.
Fatio, Louise (1954). *The Happy Lion.* Scholastic.
Flack, Marjorie and Kurt Wises (1933). *The Story About Ping.* Penguin.
Foreman, Michael (1969). *The Great Sleigh Robbery.*
Littledale, Freya (1980). *Snow White* . Scholastic.
Hoff, Syd. (1959). *Julius.* Harper & Row.
Hughes, Shirley (1977). *David and Dog.* Prentice-Hall.
Hutchins, Pat (1968). *Rosie's Walk.* Scholastic.
Kellogg, Steven (1973). *The Island of Skog.* Dial.
Leaf, Munro (1936). *The Story of Ferdinand.* Viking.
Lobel, Arnold (1986). *Ming Lo Moves the Mountain.* Scholastic.
McPhail, David (1980). *Pig Pig Grows Up.* Scholastic.
Mayer, Mercer (1981). *Terrible Troll.* Dial.

Ness, Evaline (1966). *Sam, Bangs & Moonshine*. Henry Holt.
Parkes, Brenda and Judith Smith (retold by). *Three Little Pigs*. (1985). Methuen Australia.
Peet, Bill (1965). *Kermit the Hermit*. Houghton Mifflin.
Rey, H.A. (1952). *Curious George Rides a Bike*. Scholastic.
Schmidt, Karen (1985). *The Gingerbread Man*. Scholastic.
Steig, William (1974). *Farmer Palmer's Wagon Ride*. Farrar, Straus, and Giroux.
Steig, William (1968). *Roland the Minstrel Pig*. Harper & Row.
Taylor, Mark. (1966). *Henry the Explorer*. Little, Brown.

MONSTERS

Goals

For this project we had several interlocking goals:

Curriculum goals

- To develop the children's reading, writing, speaking and listening abilities in an integrated manner.
- To share with the children regularities in the world of literature that may have eluded their attention.

Professional goals

- To integrate three teaching techniques into a single unit of work: posters, interviews and bureaucratic forms (see *Literacy Through Literature*).
- To integrate the process approach to writing into daily activities (Graves, 1983).
- To test the application of our teaching model (see pages 143-146).

WOLF WANTED

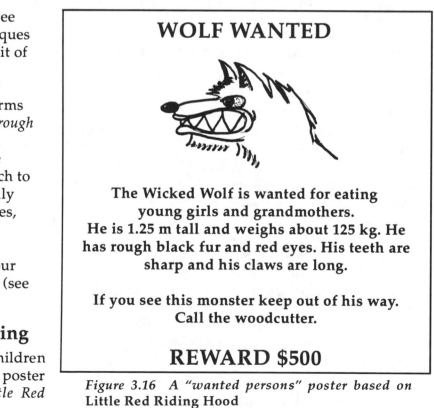

**The Wicked Wolf is wanted for eating young girls and grandmothers.
He is 1.25 m tall and weighs about 125 kg. He has rough black fur and red eyes. His teeth are sharp and his claws are long.**

**If you see this monster keep out of his way.
Call the woodcutter.**

REWARD $500

Figure 3.16 A "wanted persons" poster based on **Little Red Riding Hood**

Lesson 1: Modeling

We showed the children a "wanted persons" poster for the wolf in *Little Red*

Your name ______________

WANTED PERSONS REPORT FORM

Who is wanted? ______________

Why are they wanted? ______________

____

Appearance

Height ________ Age ________

Weight ________ Body covering ________

Hair ________ ________

Dangerous parts

Eyes ________ ________

Habits: What does this creature do? ______________

____

Action: What should you do if you see this creature?

____

Cautions to be taken: ______________

Reward offered? How much? ______________

Signature ______________ Date ________

Figure 3.17 A "wanted persons" report form

Riding Hood (figure 3.16) and read the wording aloud. We then asked them to identify which information had been taken from the story and which had been added by the person who made the poster.

Modeling the process. We then read aloud *The Three Billy Goats Gruff.* On an overhead projector we showed a copy of a "wanted persons" report form (figure 3.17) and recorded oral suggestions for slightly fewer than half the items on the form.

Guided practice. We asked the children to complete the information independently, with liberal assistance available from both us and their peers.

We closed the lesson with an oral sharing of some of the ways the form had been completed.

Teacher Talk	Children's responses	Information recorded
Who is wanted?	The troll	The troll
Why?	Trying to eat people. Eating billygoats. Stopping people from going over the bridge.	He is wanted for stopping people from going over the bridge, and trying to eat them.

Figure 3.18 A teacher/class interchange while filling out a "wanted persons" report

Lesson 2: Supervised Practice

We read *The Story of Ferdinand* aloud and gave each child a copy of the "missing persons" report form (figure 3.19). We asked the children how they would fill out the "missing person" form if they were Ferdinand's mother. We accepted oral suggestions for slightly less than half the items, then the children completed the form independently. We closed the lesson with an oral sharing of their responses.

Your name ____________

Missing Person Report Form

Who is wanted? ____________

Home address: ____________

____

Appearance
Height ________ Age ________
Weight ________ Body covering ________
Hair color ________
Eye color ________

Intended destination: ____________

____

Where was this person last seen? ____________

____

If found, please tell: ____________

Address ____________ Phone ________

Is a reward being offered? If so, how much?

____

Figure 3.19 A "missing persons" report form

Lesson 3: Supervised Practice

We read aloud *The Creature in the Forest* and asked the children to complete a "wanted persons" report for the dragon. Next we asked them to create a poster based on the information on the form. This phase required extensive oral discussion and modeling. Items of information from the form were to be cast into sentences and sequenced into flowing prose. We made frequent reference to the wicked wolf model.

The children found this difficult to do. Even competent children would produce sentences such as:

Body covering is scales. Dangerous parts are claws and teeth . . .

rather than:

It is covered with scales and has dangerous claws and teeth.

We found it difficult to explain how discrete items of information could be incorporated into a coherent prose statement. We simply kept modeling the process and suggesting rewording.

Lesson 4: Independent Application

The children chose a book from a monster library (a bibliography is provided at the end of this section) and undertook to do either a missing person or a wanted person report, using the appropriate form. They each then created a poster.

We had a cork board at the back of the room, divided into four labeled sections: Human Horrors, Fabulous Beasts, Fearsome Animals and Mind Monsters. We drew these labels to the children's attention and provided a brief definition of each.

We asked the children to place the dragon (from *The Creature in the Forest*), the troll and the wicked wolf. Since we hadn't yet encountered a Mind Monster, that was left blank.

Literary monsters	
Human horrors	A human horror is any fearsome creature in a story that is a distorted version of a human being. Human horrors include giants, trolls, goblins, ghouls, ghosts, and devils.
Fabulous beasts	A fabulous beast is a fearsome animal that never was. Fabulous beasts include dragons, basilisks, gryphons, chimeras and cockatrices.
Fearsome animals	A fearsome animal is one which occurs in nature but which regularly appears as a monster in stories. Fearsome animals include wolves, bears, tigers, lions, foxes and snakes.
Mind monsters	A mind monster is a figment of someone's imagination. They include nightmares and hidden fears that spring unbidden from the unconscious.

Figure 3.20 A classification scheme for literary monsters

As the children completed their posters we asked them to place them in the section of their choice. This required some considerable deliberation. And since someone had made a poster for Sendak's *Where the Wild Things Are* we had an opportunity to discuss Mind Monsters as well.

The creation of the poster required wording and a picture. Graves suggests that drawing is a fine *pre-writing* activity for children, and we encouraged pictures first. The regular classroom teacher wisely suggested we let each child decide the sequence.

Lesson 5: Independent Application

We asked each child to select a book with a monster in it, then form pairs and label themselves A and B. They decided whether they wanted to produce a "wanted" or a "missing" poster and we gave them the appropriate forms.

Child A in each pair then interviewed Child B and recorded the answers on the form. (In theory Child A hadn't read the book Child B was reporting on, although in actual practice many of them had read every monster book in the room.) Then the roles reversed and Child B interviewed Child A. A wanted person report form is shown in figure 3.21, and a wanted poster in figure 3.22.

The children created rough drafts of the "copy" (planned wording) for individual posters based on the information provided by their partners. These were checked by the people who had been interviewed and by the regular teacher for completeness, clarity and conventional spelling. The children then put the rough draft into final form and added pictorial information. The resulting posters were added to the classified display.

Lessons 6 and 7: Independent Application

This type of collaboration was new to the children and several were confused and concerned about ownership of the resulting posters. So we repeated the lesson using fresh stories and fresh partnerships. Soon joint ownership was accepted.

Meeting the Goals

Curriculum

Developing reading, writing, speaking and listening in an integrated manner. The project had provided many opportunities to exercise each of these skills in a highly goal-oriented context.

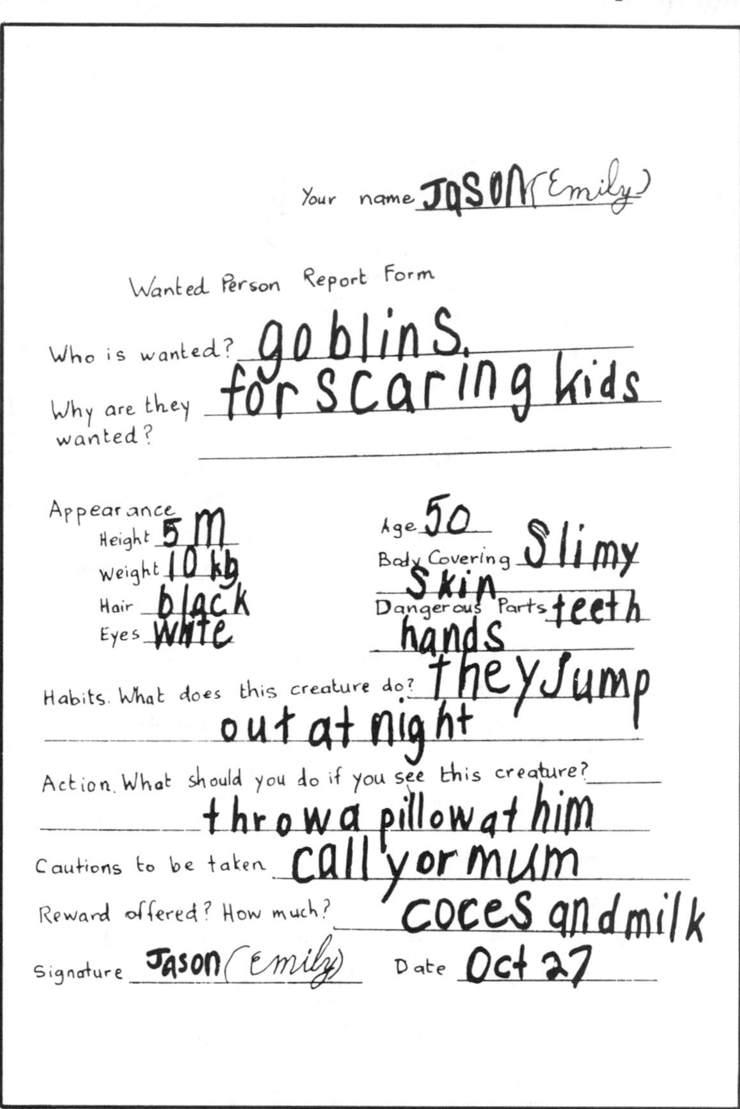

Your name JaSon (Emily)

Wanted Person Report Form

Who is wanted? goblinS.

Why are they wanted? for scaring kids

Appearance
Height 5 m
Weight 10 kg
Hair black
Eyes wite

Age 50
Body Covering Slimy Skin
Dangerous Parts teeth hands

Habits. What does this creature do? theyJump out at night

Action. What should you do if you see this creature? throwa pillowat him

Cautions to be taken. call yor mum

Reward offered? How much? coces andmilk

Signature Jason (Emily) Date Oct 27

Figure 3.21 A Wanted Person Report filled out by Jason from a book read by Emily

Regularities of literature. The children's initial uncertainty in classifying fictional beasts showed that the recurring categories of monster hadn't come to their attention yet. But they soon became adept at identifying any given fearsome creature.

Professional

Once we had overcome the difficulty of translating information, the use of bureaucratic forms and interviews leading to a poster worked well. Our biggest surprise was the realization that the steps in the writing process hadn't been at the forefront of anyone's attention. We had all simply adopted it as a normal working procedure. Yet we believe that at this practical and unconscious level process writing is at its most effective.

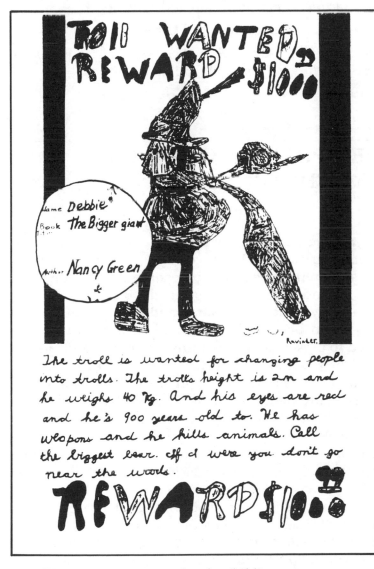

Figure 3.22 An example of a child's poster

In general, the teaching model held up well. We didn't stride through it relentlessly but were able to backtrack and reteach when unexpected difficulties arose.

Bibliography of monster books

Ambrus, Victor (1980). *The Valiant Little Taylor.* Oxford University Press.

Appleby, Susan, illustrator (1984). *The Three Billy Goats Gruff.* Scholastic.

Crowe, Robert (1976). *Clyde Monster.* Dutton.

Faulkner, Matt (1986). *Jack and the Beanstalk.* Scholastic.

Gackenback, Dick (1978). *Harry & the Terrible Whatzit.* Scholastic.

Grimm, illustrated by Paul Galdone (1982). *Hansel and Gretel.* McGraw-Hill.

Grimm, illustrated by Freya Littledale (1980). *Snow White.* Scholastic.

Grimm, retold by Hogrogian (1983). *The Devil with the Three Golden Hairs*. Knopf.

LaFontaine , illustrated by Brian Wildsmith (1976). *The Lion and the Rat*. Oxford.

Leaf, Munro (1936). *The Story of Ferdinand*.Viking.

Mayer, Mercer (1968). *There's a Nightmare in My Closet*. Dial.

Peet, Bill (1984). *Cowardly Clyde*. Houghton Mifflin.

Sendak, Maurice (1963). *Where the Wild Things Are*. Harper & Row.

Steig, William (1982). *Doctor de Soto*. Scholastic.

Steig, William (1968). *Roland the Minstrel Pig*. Harper & Row.

Stieg, William (1969). *Sylvester and the Magic Pebble*. Simon and Schuster.

Steig, William (1977). *The Amazing Bone*. Farrar, Strauss and Giroux.

Viorst, Judith (1973). *My Mama Says There Aren't Any Zombies, Ghosts, Vampires, Creatures, Demons, Monsters, Fiends, Goblins or Things*. Macmillan.

TIME-SLIP FANTASIES: PLANNING FOR THE UPPER ELEMENTARY SCHOOL

Introduction

In this section we present our planning for a unit we think would be suitable for children in the upper levels of elementary school. We haven't yet taught this unit.

We selected well-written novels that reflect the spread of reading ability commonly encountered in a sixth grade class, including books from Canada, the United States, Australia, and Great Britain. It's a fairly arbitrary selection and other suitable titles could easily be added. It happens to be heavily weighted in favor of female protagonists but could be modified to present an equal number of boys and girls.

We also planned for a spread of routines. Those described for Pearce's *Tom's Midnight Garden* fit with the nature of the text; however, other routines arranged in alternative sequences would serve equally well. Our whole-class work with this book would provide a review of routines already familiar to the children as well as introduce new ways of responding to novels.

The motivational focus would provide an overall purpose for the activities: the children would select and develop their analyses so their assigned novel would come to illuminate this purpose.

We've only hinted at the inevitable discussions that will develop around the philosophical conundrums raised by the idea of slipping through time.

The time required depends on the length and frequency of the lessons. With one-hour lessons daily the project would take about three weeks.

Overview

You will read *Tom's Midnight Garden* aloud to the class over a period of three weeks, then divide the children into five groups. Each group will read an assigned novel and, through the use of selected analysis routines, share with the rest of the class various aspects of the story. The objective is to convince the rest of the class that their novel is worthy of a "time-slip award."

The class will compare the six novels using a comparison grid and vote to determine which book will receive the certificate of merit.

Objective

To enable the children to discover that books in a sub-genre have similar structures.

Materials

One copy of *Tom's Midnight Garden* and six copies of each of the following (or similar titles):

Charlotte Sometimes (Farmer)
The Root Cellar (Lunn)
Playing Beatie Bow (Park)
Conrad's War (Davies)
Time at the Top (Ormondroyd)

You will also need a library of time-slip fantasies (see the bibliography at the end of this section for suggestions).

Motivational focus

The class must select the best time-slip fantasy.

Procedure

Introduction

Initiate a discussion on the possibility of time travel:

- If you could travel through time where/when would you go? What would you do?
- If you traveled to the early colonial days what advantages would you have with your knowledge of the future and your ignorance of their customs? What disadvantages would you have?
- If you traveled into the past and made a change, would it change the future?
- If you can travel into the future, has the future already happened? Is everything predetermined? Do we have free will?
- If you can travel into the past is the past still happening?

At the close of the discussion ask the children to write a brief statement of their ideas about time travel. Collect their papers and place them in a sealed "time capsule" for the duration of the project.

Whole class work

Provide an overview of the project and begin reading *Tom's Midnight Garden* aloud. As the reading proceeds over the next three weeks conduct the following routines with the whole class:

Chapters	Technique	
1-3	Countdown	A plot profile is developed as the story progresses ↓
4-5	Mapping	
6-7	Literary letter	
8-9	Summary cloze	
10-11	Literary journal	
12-13	Reacting to propositions	
14-16	Book bingo	
17-18	Lazy letter	
19-20	Character grid	
21-22	Word webs	
23-24	Rating scales	
25-27	Sociogram	
Complete story	Story grammar	

Introduce the routines at the conclusion of the chapters listed. The content covered may include any part of the book up to the point where the reading stopped.

Group work

At the same time, the children are working in groups to share an assigned novel. Group responsibilities are:

1. Read the novel by a specified date.
2. Prepare four analyses that will inform the rest of the class about the novel, using any four routines.
3. Prepare statements to be entered into the comparison grid (figure 3.23).

Classroom organization will be:

- ***Presentations.*** Have each group in turn present an analysis.
- ***Comparison grid.*** Have each group present its entries for the comparison grid.
- ***Voting.*** Prepare voting slips and conduct the vote. The children can't vote for their own novel; they choose the book they now most want to read.

novel	*Tom's Midnight Garden*	*Charlotte Sometimes*	*The Root Cellar*	*Playing Beatty Bow*	*Conrad's War*	your choice
central character						
age						
sex						
companion						
locality 1						
locality 2						
portal						
direction of travel						
historical connection						
personal growth						

Figure 3.23 A time-slip comparison grid

- ***Award.*** Prepare a sufficiently elaborate certificate for the best time-slip fantasy and present it to the winning group.
- ***Attitude.*** Again ask the children to write a brief statement of their ideas about time travel.

Opening the time capsule

Invite the children to share with the class any changes that have occurred in their attitudes as a result of the unit.

Extensions

You may want to assemble a small library of time-slip fantasies for the children to read independently. Some may wish to share books they read with the class and add them to the comparison grid.

Criteria

You might also help the children develop a list of criteria ("rules") both for novels and for time-slip fantasies. If so, have the groups demonstrate that their assigned novels meet all or most of the specified criteria.

Specimen criteria:

Novels	Time-slip fantasies
1. Interesting plot.	1. Provides an explanation for the method of time slippage.
2. Convincing characters.	2. Provides a historical connection beyond the time-slip.
3. Further 4. criteria 5. offered by 6. the children.	3. Further 4. criteria 5. offered by 6. the children.

Time-slip bibliography

Bond, Nancy (1973). *A String in the Harp.*Macmillan

Davies, Andrew (1980). *Conrad's War.* Dell.

Doty, Jean S. (1980). *Can I Get There By Candlelight?* Macmillan.

Farmer, Penelope (1969). *Charlotte Sometimes.* Dell.

Houghton, Eric (1980). *Steps out of Time.* Lothrop.

L'Engle, Madeleine (1973). A Wrinkle in Time. Dell.

L'Engle, Madeleine (1979). *A Swiftly Tilting Planet.* Dell.

Lively, Penelope (1974). *The House in Norham Gardens.*Dutton.

Lunn, Janet (1983). *The Root Cellar.* Penguin.

Melling, O.R. (1985). *The Druid's Tune.* Penguin.

Norton, Andre (1976). *Wraiths of Time.* Ballantine.

Ormondroyd, Edward (1963). *Time at the Top.* Bantam.

Park, Ruth (1980). *Playing Beatie Bow.* Atheneum.

Pearson, Kit (1987).*A Handful of Time.* Viking Canada.

Stolz, Mary (1975). *The Cat in the Mirror.* Dell.

Taylor, Cora (1988). *Yesterday's Doll.* Scholastic. (Also published as *The Doll* by Western Producer Prairie Books)

Utley, Alison (1981). *A Traveller in Time.* Faber.

Walsh, Jill Paton (1980). *A Chance Child.* Avon.
Wells, H.G. *The Time Machine.* Bantam.
Wiseman, David (1981). *Jeremy Visick.* Houghton Mifflin.
Wiseman, David (1982). *Thimbles.* Houghton Mifflin.

There are many other types of time-slip stories. Groups of children are whisked off to mythic kingdoms to become involved in quests; visitors from other times arrive in the present and cause numerous problems; some characters flit up and down the space-time continuum in a series of episodic adventures. Ruth Lynn's *Fantasy for Children* (1983), under the heading "Time Travel Fantasies," contains 147 annotated entries.

THE LITTLE MISS MUFFET PROJECT

Purpose

This was a simple empirical research project to help us determine the degree of learning that resulted from whole language instruction.

The children

We worked with a class of 27 first graders in their second month of school; they had received 35 days of instruction when we started. They came from a predominantly middle-class neighborhood ,with a racial mix common for that area, and had a normal range of ability.

The research design

Their classroom teacher, who normally used a skills-based basal reader, agreed to maintain her regular program and provide no further instruction with *Little Miss Muffet* beyond permitting the children to play during free periods with the material we provided. We hoped we'd be able to conclude that any growth in *Little Miss Muffet* vocabulary was due to the whole language instruction.

We gave both the experimental class and a control group in the same school a word identification test (figure 3.24). We read aloud one word in each row and used it in a sentence. Then we repeated the word and asked the children to check (✓) it. Target words are checked in the example.

The text

The text of *Little Miss Muffet* was written on individual cards of equal length (see Sight vocabulary, page 18).

Measurement of learning

Measuring progress in literacy is a complex undertaking (see Chapter Five). The number of words a child can identify from a given body is only a *rough* indication of *one* aspect of that child's competence in literacy. We used this test because it's simple to prepare and easy to administer, and responses are unambiguously right or wrong. We were concerned nevertheless about giving young children a task they might not, initially, be able to do and indeed, in spite of our reassurances that whatever they did would be all right, one child cried because she couldn't answer all the questions on the pretest.

We used items (a), (b) and (c) to demonstrate the procedure. Items 1-8 require gross discriminations; items 9-16 have initial letters in common and thus require finer discriminations. We administered the same test at the end of the project.

(a)	house	dog	man	pig
(b)	rug	fire	about	pen
(c)	bill	band	bag	bent
1.	away ✓	Miss	little	sat
2.	her	frightened ✓	eating	there
3.	who ✓	came	a	big
4.	beside ✓	spider	and	sat
5.	little	away	Miss	down ✓
6.	her	frightened	sat ✓	which
7.	eating	and✓	there	a
8.	came	spider ✓	big	and
9.	boy	bat	big ✓	ball
10.	a ✓	an	o	i
11.	cut	came ✓	crab	cent
12.	this	thing	there ✓	the
13.	eel	egg	elbow	eating ✓
14.	horse	help	his	her ✓
15.	sat ✓	sing	stand	soup
16.	mum	many	make	Miss ✓

***Figure 3.24** A word identification test based on vocabulary from "Little Miss Muffet." Target words are checked*

Instructional time

We taught for 15 minutes once a day for nine school days, for a total of 135 minutes of instruction.

Teaching Procedures

Shared reading

- Teacher modeling
- Pointing/tracing
- Visual tracking by the children
- Unison reading: normally, softly, angrily, loudly, as though afraid.

Text identification

- We traced and framed lines, phrases and words to be identified by the children.

- We named lines, phrases and words to be framed or traced by the children.

Text manipulation

Word removal and replacement. We removed words from the rhyme and replaced them with blank markers. These we randomly displayed at the foot of the chart and asked the children to:

- identify the missing words
- identify and replace the appropriate words
- read the reconstructed text.

Word transposition. We transposed words, usually nouns. For example:

Little Miss Muffet sat on a spider
Eating her whey and curds,
There came a big tuffet
Who sat down beside her . . .

We asked the children to locate and replace the misplaced words.

Word substitution. We presented alternative versions of the rhyme:

Little Mr. Pair
Sat on a chair . . .

We randomly displayed the displaced words *(Miss, Muffet, tuffet)* at the foot of the chart and the children replaced appropriate words.

Letter substitution. We introduced variant spellings to form deviant versions:

Little Miss Puffet
Sat on a buffet . . .

The children read the text orally in unison but were to stop, remain silent and raise their hands when they came to a word they believed to be wrong. The word that should appear was identified, the word that actually appeared was pronounced, the offending letter named and the appropriate correction made. The children regarded any disturbance of the text as highly amusing.

Text reconstruction. We distributed the complete text of the rhyme on individual cards so that each child held one word. We encouraged the children to show their word to a friend if they needed any help identifying it. We then reconstructed the text as a group. We suggested unsupervised text reconstruction, individually or in small groups, as an option during free periods.

Word identification: justification

When a particular word was correctly identified we frequently asked the children to say how they knew. They usually referred to the initial letter but exceptions occurred, as shown in figure 3.25.

Dictated spelling

Sometimes we removed the missing words from view and asked the children to suggest spellings for them. Any correct letter the children suggested was set down in its appropriate position. We didn't ask what letter came next, just what other letters were needed. Children often provide letters in order of saliency rather than sequence.

We were a little uncertain how to deal with wild guesses but one strategy we used was to "store" incorrect letters below the word being built on the chalkboard ("let's save that one to see if we need it"). When the word was generally deemed complete we compared it with the original and noted any leftover letters. We exploited teaching opportunities presented by errors (figure 3.26) whenever it was possible to discern the source of the child's confusion.

Miscues by Millie

On the third day an apparent "loss" of voice produced a series (figure 3.27) of messages to indicate that our friend Millie would read to the children that day.

However Millie, being a particularly bucolic bovine hand-puppet, wasn't excep-

Word being identified	Justification
Muffet	It's got an M [letter name]
Spider	It starts with /s/ [Phonemic approximation]
her	It has an *r* [letter name] at the end.
tuffet	It's got two *t*s [letter name] in it.

Figure 3.25 Justifications offered by grade one students after correctly identifying a word

Expected response	Observed response	Teacher's response
Muffet	*tuffet*	Word cards for *Muffet* and *tuffet* were compared and contrasted.
beside	*down*	Letters *d* an *b* compared and contrasted.
sat	*spider*	Word cards for *sat* and *spider* were compared and contrasted. "Which letter tells us to make the /t/ sound in *sat*?"

Figure 3.26 Examples of teaching opportunities presented by children's errors

tionally adept at reading herself and somewhat prone to error. For example, "Little Miss Muffet sat on a tuffet" became "Little Miss Muffet sat on a frog."

The children were quick to notice deviations from the text and vociferous in their corrections. Unfortunately Millie was not only stupid but stubborn. She insisted that the word was *frog*. The children were equally and vehemently insistent it was *tuffet*. Millie reluctantly bowed to the opinion of the majority.

Towards the end of the lesson one little girl in the back row noticed that Millie's voice continued to utter from the teacher's mouth despite the fact that Millie's lips had ceased to move. However, Millie stoutly maintained that only she, and not her operator, was able to speak.

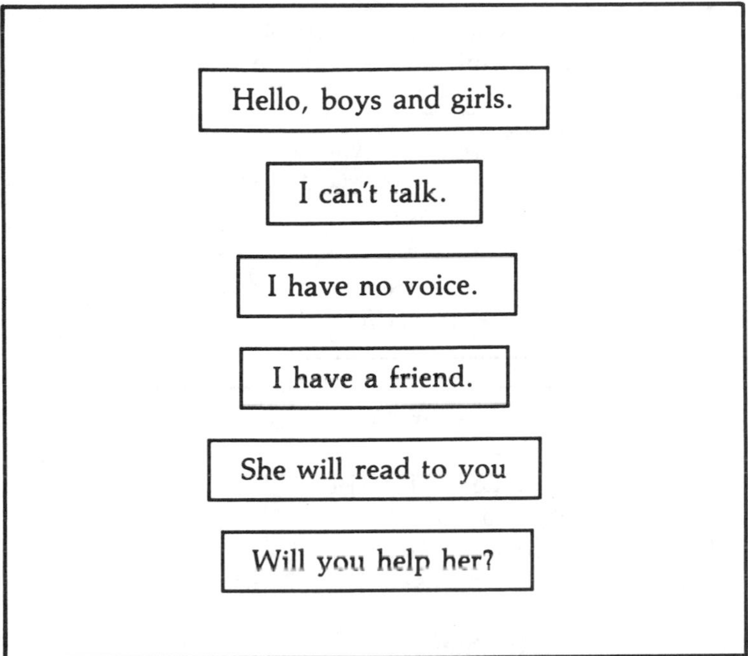

Figure 3.27 Written messages used to rationalize the presence of Millie

Millie stayed on for the remainder of the project and was occasionally asked to read. Unfortunately there was little improvement in either her reading or her acceptance of correction.

Transfer

Each of the following routines required the children to read the vocabulary of the rhyme in a new context.

Yes or No

A set of statements (figure 3.28) was written on 30 x 20 cm cards. As far as possible they reuse the language of the rhyme without introducing too much new vocabulary.

We provided the children with two small cards, one pink and one white. They wrote YES on the pink card and NO on the white. The children were to read each statement silently and indicate whether it was true (show pink) or false (show white). We modeled the procedure with the first three statements:

- The statement was read orally, in unison.
- We turned it into a question.
- A volunteer provided the answer orally, and the children held up the appropriate card.

Some of the untrue statements evoked considerable giggling and cheerful disgust.

"Who" questions

A set of questions was written on cards (figure 3.29). Again each child was provided with two small cards. On one they wrote *A big spider*; on the other, *Little Miss Muffet*. Again the first three questions were modeled orally, and subsequent questions were shown silently. The children indicated the correct answers by holding up the appropriate card.

Clues

The clues and answer cards shown in figure 3.30 were put on cards as before. The children cut their answer cards along the lines to form six smaller cards, then held up the appropriate card as we showed each clue silently. They spent several minutes of intent "time on task" (see page 146) as they tried to match the meaning of what they saw with the appropriate word or phrase from the array of answers spread out on their desks.

How to Reduce Guessing: The Cashflow Game

We noticed during the preceding activities that some of the less able children were guessing at random, so we introduced

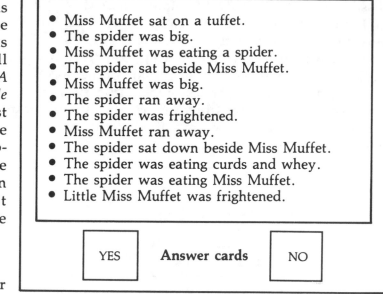

- Miss Muffet sat on a tuffet.
- The spider was big.
- Miss Muffet was eating a spider.
- The spider sat beside Miss Muffet.
- Miss Muffet was big.
- The spider ran away.
- The spider was frightened.
- Miss Muffet ran away.
- The spider sat down beside Miss Muffet.
- The spider was eating curds and whey.
- The spider was eating Miss Muffet.
- Little Miss Muffet was frightened.

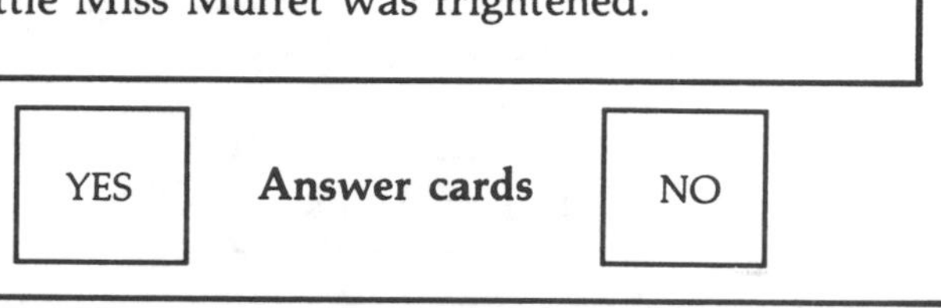

Figure 3.28 Yes/No statements and answer cards based on "Little Miss Muffet"

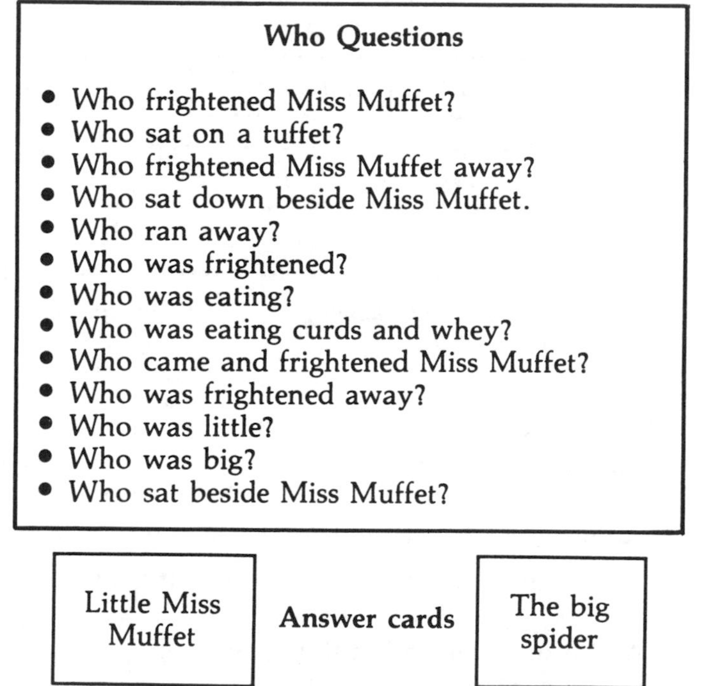

Who Questions

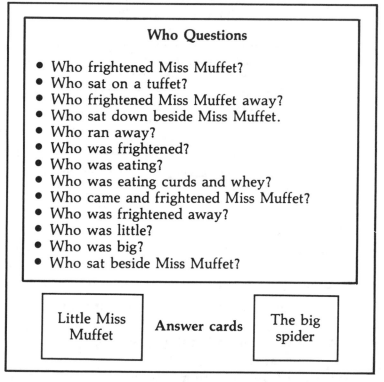

- Who frightened Miss Muffet?
- Who sat on a tuffet?
- Who frightened Miss Muffet away?
- Who sat down beside Miss Muffet.
- Who ran away?
- Who was frightened?
- Who was eating?
- Who was eating curds and whey?
- Who came and frightened Miss Muffet?
- Who was frightened away?
- Who was little?
- Who was big?
- Who sat beside Miss Muffet?

Figure 3.29 "Who" questions and answer cards based on "Little Miss Muffet"

Clues

- I sat on a tuffet.
- I sat down to eat.
- I go with curds.
- I was frightened.
- I sat down beside Miss Muffet.
- I go with whey.
- I ran away.
- A big spider sat down beside me.
- I am little.
- I am big.
- Little Miss Muffet was eating us.
- I frightened Miss Muffet away.
- Miss Muffet sat on me.

Little Miss Muffet	The big spider	tuffet
curds and whey	whey	curds

Answer cards

Figure 3.30 Clues and answer cards based on "Little Miss Muffet"

Figure 3.31 Child's desk arrangements for a cashflow game

the cashflow game to promote more deliberate responses. We provided the children with ten counters each. Five they placed on a book; these belonged to them. The remaining five they simply put on their desk; those belonged to us. Whenever the children answered correctly they transferred a counter from the desk to the book; incorrect answers made the "cash" flow in the opposite direction. We had more counters available in case the children won all five of ours — and they were delighted by our chagrin when they did so.

This procedure appeared to work well except for the least adept children, who wisely checked to see what everyone else was doing before making a response.

Individual Reading

We provided each child with a normal-sized copy of the Muffet rhyme and we all read in unison. We framed various phrases and words in preparation for the following writing activity.

Writing

We asked the children to label the following items on the picture provided:

Little Miss Muffet
big spider
tuffet

Amy's response is shown in figure 3.32.

Individual Needs and Independent Activities

As we worked with the children it became clear that some learned the visual form of the rhyme rapidly and could identify any word, in context or in isolation. At the other extreme were some who guessed wildly and appeared to find it difficult to sustain attention during whole class instruction.

Since we were interested in the efficacy of the whole class instruction we didn't make modifications for the extreme cases. However, any of the teaching material could also be used for small group instruction or independently by the children.

All the material prepared for this project was made available to the children during free periods. We assumed that three children could work with each — the pocket chart, Millie, the yes/no game, the "who" questions and the clue cards — thus occupying 15 in small group work. If similar material were available for one other familiar rhyme, there would be more than sufficient material to keep a significant portion of the class productively occupied with only general supervision, leaving you free to work with small groups and individuals. Combining free play with familiar materials

Little
Miss
Muffet
spider
big
tuffet
Little Miss Muffet
Sat on a tuffet,
Eating her curds and whey.
There came a big spider
Who sat down beside her
And frightened Miss Muffet away.

Figure 3.32 The text and picture of "Little Miss Muffet," labeled by Amy , grade one

with modified small group instruction in this way is one means of meeting individual needs.

Skills Development

Skills development is controlled by the words selected for substitution and the letters selected for manipulation. From our analysis we determined that we had covered the skills shown in figure 3.33.

Storage and Retrieval

Putting texts on individual word cards has the enormous advantage of making it very simple to manipulate. However, the practice generates large numbers of loose cards which, if they become disorganized, are transformed from a resource into a headache.

For the Little Miss Muffet project we developed what we thought of as our Little Miss Muffet teaching kit (figure 3.34). We began with a simple manila folder, writing the complete text of the rhyme on the outside. We taped sturdy envelopes on the inside to form pockets: one held the text of the rhyme, one the word substitutions, one letter cards, one blank word cards and blank space cards in a contrasting color. The yes/no, "who" and clues cards we kept inside the folder. We could easily store the whole package in a file drawer.

High frequency words		**Enrich-ment**	**Sound/ symbol**
Text	*Transfer activities*		
little sat on a eating her and there came big who down away	was the ran go I am me to	Miss Muffet tuffet curds whey beside frightened	p/m b/s e/a s d h t er fr sp

Figure 3.33 Little Miss Muffet Project: skill development

Caveat

Since we were trying to control the children's exposure to a specific vocabulary and to measure one aspect of their language growth, the project doesn't represent what we believe to be good teaching practice. In particular two things prevented optimum instruction.

First, the project concentrated on a single rhyme. In normal practice *Little Miss Muffet* would be but one item in a small but growing repertoire of rhymes, poems and rhythmical stories. Second, instruction was concentrated into a single 15 minute period per day. Our normal practice is to distribute whole language activities throughout the day.

But the purpose of the project wasn't to demonstrate that whole language was *better* than the program being offered to the control group, but simply to determine whether or not a whole language program resulted in the achievement of expected results. The control group provided a base line. Since those children hadn't been exposed to the *Little Miss Muffet* vocabulary it was reasonable to expect they wouldn't learn any of it.

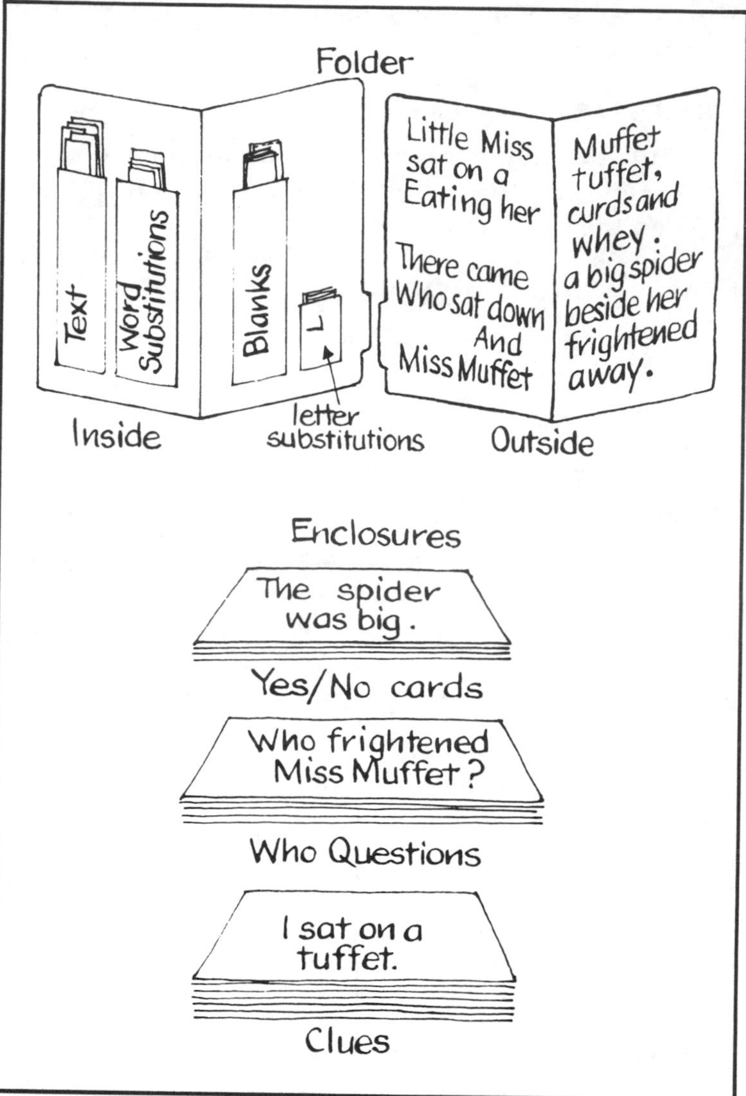

Figure 3.34 The "Little Miss Muffet" teaching kit

Evaluation

The results, shown in figure 3.35, indicate that the experimental group made a slight gain while the control group made essentially none. It's interesting to observe that the gains made by the experimental group occurred among words requiring more refined discriminations. This may indicate that instruction helped some of the children become slightly more discriminating in word identification.

The results aren't as dramatic as we would have liked. However, when you consider that 135 minutes doesn't amount to half a day of instruction, the modest gains aren't surprising.

The numbers of children involved don't make statistical analysis worthwhile. The figures presented and the conclusions drawn from them must be regarded only as very tentative possibilities.

	Pre-test			Post-test		
	gross	fine	*total*	gross	fine	*total*
Experimental	6.9	4.6	11.5	6.8	7.3	13.1
Control	5.6	4.5	10.1	6.7	3.8	10.5

Figure 3.35 Mean number of words correctly identified by children in grade one

But beyond statistics, it's difficult to document the numerous occasions when the classroom was filled with laughter; or the number of times a momentary hush fell over the children as they pondered their choice of an answer card; or their derisive watchfulness as they witnessed Millie's miscues; or their delight in winning all the *our* counters. We believe that if all children had a history of such occasions associated in their minds with "learning to read," more of them would more readily become habitual readers.

THEORETICAL REFLECTIONS

The Role of Direct Instruction

The term *direct instruction* has become anathema to many whole language teachers because it's associated with an extreme position regarding the isolated teaching of discrete parts of superficial aspects of language (Carnine and Silbert, 1979). Our attitude is ambivalent. We endorse the directness of instruction but reject the isolation of skills.

The revelation by Durkin (1978-79) that the teachers in her study spent very little time instructing has had a great impact on education. Carnine and Silbert take the position that if we expect children to do something we should be prepared to show them how to do it. We have no argument with their basic premise that children should be shown how to do what we expect them to do. But they have taken the traditional basal-reader approach at face value and have suggested systematic ways for all the multifarious skills to be taught. They are addressing the surface structure of language when we feel instruction should address the mid-level strategies instead.

A General Teaching Model

We've adopted the following general teaching model, one that can easily be adapted to fit the situation and the various activities being taught. For young and unskilled children, and for complex processes, we prolong the modeling and guidance phases. When teaching a simple activity to young children we often omit the elicitation of "rules."

Modeling

We provide one or more completed examples based on material already familiar to the children.

Discussing the model. We draw significant aspects of the example to the children's attention.

Modeling the process. When the activity is complex and involves several steps we itemize, describe and explain the steps involved.

Levels of response. With older children we model the various quality levels of response, giving examples of "A," "B" and "C" levels and explaining the characteristics that differentiate one level from another.

Origin of the examples. Where possible we use examples produced by children working under the same conditions as the group we're currently working with — usually children from the previous year. Or we might coach slightly older children, individually or in a small group, and use their work. We may even bring in the older children to explain how they tackled the task, to describe problems they encountered and to answer questions from the younger children. Another possibility is to coach one or more of the children we're currently working with. The temptation is to use the most competent children as models but we've found we can create additional social benefits and increases in self-esteem if we use less able children to demonstrate a new idea or procedure.

Guided Practice

A guided practice lesson is teacher-centered, whole-class and orally based. We walk and talk the children through all the steps involved. If we do break the procedure down into smaller steps we try to ensure that the children understand how each step relates to the whole.

When working with inexperienced and/or less able readers we may go through the guided practice phase with several different stories, poems or expository passages.

The Elicitation of "Rules"

Helping the children to observe regularities, patterns or defining characteristics may occur at various points in the teaching sequence. We are guided by two principles:

- Learners must have a sufficient number of experiences to base generalizations on.
- The less competent and less experienced the learners, the greater the number of concrete experiences they need before they can be expected to make a generalization.

Providing rules too soon. Student-teachers often begin teaching something new by presenting definitions of a procedure or concept. A definition is an abstraction based on a generalization made across numerous concrete examples of a concept. But it's hard to understand or learn from an abstraction before extensive experience with concrete reality. For example, children will learn the essential characteristics of a picnic much more readily by going on three or four different kinds of picnics than by listening to a definition.

Inexperienced teachers also often attempt to establish rules after presenting a single example. Children can't generalize from one example. Any example, in addition to the essential defining characteristics and relationships, will have attributes that can be changed without changing the essential nature of the process or concept. Children who have their first picnic sitting on the grass in the park may associate picnics with eating on the grass in the park. They'll need experience with picnics on beaches, in city squares or in a garden before they appreciate that picnicking involves eating food away from home in the open air and that parks and grass are optional characteristics.

The actual timing of establishing rules for any given procedure varies considerably. If the modeling process has involved the use of numerous examples, "rules" can be elicited after the first guided practice session. If the children are inexperienced or the procedure is complex, they usually can't be established until after two or three guided practice sessions.

Rules versus "rules." Rules are directives issued by authorities and are, theoretically at least, perfect and thus immutable. "Rules" are tentative generalizations based on perceived regularities observed by the learner. We can provide examples of "rules" but we try to get the children to establish their own. Within reason we will accept a "rule" we feel is inadequate, trusting that the children's subsequent experience will lead them to revise it during the review sessions we hold periodically. We much prefer this participatory procedure since in the long term it's more helpful to the children than the admittedly efficient, though authoritarian, process of teacher-provided rules.

Supervised practice

Supervised practice sessions are still whole-class, orally based procedures but they are less teacher centered. We read a story, poem or exposition to the class and have the children work independently or in pairs as they apply the newly acquired technique to it. The number of supervised practice sessions will vary with the sophistication of the children and the complexity of the technique.

Independent application

In this final phase our direction is almost entirely withdrawn. Each child individually selects a book or passage and applies the technique to it.

It is at this stage that the value of multiple examples and tentative "rules" become apparent, since the texts the children select may not quite fit examples provided earlier or follow the "rules" elicited. The children need to approach this phase with openness and flexibility so they can modify the principles evolved from earlier experience to fit the new situation.

With young and inexperienced readers it's sometimes wise to limit the range of choices. Given free range of the school library, some children may select wildly inappropriate texts and become frustrated in working with them. We usually provide a limited selection of texts that we've previewed and judged to be useful for the procedure we're working with and roughly at the reading level of the children we're teaching. We give special consideration to the less competent readers, identifying for them a subset of easy books.

Extensions and creative variations

Once the children are familiar and comfortable with the technique we may introduce more complex variations. This is the time we feel we can come close to modeling creativity. After introducing two or three variations we invite the children to explore and share their own ventures. We're often delighted by their inventiveness and frequently incorporate their ideas into our teaching repertoire.

Independent selection and application of techniques and tools

When the children have a repertoire of five or six techniques we permit them to select both the book and the technique they wish to apply to it. At this point the class starts to become self-sustaining and we can truly take on the role of counselor and facilitator, helping the children achieve goals *they* have set. We encourage others to try creative modifications developed by individuals but continue to introduce new techniques via the more directed approach.

Caveat

This kind of orderly writeup of our procedures never seems to reflect what we actually do. The formal explanation is much more tidy and self-conscious than our actual planning and teaching performance. We really do do all the things we describe, but we may not do all of them all the time. Some may be omitted, some repeated, some forgotten (!) and some restructured. Nor does the formal exposition catch the excitement, the laughter, the sense of adventure and simple sense of fun that often infuses the projects we pursue.

Application of the model

Earlier in this chapter we described several projects that exemplify the principles discussed above. The "Monsters" section shows how we've incorporated this teaching model into a particular project.

Devising Instructional Activities

We often notice that children are less than fully focused on their classroom assignments, or on us when we're addressing them, and wonder how much time they are spending "on task." We relish the times when they are totally absorbed in the tale or the task during story time and assigned work periods. They are still. Their gaze is steady and focused. There's an air of serenity about them. These are moments of steadfast intent.

Such intent is readily apparent in chess players, musicians and mathematicians when they are deeply immersed in their occupations. We've also witnessed it in plumbers, electricians and carpenters. It's an intense preoccupation that rises above time, hunger or fatigue. It's one of the conditions we strive to engender in the children we teach, although we succeed far less frequently than we'd like. The quiet calm of the learner isn't a constrained silence imposed by authoritarian control. It's unconsciously self-determined, a reverie the individual slips into.

Many routine activities, like driving a car, listening to the radio, ironing or digging in the garden commonly demand less than our full attention, though each is capable of doing so — for instance, driving on icy roads in foggy weather. Unfortunately too many classroom activities fall into this category. Copying exercises from the chalkboard before completing them is a good example. We asked one third grader to tell us orally what word was required for each blank on his sheet and he rattled off the correct answers in about 10 seconds. It took him, and most of his peers, 45 minutes to execute the mindless, mechanical aspects of the task. In the meantime his mind remained open to distractions from friends, activities outside the window, internal physical conditions and the texture of the desktop.

Eliciting steadfast intent

Moments of steadfast intent occur when learners feel empowered, competent and motivated — all interconnected.

Empowerment. Learners must feel some sense of self-direction. It's possible for them to become absorbed in following someone else's directions but absorption is more likely to occur if they've determined for themselves what they'll do and how they'll do it.

Competence. Learners must feel secure enough to proceed even when problems and novel situations arise.

Motivation. Learners must want to engage in the activity. The execution of the task should be intrinsically rewarding. Working for points, marks, verbal approval or other rewards, or to avoid the teacher's displeasure, are all distracting.

As teachers our aim should be to increase the moments of steadfast intent. When tasks are within the range of their capabilities we should permit, encourage and expect children to make executive decisions. We should make sure that everyday situations arise in which they have to make up their own minds about how to proceed.

We should try to ensure competence. After showing the children how to execute a task, guiding them along the required steps and providing them with supervised practice time, we should encourage them to proceed independently.

We should try to provide activities they like to do. That seems obvious, but when we look at some of the stultifying activities that masquerade as instructional exercises we wonder if the authors ever asked themselves how children would feel about doing them. We start from the simple premise that children like to play. Play involves manipulation, control and invention. We try to select activities that include these characteristics and at the same time contribute to the instructional goals we've identified.

The story world and the real world

Tolkien has said that the job of the fantasy writer is to create a consistent secondary world (Carpenter and Prichard, 1984). In fact all storytellers use words, written or spoken, to create in the minds of their readers or listeners a gauzy representation of something that was but is no longer, something that might be or might have been, something that never was but should have been.

Examination of traditional comprehension questions designed to promote understanding shows that most of them ask children to consider only the story frame: "Why was Snow White's mother jealous?" or "Why did the huntsman spare Snow White's life?" Only occasionally do questions reach out. "Would you have liked Wilbur as a friend?" or "If you were to ask Charlotte one question what would it be?" invite the child to participate in the secondary world created by E. B. White.

We've found that questions that take concepts or situations from the real world and apply them to the story world produce appealing activities that also promote good levels of understanding. Imagining how a given story character might respond if interviewed on television, drawing a map of the setting or making a "wanted" poster for the villain all apply real-life situations or constructs to the story world.

For all children the activities and implicit concepts should be within their level of maturity. For older children the systematic application of real-world values to the story world can lead to original insights. A close examination of how Robert O'Brien treats males and females in *The Secret of NIMH* (Hardcover title: *Mrs. Frisby and the Rats of NIMH*) reveals a distinct tendency towards male chauvinism (see page 231). A close look at C. S. Lewis's *The Lion, the Witch and the Wardrobe* reveals a very authoritarian power structure and a predilection for violence as a means to the solution of differences.

Sometimes the introduction of real world issues shows that significant areas of human behavior have been ignored by the author. If we ask of Tolkien's Hobbit world "How did Bilbo make a living?" or "How do Hobbits fall in love?" or "Why is there no moral issue related to the killing of Orcs?" we begin to realize that Tolkien simply doesn't address these issues.

It's possible to be too demanding and so destroy the fabric of fantasy, but we've found that, used with caution and restraint, applying constructs from the real world often produces novel and useful ways of taking a fresh look at the world of story.

CHAPTER FOUR

PRESENTING THE NOVEL

TO TEACH OR NOT TO TEACH?

We worded the title of this chapter carefully. "Teaching the novel" carries inappropriate connotations. When we teach children about volcanoes, Russia or the water cycle we acquaint them with a body of knowledge that is relatively stable. People might have opinions about the USSR's political system but the name of its capital, its area and the demographics of its people are not matters of dispute.

That model of teaching doesn't work well for novels — or any other form of aesthetic writing. There is no body of immutable, received knowledge about a story. The name of the author and the words on the page may not be a matter of personal taste and judgment, but the effects the author's words have on the reader very much are. Our role is not to impose on young readers the "approved" interpretation but to model some of the possibilities for interpretation and encourage the children to explore and develop taste and judgment. This is not to say that any opinion is as good as any other, or that no progress is expected. Any adult will feel quite capable of judging one response as superficial and another as more mature. In general we expect children's responses to grow more complex, more insightful, more tentative and more adequately supported by reference to the text, life experiences or other reading.

Our approach is to try to show children how to examine the novel. We say, in effect, "See what you can discover about the novel, about yourself and about life by looking at the story in this, that or another way."

Novels can be presented in several ways. Because they are long and take time to work through, children can't became acquainted with a whole book in a single sitting (except through a screen presentation). At any given point in the unit you must be aware what portion of the book has been covered and what story information is not yet available to the children.

Some approaches assume the whole novel will be read before the children undertake activities. Post-reading activities may be very useful, but they are limited in three ways. First, they leave untouched activities that might be undertaken during the reading — or more realistically, in the spaces between sequential readings. Secondly, the very structure of a novel enables readers/learners to engage in enlightening activities *as* they experience the novel, when they stop reading to reflect and share reflections with others. Thirdly, children need to learn to think and react during the reading of the novel. Readers are active while reading; they don't wait until the story is finished before they form opinions, generate hypotheses or make judgments. Children need guidance in the complex kind of thought processes that are possible when they read stories.

As adult readers reading for personal pleasure we speculate on possible outcomes, critically compare our predictions with the author's choices, evaluate the wisdom of decisions made by the characters, draw analogies between situations in the story and in our own lives, or compare the book with others we read earlier. And everyone enjoys discussing a story with someone else who's reading it too. All these activities we can do after the book is finished, of course, but they are most engaging while our (re)construction of the story is still in flux.

As teachers we can guide children as they learn these pleasures in a group of their peers. The following sections discuss the advantages, disadvantages and limitations of these seven commonly used ways of presenting the novel.

- Reading aloud (by the teacher) while children follow in their own copies
- Reading aloud by children
- Reading aloud from a single copy as the children listen
- Assigned independent reading
- Assigned supervised reading
- Screen presentations
- Audio recordings.

READING ALOUD WHILE CHILDREN FOLLOW IN THEIR OWN COPIES

Advantages

Modeling

Some educators still say that reading aloud to children as they follow along in their own copies promotes laziness and retards independent growth. We strenuously disagree. Reading aloud allows teachers to extend the value derived from shared reading experiences into the higher grades. These experiences are already common in the primary years. Less able readers who need massive amounts of expert modeling benefit most. A page of solid print over which they themselves might labor, stumble and fall is brought to life through the vibrant, living voice of an expert reader. And we don't use the word "expert" lightly. Teachers are the best readers in elementary classrooms. You may feel inadequate when you compare yourself with gifted colleagues or professional readers, but you are certainly ahead of most five to 13-year-olds. On the other hand, if you have accomplished child readers in your school, by all means make judicious use of them.

Social cohesion

It's difficult to describe the sense of community created by the oral sharing of a novel, but anyone who has participated in it knows how real it is. The trials and tribulations of the protagonists seem to draw children together in the same way unexpected hardship creates a sense of cohesion among strangers traveling together.

Teachers and children often allude to aspects of shared stories to make a point or crack a joke. A visitor asked one woebegone child sitting outside the principal's office what was wrong. The tearful answer was, "I'm having a terrible, horrible, no good, very bad day." The visitor had also read Judith Viorst and knew what the child meant.

Control of story information

Speculating on how things will turn out is one of the most enjoyable activities when sharing a story in a group. Children enjoy suspense, and they delight in discovering that their speculations were correct. We've watched in admiration as children applied their knowledge of the world and of stories to predict how the plot will progress. However, the process works well only when children are truly ignorant of the outcome of the story, a fact that argues strongly for reading it aloud to them.

Eliminating reading differences

Reading aloud to children eliminates concerns related to differences in reading ability and permits you to address the children's *interest* levels, which for the lower two-thirds of the class is likely to be significantly higher than their reading levels.

Demonstrations of the expert use of language

Each time children are read to they are exposed to a demonstration of language being used by an expert. Just as they learn from watching how top-class athletes perform, so they will learn how to use language better by observing its use by accomplished authors. Applebee (1978) showed that when young children hear many stories they develop a *tacit* understanding of how stories work, an understanding fundamental to the understanding of new stories (Johnson and Mandler, 1977).

Good literature also promotes vocabulary development. A good tale usually uses a wide range of vocabulary, and hearing a new word in a meaningful context is probably the most common way of expanding vocabulary. And this growth applies to other forms of expression. Hearing good language provides opportunities for the children to become acquainted with all the other means authors have to tell a story: simile, metaphor, flashback, irony, symbolism, character development and plot structure. These stylistic devices aren't learned by doing isolated exercises but from seeing them deployed in the service of telling a tale.

Explanatory comment

Reading aloud to children provides them with a source of supplementary information they can call on *at their discretion.* If a story contains something they don't understand they can ask questions. Preschool children ask questions all the time but tend to stop when they come to school, since they don't always feel safe doing so. Story hour should be a particularly relaxed time where no one feels at risk. Sensitive readers will also read their audience, sense a lack of understanding and stop to provide needed explanations.

Where you anticipate a lack of background knowledge, you can provide additional information by means of editorial comments, and draw parallels to the lives of your listeners. We were reading the opening chapter of *The Lion, the Witch and the Wardrobe* to a grade six class and stopped at the point where Lucy is invited back to Mr. Tumnus's home. We asked the class if they thought Lucy would go with him and what they thought of the wisdom of her decision. The children were unanimous in predicting that she would go, but all agreed it was very foolish to go off into the woods with a stranger.

However, interventions should be few and brief. Reading a story aloud creates an illusion which good readers can break and remake at will. In general we follow the lead of the class. If the children appear puzzled or ask questions, we offer our insights. Otherwise we place our trust in the authors we've chosen and let them tell their stories.

Particular advantages as children follow along in their own copies

When each child has access to the text a multitude of related activities become possible: rereading to support or deny a thought, scanning the text to locate an item of information, using context to determine the meaning of a word. The children can consult the text for their varied related interests.

Disadvantages

The major disadvantage is that you are active and the children are relatively passive. The value of your modeling makes this situation tolerable, although we move the children on to readers' theater as soon as possible (see Readers' Theater, page 82). Modeling has least value for the more accomplished readers, and these we try to incorporate more actively as soon as we can.

Reading aloud also consumes a good deal of class time. While the investment of time contributes to the classroom sense of community, it also limits the number of novels that can be covered in a year.

Limitations

Enough copies of the book need to be available for everyone, although we've worked successfully sharing one book between two (15 copies for 30 children).

The books must be fairly close to the children's instructional reading level, ideally just beyond. If they are too far beyond, the children are likely to lose track of your reading and thus lose the benefit of your modeling. Unfortunately the range of reading ability normally encountered in a class precludes such a nice arrangement. In any case, standard readability formulas are insufficiently precise. We suggest you simply select a book likely to challenge the average readers in your class, accepting the dangers that some less able children will be over-challenged, some others under-challenged.

READING ALOUD BY CHILDREN

We discussed the problems with traditional practices and offered an alternative under Round Robin Reading versus Readers' Theater (page 87).

READING ALOUD FROM A SINGLE COPY AS THE CHILDREN LISTEN

Advantages

This has all the advantages of having the children follow in their own copies, except for modeling and returning to the text to substantiate a point. It creates a sense of community just the same, allows you to control the story information (making prediction possible), eliminates problems caused by differences in reading ability, demonstrates expert use of language and permits explanatory comment. The main advantage is that it's based on the reality of most classrooms. Many schools have good libraries but they normally carry only one or two copies of a given title. Reading aloud as the children listen is the most viable way of making a story available to all children at the same time.

Disadvantages

It has all the same disadvantages as well: the children are passive, there is less value for the most competent readers, and the practice is time-consuming.

Limitations

A limited amount of modeling takes place. The children hear various moods and characters created by modifications in your voice, but they don't see the print as the basis of the presentation and thus can't make a connection between the marks on the page and a living human voice.

ASSIGNED INDEPENDENT READING

You could assign a novel to a class or group as an independent activity, setting a deadline for all or part of it to be completed. The reading can be done at the children's discretion: lunchtime, free choice time, at home.

Advantages

It's relatively quick and need not consume instructional time. The children can read as quickly or as slowly as they want.

Some individuals may choose to reread certain passages. The practice brings them one step closer to independence. The children are free to think about those aspects of the story that have special significance for them.

Disadvantages

Invariably a raggedness develops. Jim forgot to take the book home. Jessica forgot to bring hers back. Jill thought she had to read only the first two rather than the first three chapters, and so on, *ad nauseam*.

Limitations

Only a *limited* sense of community develops, that curious sense of reassurance that comes from learning that images and moods created in the privacy of your head are shared by others.

The anticipation of outcomes doesn't work nearly as well either. It would be a very self-disciplined class indeed that could stop reading at the end of chapter three at your behest, particularly if that happens to be a suspenseful point in the story.

ASSIGNED SUPERVISED READING

In this presentation children are given a specified amount of class time to read a specific portion of the text.

Advantages

You can be reasonably sure that everyone does some reading.

Disadvantages

Some children will read easily, quickly and well. Less able children may be completely frustrated by the same text.

Some children will finish early and must be given unrelated filler activities. Others won't have finished when you decide it's time to talk about what has been read.

Limitations

While some portions of the novel can be read during class time, the size of the task, particularly for young or inept readers, makes it a very time-consuming activity.

SCREEN PRESENTATIONS

Screen presentations include film, video cassette, filmstrip and filmstrip/cassette combinations.

Advantages

Media forms, given adequate machinery and technical know-how, are relatively painless to present and receive. A good production may act as a model for showing how printed words can be translated into voice, gesture, action, locale and artifact.

Disadvantages

One perceived disadvantage probably says more about our work ethic than about the value of film. Many teachers feel that simply watching a story unreel itself on a screen is too easy. Reading is more like work and thus justifies its place in school. None of this is necessarily true. A good film can be as emotionally or intellectually demanding as a good book. There was a time when novels were also regarded as frivolous diversions, not suitable fare for the curriculum — as unthinkable as learning to watch soap opera or sitcoms would be today.

A more fundamental disadvantage has to do with the different abilities of text and film to tell a story. Film handles action and description very well. It shows us how the characters look, what they wear, what they do, and where they do it. A picture is indeed worth a thousand words — but only sometimes. Film does a very poor job on introspection and editorial comment. Two pages of self-doubt and indecision may be portrayed as a two-second pensive expression on the screen. Film and text are very different media and sometimes it isn't possible to translate adequately one form into the other.

Limitations

You'll be restricted to those stories that have been produced in a non-print form and that you can lay your hands on. While an increasing number of children's books have been made into feature length films, not all are available for rent, nor are funds for such rental always available. Video cassettes are making film renditions more available for use in the classroom.

Film, in general, is much more concrete than text. Moods, gestures, expressions, appearances, only hinted at by the author and filled out by the reader are completely specified by the actor or film director. Many readers express dissatisfaction with film versions of familiar stories because the director's interpretation didn't match theirs.

AUDIO RECORDINGS

Advantages

Records or cassettes have many of the advantages of live oral readings. They eliminate reading differences, appeal to the interest level and create a sense of community. In addition, the children are exposed to the voices of some of the finest readers in the world. Nichol Williamson's reading of *The Hobbit* is an outstanding performance. Some readings use separate voices for each character and add sound effects and mood music so the reading is transformed into a radio play.

Recorded versions can be replayed as often as anyone wants. You may want the class to reconsider a certain portion; individual children may want to hear a favorite part again or review a section they missed or failed to understand.

Disadvantages

Today's children, and many teachers, have a long history of visual stimulation. Often children don't attend well to a recording. One group of children asked their teacher to switch off E. B. White's reading of *Charlotte's Web* and read it herself. A live reader adds body language, gestures, expressions and eye contact, important aspects of the story-sharing process.

A major disadvantage is that most audio recordings are abridgments. Novels are long works of art that may require several cassettes for the complete version, and that creates a marketing problem. However, an abridgment is a very unsatisfactory substitute for the real thing. A novel, like a symphony or a painting, is a statement of artistic expression that provides the listener/reader/viewer with an aesthetic experience. We wouldn't offer children a simplified version of Beethoven's Fifth Symphony nor would we introduce "The Last Supper" by means of a cartoon.

If you accept Rosenblatt's notion that a poem or story is an experience created by the reader/listener's processing of the text (see A Transactional View of Literacy, page 26), then the experience of an abridgment will always fall far short of what the author intended.

BALANCING OPTIONS

Each method for presenting the novel has advantages, limitations and disadvantages. The combination that seems to work best for us is to read aloud with the children following along in individual copies. We start off accepting the major burden of the reading but incorporate class members by means of readers' theater as the story progresses. At the same time we make available for independent reading a group of stories that are thematically or structurally related to the novel being read aloud, and the children share their reactions to them with the class. We use screen or audio versions, where available, as adjuncts: screen versions for comparison, and audio presentations for self-selected private listening.

We include assigned *independent* reading as small group work. Assigned *supervised* reading is for short passages only, usually involving rereading to find evidence in support or denial of particular points.

RESOURCE GUIDE

Chapter Nine contains a teacher's resource guide based on *The Secret of NIMH* (first published as *Mrs. Frisby and the Rats of NIMH*). It's important to note that this is a *resource for teachers.* It is not a study guide for children. Its length and complexity are due in part to the fact that we've not presumed to know how you might present the novel. Your approach will determine which resources will be of most value. If you plan to read aloud from a single copy, the section on Anticipating Outcomes will be very valuable. If you assign the novel for independent reading, then some of the activities in Related Activities will be useful.

We also don't expect you to assign every activity in a given section. We would present suggestions to the children and allow them to choose one or more.

In general, we repeat, the guide is for teachers, but we do provide examples of activities and exercises that might be placed directly in the hands of the children. We hope you'll select from them with the needs of your particular class or of a particular child sharply in your mind.

We provide background information in Critical Review and Analysis: Literary sociogram. Where such information entails instructional opportunities we provide teaching suggestions.

The Prereading Discussion and Prereading Activities sections will help you create a receptive frame of mind for dealing with the novel. Prereading Discussion is designed to be conducted orally under your direction; Prereading Activities is designed to be conducted independently by children working individually or in small groups. The latter also lists examples of resources, but we anticipate that you will identify and obtain locally available resources.

We designed the Anticipating Outcomes technique to be conducted by the teacher as well; it works best when you read aloud from a single copy while the children listen.

We've planned the points of intervention in Related Activities around the rhythms of the story rather than mechanically after each and every chapter. The first occurs at the conclusion of chapter 3 when the setting has been established, the characters have been rendered worthwhile and vulnerable, and a threat by powerful forces looms over them.

Developing Insight we designed for use when the reading is finished; it's intended to promote reflection on one of the undercurrents of the story.

With Vocabulary Development, we encourage children to examine how the author has used certain words. Through examining and interacting with expert models they will readily increase the size of their vocabularies.

We designed Board Game: Pursuit! to summarize the story and promote detailed comprehension. The game board reflects a grammar of the story. The question cards are designed to encourage various kinds of comprehension.

Related Reading lists resources to use if you want to develop a unit along the lines of the time-slip fantasies described on pages 128-132.

IT LOOKS LIKE FUN — BUT WILL THEY LEARN?

Ms Meryan Page in Victoria, BC (Canada) gave two grade seven classes a cloze test and asked them to write a passage entitled, "My Favorite Character." With one group the unit was taught for three hours a week over a period of six weeks. The control group carried on with its regular reading program.

Reading

Figure 4.1 on the next page shows the results of the cloze test. The small number of children in the sample makes a sophisticated statistical analysis pointless, but the results at least suggest that the "novel" group made more progress than the others.

Writing

A panel was asked to judge each piece as average, below average or above average for grade seven students, without knowing which passage came from which group. Each rating was then weighted:

below average	-1
average	0
above average	+1

Figure 4.2 shows the results of the weighted scores. Once again the small numbers render statistical analysis inappropriate but it would appear that the panel tended to rate the post-test writing of the experimental group more highly.

	Pre-test	Post-test
Experimental (N = 29)	9%	45%
Control (N = 28)	9%	18%

Figure 4.1 Percentage scores of grade seven students on a cloze test (N = number of students)

	Pre-test	Post-test
Experimental (N = 29)	− 14	+ 10
Control (N = 28)	− 4	− 4

Figure 4.2 Weighted ratings of passages written by grade seven students

Attitude

Ms Page assessed the attitudes of the children towards the various activities of the project. Eighty-three percent reported that they liked doing the unit "quite a lot." Before the project only 50% of the class said they liked to read. At the conclusion 65% indicated that their attitude towards reading had improved. This figure doesn't include the six students (20%) who rated reading at the top of the scale at the outset of the project (see also figure 5.12).

Conclusions

We tentatively conclude that the children made adequate or more than adequate progress in reading and writing, that they liked doing the project and that there was an improvement in their attitude towards reading.

Limitations

It's possible that other variables could account for the differences. We need numerous similar studies, however limited they may be. Human interactions are complex and we must learn through the consistencies perceived across many varied experiences. Rigid "control" of variables may work well with falling bodies but is already suspect with beans and works very poorly with human beings.

THEORETICAL REFLECTIONS

Language Generation and Language Enrichment

Reading and writing are skills. Downing and Leong (1982) argue that reading is a unitary skill — we could conceptualize hierarchies of sub-skills, but in use these are so highly interrelated as to meld together into a single competency. Skills are acquired through a balance of instruction and practice. Learning to type, play the piano, send Morse code or knit may require some initial instruction, but for smooth integration of skilled performance extended practice is required. The need for practice in learning to read and write provides the underpinning for such opaque and circular slogans as "Children learn to read by reading," or "Writers learn to write by writing."

Language Generation

Language *generating* activities require, encourage or permit children to use the language they already have. Brainstorming, story completion and discussion provide opportunities to use language. Of course new words or language constructions may be encountered in seeing and hearing the language of others, and language growth will occur, but the infusion of enriching language isn't planned.

Using language should be a major aspect of the language arts program. However, merely giving children assignments doesn't represent good practice, as Durkin (1978-79) points out. While children should have numerous opportunities to write a new version of a poem, write to an author or turn a story into a play, they need first to be shown how to do these things.

Language Enrichment

So activities designed to *enrich* the language of the children, that require them to interact with others whose language is beyond their level, are also important. In the family this enrichment occurs naturally. A three-way conversation among two adults and a ten-year-old provides almost continuous modeling of mature language and has a built-in expectation that the child will understand and respond to that language. But in classrooms teachers are outnumbered thirty to one by relatively immature speakers who tend to offer less than competent models for each other. We can provide much valuable modeling, but our influence is likely to be limited by the size of the group and the impossibility of maintaining a dialogue with each child.

There are many partial solutions to this dilemma, including the introduction of more mature language users (visitors, parents, aides or older students) and the use of various forms of media. The most common is the use of printed texts, examples of sophisticated language that demonstrate to the children the many ways language is used.

Some of the principles that follow apply to both language generating and language enrichment activities, even though they were selected as activities specifically intended to expand and enrich the children's language.

The Interaction of Language Generation and Language Enrichment

Language generating activities and language enrichment activities overlap and interact synergistically — each enriches and benefits the growth of the other. Increased writing competence seems to benefit reading. Improved reading competence leads to wider and more challenging reading and exposure to an expanded range of writing techniques and vocabulary. Writing techniques encountered in reading often contribute to improvement in writing, which leads to further improvements in reading.

Language enrichment activities quite naturally involve much use of already familiar language. As the children struggle to express their opinions regarding a challenging story or poem they will incorporate some of the author's language but will also use much they knew already.

Natural Texts for Language Instruction

The goal of any language program is to help the learners become competent language users. For reading, the children need access to the written word: real books, real magazines, real newspapers and all the other forms of literature used in our society.

Often the first encounters with print in school consist of bizarre forms of literature that are quite unlike any other forms of writing. The early stages of controlled-vocabulary basal readers contain mutilated and impoverished forms of writing that ill-prepare children for dealing with real literature. At the upper primary levels, the language of the readers is usually more natural but the accompanying exercises frequently expect the children to respond mechanically to meaningless fragments of mutilated language.

Whole language advocates take the common-sense view that children can best be introduced to written language by being exposed to real examples of literature, natural texts written for purposes other than instruction, like nursery and other rhymes, poems, fairy tales and folktales. Language that has a strong rhythm and natural repetition and is robust enough to withstand repeated presentation is desirable. At the upper primary levels the contents of the school and classroom library provide the vehicle for language instruction.

Considerations for Individual Learners

Instruction should empower the learner

Learning to talk gives children a greater measure of control over their own lives. Learning to read and write should do the same. Learning to predict while reading will benefit readers for the rest of their lives. Learning to mark a vowel as long or short endows the learners with nothing. Learning to divide words into syllables offers no increase in social power. Learning how to write a letter of application will be of repeated value.

Instruction should meet individual needs

We have tried individualized instruction and have abandoned it in regular classrooms because it's almost impossible to manage. If we give each child a battery of diagnostic tests and then assign deficit-mending activities, we become merely assessors and assigners. Time for face-to-face interaction is gobbled up by paper shuffling. Nevertheless, the necessity for meeting individual needs remains. The mistake we made in the past was assuming that we could find out what each individual needed and provide appropriate instruction. We can't and we don't.

When we use a whole language approach we find that we can go some way in meeting individual needs by providing whole-class instruction with open-ended assignments. Assignments that invite divergent responses permit the children to respond at their own level of competence. Bright children are more likely to make detailed, insightful or imaginative responses. Less able children may make less creative responses but their responses will represent real growth for them nevertheless. Some need will remain for more personal and more extended instruction in small groups for the least able children.

Instruction should respect the autonomy of the learner

It is ironic that in a democratic society we have developed curricula which appear to have been tailor-made for a totalitarian despot. We have broken up language into discrete skills and arranged those to form a rigid teaching sequence. We have determined what will be learned, how it will be learned and when it will be learned. We then expect youngsters to emerge from such a regimen able to make mature, reasoned and independent decisions on how society should function. Convergent activities constrain and constrict. Divergent, open-ended activities endorsed by advocates of whole language place some measure of responsibility for learning on the learner and thus respect and promote the growth of autonomy.

How Should We Intervene?

Interventions should involve the meaningful use of language

The meaningful use of language starts with the use of natural texts, which always use language meaningfully. The activities we plan around such texts should also treat language meaningfully. Breaking words into syllables or making spelling lists of isolated words is treating language in a non-meaningful fashion. Meaningful activities focus on the people, the places and the events described in the text. They deal with the characters, their plans, their hopes and their reactions.

Interventions should be attractive

It is in our interest to devise or employ activities that children like doing because then our energies will be working in productive directions. Every published program promises enjoyment but even a cursory examination of the skills activities reveals that many of them don't deliver.

Interventions should focus first on global aspects and progress to specific details

We've known for a long time that oral language is learned through a process of progressive discrimination. Children begin with a vague, immature but whole idea of how to talk and gradually refine their ability in the direction of the adult speech community. Clay (1979) and Holdaway (1979) offer evidence that learning to read follows the same pattern. Harste, Woodward and Burke have done the same for writing (1984). During instruction, children should interact first with the complete text. Attention should then be drawn to ideas, sentences, lines, phrases, words and spelling in that order.

Activities should involve a thoughtful and sensitive engagement with the substance of the text

Songs should be sung, poems recited and chants chanted. Stories can be predicted, told and discussed. A good rule of thumb for choosing related activities is to ask ourselves what we do before, during or after reading a piece of literature at home. If we find it useful to mark all the diphthongs on the front page of the newspaper, then it may seem reasonable to ask children to do the same thing. If we find it valuable to share with others our reactions to what we've read, then it seems reasonable to have children do the same sort of thing.

Activities should involve the communication of something of substance to a significant audience

Mechanical exercises found in workbooks communicate "nothing to no one for no purpose." Filled-in blanks marked right or wrong say nothing. The key to real communication is the identification of an audience. Once this has been done all else tends to fall into place.

Plays are presented to other classes, invitations are sent home, letters go to pen pals. Sometimes activities are worth doing for their own sake. Songs may be sung for the pure pleasure of singing together; no audience is necessary. The same may be said for choral speaking. However, an audience always provides a motive and focus for language activities. Rehearsal for the performance provides the repetition necessary for learning to occur. Publishing writing is performance.

Activities should encourage or require the substantiation of opinion or interpretation or judgment by reference to the text

Activities related to a text must ensure that children interact with and manipulate the language of that text. Some of the author's language will come under the learner's control, and the learner's language competence will be enhanced.

Instruction should contribute to specifiable skills

Both reading and writing are rather like riding a bicycle. While biking can be broken down into separate "skills" of steering, balancing, pedaling, etc., the skills together wouldn't give an adequate description of riding a bicycle. It certainly wouldn't make any sense to teach each skill separately. All the skills are in a dynamic relationship with one another. Steering is possible only if one's balance is maintained. Balancing is easier if pedaling is vigorous. Everything is more difficult when the bike goes too slowly. The same kind of dynamic interaction occurs in reading and writing, although most teachers and most current instructional materials presuppose reading as a skills-based activity. Most teachers will be held accountable by administrators and parents who perceive reading as skills. Most evaluation instruments are developed from a skills model. Until a general re-education regarding language has been accomplished, it seems necessary to be able to defend whole language instruction from a skills-based point of view.

Skills-based basal readers identify a skill and offer materials and exercises which promote that skill. We have serious reservations about such an approach. It leads to the creation of an artificial language of instruction wherein children are asked to do things with language (such as filling in blanks) that they are never required to do in the real world. A skills approach has children dealing with one skill at a time: one reading exercise may deal with the identification of main ideas, another with sequence, a third with prediction. Writing exercises may require attention to commas, speech marks or subject/verb agreement. But real reading and real writing require a balanced attention to many aspects of language simultaneously. While reading, the reader must note main ideas and understand sequence and predict and perform numerous other tasks all at the same time. Such skills are in a dynamic relationship with one another. Sequence requires prediction, which in turn requires the identification of main ideas, which is related to many other aspects of reading, ranging from decoding to critical appraisal. If one of these skills is lifted from the living process in which it functions, the nature of the skill changes and the learner learns something that isn't required in real reading or writing. Meanwhile, the real demands of literacy go untutored.

Instruction should contribute to an increased capacity for clarity and precision of expression

Any language program should increase the ability of learners to express themselves in oral and written forms. Children should be able to explain, describe, defend, dispute or analyze a topic in either speech or writing. Competence is developed by trying to convey something of significance to someone who cares:

- trying to convince the principal to keep a threatened extramural program
- writing a thank-you letter to an honored guest
- appealing to the town council in defense of a natural wilderness area

One doesn't learn to do those things by filling in blanks in scraps of isolated, meaningless artificial language and submitting them to a tired teacher who will merely mark them right or wrong. Language skills are honed when people try to express something they care about to someone the topic has relevance to. Children need real topics, real purposes and real audiences.

The activities should be suitable for learners to apply to self-selected texts

We don't want children to work only under our direct supervision as they complete assigned tasks. We want them to develop a sense of responsibility so they grow in their competence to choose for themselves the tasks they'll undertake.

The instructional sequences we use begin with a high degree of teacher modeling and direction, then that support is gradually withdrawn until the learners begin to function independently. We use the same approach in kindergarten, grade one, the upper primary grades, secondary school and graduate school. As far as language enrichment activities are concerned, we expect that each learner will eventually be able to go to the library, select a text and apply to it the technique we've taught. With young or less able learners we use simple texts and simple, concrete activities. With mature or highly competent learners we use more abstract and complex activities applied to complex texts.

It is through the self-selection of texts that we feel most secure about meeting individual needs. Some measure of individualization occurs in whole-class, whole-language activities, but when children are working with texts and on tasks they have chosen for themselves we feel quite certain that each one is working near to his or her capacity.

It's worth repeating: children shouldn't simply be given untutored assignments (Durkin, 1978-79). In whole class instruction they receive guidance on the technique; then they have an opportunity to apply it to material more closely suited to their own individual interests and needs.

The Teacher

While it is right that most of our attention and concern should focus on the children, teacher welfare is also crucial. A tired, over-stressed teacher rarely offers good instruction.

Preparation time should be modest

It's sometimes frustrating to think what might be possible if only time, material and energy were available. Many schemes have been promoted which, while excellent in concept, require more than most teachers are able to give. Perhaps the most famous is team teaching. Given dedicated teachers who were willing to put in 25 hours a day, the program worked wonderfully. But it didn't turn out to be generally viable. Most teachers have reverted to self-contained classrooms.

We've kept preparation time in mind, rejecting or adapting anything that involved elaborate or time-consuming preparation. One principle we followed: if the activity was simple enough for children to apply independently, it was usually modest in the preparation demands as well.

Some of the activities we've proposed demand a considerable amount of classroom time. We offer no apology for that. The process of providing multiple models, explanations and guided practice takes time. Some steps could perhaps be eliminated but only at the price of quality instruction.

The program should allow you to modify instruction to suit the needs of individuals, groups and the class as a whole

All programs claim to meet the needs of individuals. But we find that the so-called management schemes in basal readers do so in only the most crude and superficial manner, and in ways that place excessive demands on teachers.

These management schemes usually call for ability grouping, but when we look closely, the only difference between groups is the rate at which the children proceed. Everyone passes through the same material. If alternative instruction is offered it's usually more exercises of the sort that failed the first time. What you do with those children who fail the supplementary activities isn't clear. Enrichment activities are used to keep the bright children busy until the teacher can get around to them.

The testing required to determine who has passed and who has failed becomes excessive. The class is rapidly broken into five or more groups, each expected to progress independently through a program that requires the immediate and continuous presence of the teacher. The teacher becomes over-stressed by trying to be in three places at the same time in an attempt to overcome the limitations of the program.

Children vary in more than ability. They vary in interest, aspirations, values, temperament and background knowledge. It's arrogant in the extreme to suppose that someone in Toronto or New York can devise a reading program that is so powerful and so broad and so flexible that it can meet the needs of hundreds of thousands of children who come to school from a very wide variety of backgrounds. Only the teachers who meet with these children daily, who meet their parents, who know something of their lives, their hopes and their fears, can begin to marshal a program that answers to their needs.

If programs are to be provided, they should be flexible and humble in their claims.

CAMPUS VIEW PRIMARY SCHOOL Report Card		
Student: *Goldilocks*		
Subject	*Letter Grade*	*Comments*
Honesty		*Goldilocks went into the bear's house.*
Carefulness	*F*	
Sports		

Figure 4.3 A partially completed literary report card

The program should allow you to incorporate locally available resources

Everything we've said about the autonomy of children applies tenfold to you.

Teachers are qualified professionals with an intimate knowledge of local conditions. If they are provided with interlocking readers, exercises, supplementary exercises and texts they become imprisoned within that system. Modification becomes extremely difficult and professionals are reduced to technicians.

The attempt to reflect our multicultural society in basal readers is pathetic. Teachers in Northern Saskatchewan or New Mexico may be teaching children with a proud and distinctive heritage. They need to incorporate the songs and stories of those cultures into their instruction.

Programs should invite and encourage modifications. The more modifications you make, the greater your sense of ownership, and with ownership comes a sense of increased commitment. In the end, it isn't the books, the drills, the exercises and the tests that teach, but that sense of commitment provided by a teacher who cares.

So How is it Done?

The preceding list of criteria appears demanding, even intimidating. It needn't be. Almost any activity that involves children interacting socially around a meaningful text will meet most of the criteria. We'll demonstrate with one of the activities described in *Literacy Through Literature*, the literary report card. This activity was presented to a grade two class.

Introduction

- We presented the children with a partially completed report card based on *Goldilocks* (see figure 4.3). The form of the report card should be based on the report form the children are familiar with.
- We explained how we filled in the completed portion of the report card, including the grade system we used.
- We invited the children to make oral suggestions for further grades for the subjects provided.
- We invited the children to suggest further "subjects" on which Goldilocks could be evaluated and recorded them on the chalkboard.

- The children then individually completed the Goldilocks report card and orally shared their responses.

Development

- The children gathered on the story mat and we told them we would read Hoban's *How Tom Beat Captain Najork and His Hired Sportsmen* to them and afterwards we would ask them to write a report card on Tom.
- They listened while we read the story with transparent solemnity.

Assignment

- The children returned to their tables and offered oral suggestions for subjects Tom might be evaluated on. We recorded these on the board.
- We distributed blank report card forms and the children completed them, cooperatively if they wished. We provided individual help where necessary.
- The children orally shared their responses.
- The report cards were displayed.

Guided practice. The procedure was repeated over the next two days with two more stories.

Independent application. On day four the children selected a book from the library, read it, chose a character, and wrote up report cards they shared orally and displayed (see figure 4.4).

REPORT CARD: GREGORY SCHOOL Angela Whitehead, Dean		
For: *Harriet Welsch*		**Grade** *VI*
Teachers: *Miss Elson* *Miss Harris*		
Subject		**Comments**
Sensitivity	*D*	*Harriet doesn't seem to give much regard to other children's feelings.*
Friendliness	*C*	*Harriet makes very little effort to get along with children other than Sport and Jane.*
Happiness	*C*	*Harriet doesn't appear to have been very happy at school. Signs of improvement recently.*
Intelligence	*C*	*I'm sure Harriet is a bright girl, but she never does her work, so I can't give her a good grade.*
Obedience	*D*	*On several occasions Harriet has disregarded our instructions*

Figure 4.4 An example of a literary report card for a junior novel

Meeting the Criteria

The 18 criteria appear in figure 4.5 on the next page in point form, together with a judgment and justification regarding whether or not each criterion is met in the preceding activity.

MEETING THE CRITERIA

Criterion	Check if criterion is met	Justification
Language enrichment	☑	Hoban's language will delight and enrich the language of the teacher and every child in the class.
Use of natural texts	☑	Hoban wrote his story for the amusement not the instruction of children.
Empowering the learner	☑	The activity deals with interpretation of character which is a lifelong aspect of reading.
Individual needs	☑	Each child chooses what will be evaluated and the supporting explanation. Later, each child chooses his/her own book.
Thoughtful and sensitive responses to substance	☑	"Subjects" demand high-level inferences based on Tom's behavior.
Communication of substance to a significant audience	☐	Not well met. Display on the bulletin board provides mild sense of audience.
Substantiation of judgment	☑	Grades require judgment. Comments provide substantiation.
Specifiable skills	☑	The lesson involves listening of a purpose, making inferences, stating main ideas, critical judgment, and supporting details. The lesson sequence involves listening, speaking, reading and writing.
Increased clarity	☑	Global judgments must be adequately supported.
Attention to relevant aspects	☑	Children know they are to rate Tom and listen for relevant information.
Autonomy of the learner	☑	The open-ended nature of the response lets each child retain his/her autonomy.
Meaningful use of language	☑	Children make judgments and must provide information as justification.
Attractive interventions	☑	Children enjoy turning the tables on an issue that is fraught with much tension for them.
Global to specific	☑	"Subjects" encapsulate main ideas. Letter grades require global judgment. Comments require supporting details.
Simple enough for self-selection	☑	Children have little difficulty reapplying this technique to their own reading.
Preparation time	☑	Preparation involves the preparation of the Goldilocks example and a blank report card form.
Individual need	☑	The teacher can select stories that are at the level of the children in the class.
Local resources	☑	The teacher can incorporate stories that are relevant to the lives of the children in the class. The technique is prescribed but the content remains under the control of the teacher.
Total	17	Total possible 18

Figure 4.5 A checklist of criteria for whole language activities

We hope this demonstrates that a routine that fulfills all but one of the criteria needn't be difficult to prepare nor demanding to deliver. And it allows ample room for the tastes of individual teachers and children. We don't expect every activity to meet every criterion but we do intend that most of them will.

Developing Curricula

If the language arts curriculum is a body of skills to be learned, then it makes sense to devise exercises that are thought to develop these skills and arrange them into a linear sequence. But if we perceive curriculum to be a series of routines that enable children to make intelligent and sensitive responses to what they choose to read and increase their ability in self-expression in speaking or writing, then progress through the curriculum must involve increasing the size of the children's response repertoire. We can then expect that the texts chosen will become more complex and responses more abstract. Thus, early primary children might be expected to make relatively simple responses to nursery rhymes, poems, picture books and short stories, while upper primary children might be expected to engage in the analysis of plot or character in short stories and junior novels. Further examples of such routines (techniques, strategies, procedures) are described in Fox and Benton (1986), Jackson (1983), Thomas and Perry (1984), Johnson and Louis (1985) and Cashdan (1986).

CHAPTER FIVE

EVALUATION

THE PURPOSE OF EVALUATION

A tremendous mystique and a fair amount of misery surround evaluation. Answering these three questions can reduce both:

- Who is conducting the evaluation?
- For what purpose?
- What is to be done with the results?

In education, teachers, administrators and diagnosticians are the main evaluators. Each group has valid concerns, but much of the misery and misuse of test data result from the failure to keep in mind that each evaluates for a different purpose. Misery is maximized when tests and results designed for use by one group are imposed upon another.

Who is Conducting the Evaluation?

Teachers. They evaluate the *work of the children* in order to modify future instruction. They need a rich variety of verbal, numerical and visual data gathered from several sources and from a range of instructional situations over a sustained period of time.

Administrators. They evaluate *programs* to monitor quality standards or the relative quality of one program versus suggested alternatives. They need numerical indicators of central tendency.

Diagnosticians. They conduct in-depth analyses of *individuals* to identify factors that will explain the child's performance. Their results may lead to advice for the classroom teacher or a recommendation for the administrator about future instruction and some form of special program. The diagnostician gathers detailed information of the child's mental, physical and emotional makeup, the classroom setting and the home background.

Diagnosis is a large and complex topic that can't be adequately dealt with here. The remainder of this chapter will focus on teachers and administrators.

Choice Points

Teachers and administrators concern themselves with evaluation most at what we call choice points, when simple but significant and often non-reversible decisions are made. Should the children move on to the next grade? If letter grades are given, what grade should be awarded? Which children should be sent for special assistance? If the school is streamed, which stream should a given child enter? What information about a given child should be passed on to the secondary school?

Such decisions are *simple* in that they involve a very limited range of options. They are *significant* in that they tend to become self-fulfilling. Children awarded A's tend to be seen as acting like "A" children. Children labelled as "slow" or "remedial" tend to be seen as slow and in need of remediation. Children themselves begin to believe the labels placed on them. In theory, some choice point decisions are reversible, but in practice they tend not to be. The results of a wrong decision may have lifelong consequences for the individual.

A MODEL OF EDUCATIONAL EVALUATION

The Need for a Model

Teachers sometimes regard evaluation as distinct from instruction, especially since testing programs that employ standardized tests are often conducted by an (inimical)

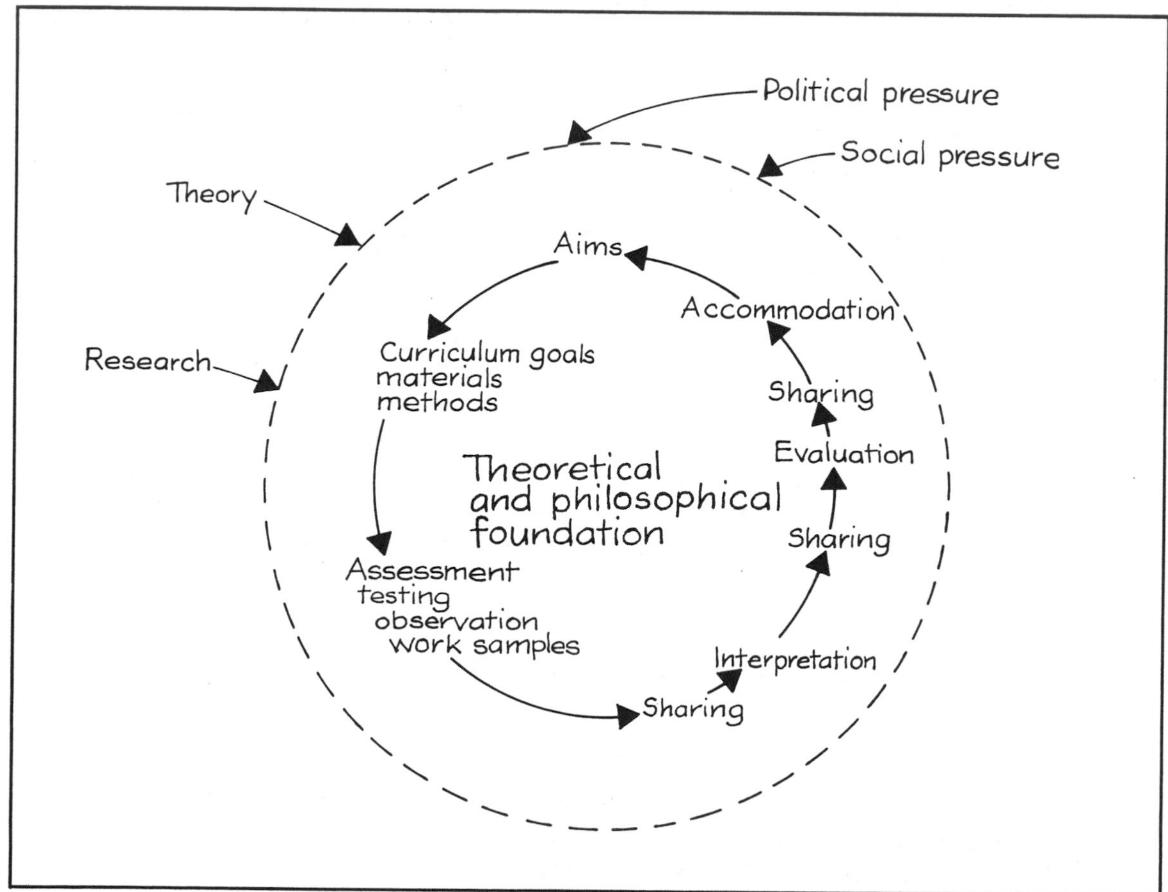

Figure 5.1 A model of the instruction/assessment process

outside agency. While the results are of major value to administrators, they have limited value for teachers. Because teachers feel the results are imposed on them, too often they disregard the results.

All members of the educational community should adopt a common model of the educational process, one that recognizes the needs of everyone and that incorporates evaluation procedures, including testing, as a component.

The Model

Figure 5.1 is shaped by and responds to a coherent philosophical and theoretical construct that describes the nature of language and the language learner, including a means of assessment that is logically consistent with the broad aims of the program and the goals of the curriculum.

Since assessment is a complex, interrelated series of steps that form a phase in a cyclical procedure, the shape is circular. The model also implies a sequence, although actual implementation may not always follow the sequence indicated by the arrows. Note that the loop is closed but permeable. *Closed* suggests that the model feeds continuously on itself to reflect the constant critical reappraisal and revision that is part of the educational process.

Permeable implies it admits information and influence from the outside in the form of political or social pressure, theoretical formulations or research findings. Entry is possible at any point: concerns may be raised about the aims of education; new teaching methods may be proposed; assessments may reveal shortcomings in the system.

To prevent visual cluttering, the dynamic relationships between elements have not been represented. But a network does exist. A change in aims implies a change in curriculum; interpretation of test results is conducted in the light of curricular goals; the evaluation of assessment results may lead to a modification of educational aims and curriculum.

Aims

Society has broadly defined reasons for including language instruction in the school system; for instance, the development of a literate citizenry capable of keeping itself informed on all matters pertaining to the healthy life of the society.

Curriculum

Broad societal aims are translated into a curriculum, interpreted in the widest possible terms:

- The *paper* curriculum resides in a written policy statement.
- The *action* curriculum resides in the teachers as they translate the paper into instruction.
- The *subjective* curriculum resides in the experiences of the learners who receive the instruction.

Assessment

This is the multifaceted process designed to gather information about the curriculum and the effectiveness of its implementation. It may take the form of testing, observation, work samples or self-report.

Sharing

Sharing occurs at several points in the system. Some interested parties may get raw assessment *data* and make their own *interpretations* and *evaluations*. Others may receive an interpretation of the data but then are left to evaluate it for themselves. Yet others — the general public, for example — may receive the information in a form that is both interpretive and evaluative. Somehow sharing must occur. Unread assessment data are a waste of public money.

Interpretation

The data must be interpreted in light of the curriculum. For example, the meaning of numbers derived from a standardized test must be related to curricular goals. Wise selection of assessment tools will generate relevant data, but relevance shouldn't be taken for granted.

Evaluation

It isn't enough to establish the meaning of assessment data; value must be placed on that information as well. Proper interpretation is crucial to appropriate evaluation.

Accommodation

Incremental adjustments in the system should occur as a result of assessment data; otherwise the assessment procedures are rendered impotent.

Driving forces

The aims of the educational system are the *raison d'être* for the whole system. Every phase must be seen as ensuring that the aims are met to the fullest extent possible. However, educational aims are not immutable. Assessment may suggest that certain aims have been overlooked or that some of those specified need to be modified. It's important, however, that the aims not be reduced to those things that can be conveniently measured.

Instruction is the active ingredient in the system. The aims of the system will be achieved by means of the instruction offered. Improvement in the system must result in improved instruction.

Assessment procedures not part of the cyclical model are more than irrelevant, they are harmful, since they consume resources that could otherwise be devoted to upgrading the system. Assessment must be seen as a phase in a self-improving cycle.

ASSESSMENT AND CURRICULAR GOALS

Assessment should cover *all* curricular goals. If the curriculum includes well-intentioned, high-sounding goals such as "The children will deepen their appreciation of their cultural heritage," then some form of assessment should be made to see how well this goal has been attained. If the program specifies that children will develop a love of literature, then the meaning of the phrase "love of literature" needs to be operationalized and some means of assessing the degree of love that students have for literature needs to be implemented. Furthermore, the results of such assessments should be valued as highly and published as widely as numerical summaries of test scores. The prestige accorded to teachers whose students do well on standardized tests should be equalled by the standing given to those whose students do indeed develop an appreciation of their cultural heritage or develop a love of literature.

Goals, however well intentioned, will disappear from the (action) curriculum or become de-emphasized if their achievements aren't assessed. A teacher's sense of self-worth is partially based on the success of the children. Teachers are rightly concerned that their students do well on (academic) assessments. If the assessments are based on a very narrow range of skills, they soon learn to prepare the children for the test. The curriculum, as actually implemented by the teacher, becomes dominated and thus controlled by the nature of the assessment procedures. It's unreasonable to ask teachers to attain one (broad) set of goals and then assess a rather narrow subset of objectives. It has become an educational truism that evaluation controls curriculum. What is tested is taught. By the same argument, what isn't assessed (and valued) isn't taught. There should be congruence in the range and spirit of the curricular goals and assessment procedures.

STANDARDIZED TESTS

Limitations

We shouldn't have an exaggerated confidence in tests — particularly standardized tests. Their densely written technical manuals and intimidating statistics may look "scientific," "objective" and precise, but they aren't.

One + two may not = three

Statistical rigor and complex arithmetic manipulations invest test data with the appearance of scientific objectivity. Even the term "measurement" papers over some very thinly supported assumptions: it brings to mind the precise, objective and reliable measurement of such characteristics as length, weight or time. A piece of cloth measured on Monday will measure the same on Wednesday and Friday, late at night or early in the morning. The act of measuring leaves the cloth the same length, and it doesn't care what the result is. Every scale of measurement will be reliable. Each unit on the measuring tape is of equal value. The centimeters between 0 and 10 are the same length as those between 40 and 50.

But measurement of reading or writing ability is quite different. Repeated measuring of the same ability will produce a range of scores. Testing when the child is alert may produce results that differ from when the child is tired or under stress. Repeated testing affects performance. The child is happy about high scores and distressed by low scores. One test of reading simply won't give the same result as another.

The unwarranted assumption of *equal intervals* deserves special mention. Huge changes occur in young children, with marked growth in reading and writing abilities apparent during their first year in school — a real reward for the teacher. Changes during the sixth year are more difficult to discern. These subjective observations lead to the conclusion that growth in literacy is negatively accelerated: the degree of change decreases with time.

Derived scores, such as grade equivalents, give the erroneous impression that progress is made through a series of measured steps of equal length. Disclaimers of these assumptions appear in test manuals but are too often buried in the fine print of the technical section.

Slim samples and broad generalizations

Evaluations are predictions. Evaluators use *samples of past performance,* restricted in both time and behavior, to make *general summary statements* about individuals for the purpose of making predictions about them.

Time sampling. Over one year children invest about 315 hours of school time in reading and writing; the assessment session may take less than one hour. Based on this slim time sample the evaluator attempts to make a statement that embraces the other 314 hours.

Behavior sampling. Readers routinely apply prior knowledge, make inferences and critical judgments, determine main ideas, predict outcomes, perceive regularities and use context, word identification and decoding. A reading test may involve little more than completing short, incomplete prose statements and selecting isolated words to fit a given prose definition. On the basis of these the evaluator makes statements that presume to embrace the children's performance regarding behaviors not actually measured.

Generalization

Assessment statements are general. Children assessed on the prose used in reading tests as reading at "the grade three level" are assumed to read poetry, novels, time tables, short stories, social studies and labels on cans also at the grade three level. It's further assumed that they will exhibit the same level of reading at home, in the classroom, on the playground, in the library, on the street, or in the front of a computer terminal. These assumptions are highly questionable. Nor do numerical descriptions of performance take into account the effect of high or low motivation for reading a particular text for a specific reason in a given context. Data gathered in the constrained, asocial atmosphere of the test session are presumed to be applicable to the social atmosphere of home, school and community.

A number

During testing sessions the children may read both silently and orally, predict, make regressions, speculate, make miscues, self-correct, hypothesize, identify words by sight, use context, and decode by syllabication or sounding out. And all this is reduced to a single number. The responses they make on the test paper are evaluated and counted to form a raw score (the number correct) which is then transformed into a derived number — for example, a grade equivalent such as 3.2.

"Noise" factors

Students may not be used to the manner of posing test questions and the form for answering them. The assumptions about language made by the test makers may be at variance with the philosophy underlying our instruction program. The thought processes required to identify correct answers may be very different from the ways students normally think with and about language. All these factors introduce "noise" into the assessment procedure and can influence scores so they don't correctly indicate the students' ability.

We can reduce the problem by familiarizing the children not only with the test procedures but with test-taking strategies, providing them with some guidance in the thinking required by certain forms of test items. Clearly they shouldn't be taught the actual test items, but they should be acquainted with questions that closely resemble them. We can model the steps involved in arriving at an answer, sharing our thought processes by verbalizing them as we solve a particular problem, provide opportunity for guided practice in training sessions and encourage the students to apply the same strategies during the actual test.

Implications for Instruction

Numerical data say very little about future instruction. If a 12-year-old child obtains a grade equivalent score of 3.2 on a standardized test, some remedial intervention may be called for. But the score doesn't tell us *what* intervention is appropriate. The results of an informal reading inventory may be much more useful, revealing that the child is overusing context, for instance, and prompting the teacher to modify specific instruction. A review of accumulated time-sampled observations may show that on the days Brian comes to school pale and irritable he's highly distractable and that his friend Jason is the major source of distraction. Data of this sort can be used to form a corrective action plan.

Progress and Precision

Technical manuals for standardized tests often give an impression that an individual's performance progresses at an even pace along a well-defined, predetermined sequence. They also imply that an individual's position along such a continuum can be pinpointed. These misinterpretations are most common when grade-equivalent scores are derived from raw scores.

Grade-equivalent scores march evenly across the page, but it's important to remember they are based on *averages*, not on individual performance. While the mean performance of a large group may advance regularly, month by month, each individual may not progress in the same regular manner. The regularity of group progress may cover a wide range of individual differences which together produce the smoothness of the observed learning curves.

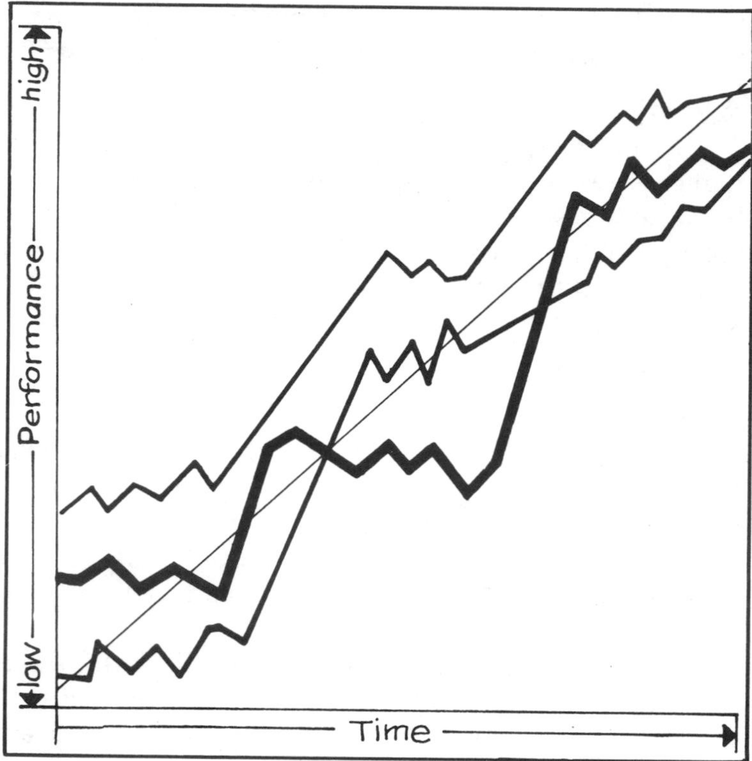

Figure 5.2 The erratic performance of three hypothetical individuals who contribute to a smooth average increase

By contrast, individual children seem to pass through a series of exploratory learning plateaus followed by sudden leaps. It's as though the learner explores in an apparently random fashion, making individual but non-incremental connections, until a sufficient number of connections result in an "Ah-ha!" reaction that leads to a marked increase in performance. New situations may require temporary regressions or plateaus to permit consolidation. And stress in areas unrelated to school may depress academic performance. Figure 5.2 shows how three hypothetically erratic individuals could contribute to a smooth average increase.

Standard error is a second source of imprecision in test scores. Since fallible human beings make and administer tests, those tests inevitably contain elements that have nothing to do with actual performance but that introduce variations in scores nevertheless. Test makers acknowledge this chance variation.

The standard error for the Reading Comprehension subtest (green level) of the *Stanford Diagnostic Reading Test* (figure 5.3) is 2.7 (Karlsen, Madden and Gardner, 1976). A student who obtains a score of 53 on this sub-test is said to have a grade equivalent score of 4.7 (seventh month of fourth year).

However, the standard error of 2.7 means that the child's "true" score has a high probability of falling somewhere between 53 – 2.7 and 53 + 2.7 — that is, between 50.3

Raw score	Grade equivalent
56	5.7
55	5.3
54	5.0
53	4.7
52	4.4
51	4.2
50	4.0

Figure 5.3 A portion of the raw and grade equivalent scores for Reading Comprehension (green level), **Stanford Diagnostic Reading Test**

and 55.7. As figure 5.3 indicates, the child's true grade-equivalent score has a high probability of falling somewhere (we're not sure where) between 4.2 and 5.3. All we can say with confidence is that the child performed on this test somewhere around a grade four level. The decimal numbers don't have the precision they seem to promise. It's meaningless to say that last month James was reading at 4.7 and now is reading at 4.9. The imprecision of the test doesn't give any assurance that real progress has occurred.

Standardized Tests: Summary

Standardized tests are useful tools for administrators since they provide a reasonable measure of the mean performance of (large) groups. Consequently they are useful in evaluating the general efficacy of programs.

But they are of very limited value to the teacher. Test scores are based on very slim samples of reading behavior. They provide limited information on individuals and at best may confirm impressions gained by other means.

CRITERION-REFERENCED TESTS

Skills Assessment

Criterion-referenced tests have both an intuitive and a logical appeal for testing reading and writing skills. It's difficult to judge what constitutes an adequate store of knowledge about a particular topic at a particular level, but it is possible to describe, at least in general terms, the expected performance in reading and writing of, say, a successful grade seven student (see figures 5.8 and 5.11).

Fine discriminations become a bit tricky, however. Distinguishing between the performance of a first grade "graduate" and a successful second grade student is relatively straightforward, but listing descriptive criteria that reliably differentiate seventh graders from those in grade six is more difficult. Objective criteria will never be adequate; qualitative judgments will always be required.

Basic Requirements

Criterion-referenced tests do a good job of assessing *basic* requirements. A school staff might draw up this list:

A successful grade seven student will be able to:

- write a personal letter
- write a formal business letter
- write a factual report
- write a short story
- *etc.*

- read and understand a story at the grade seven level with a reasonable degree of understanding
- be able to read critically
- be able to substantiate a judgment by reference to the text
- *etc.*

We can devise tasks that call for the exercise of these abilities and make a qualitative judgment of each student's performance. The subjective element is reduced if we use a pass/fail system rather than an A-F scale or percentages. We don't have to assess outstanding levels of performance, only whether the student can or can't perform the task adequately (see Grading, page 192).

From Theory to Practice

How do you devise test items that operationalize such general descriptions in a reasonable manner? What is a "grade seven level story"? How do you assess *understanding* and *reasonable degree*? You'll need to look at your instructional practices. What sort of texts are routinely used in grade seven instruction? How is comprehension promoted? What kind of performance is generally found to be adequate? The test procedures should resemble instructional activities as closely as possible.

Limitations

Criterion-referenced tests share with norm-referenced tests the difficulty of selecting test items that fairly sample and reliably represent the behavior being assessed. Literacy is a highly complex skill that incorporates a large number of activities functioning in a dynamic tension. It isn't easy to devise a few simply administered, easily scored test items that will accurately reflect an individual's overall ability in reading and writing.

Criterion-referenced tests (like standardized tests) can threaten to control the curriculum. If children (and thus teachers) are evaluated on a subset of literacy behaviors embodied in a particular test, then the temptation to teach to the test becomes very strong. As with norm-referenced tests, the action curriculum may shrink to the items on the test.

The control of the curriculum by tests and test makers can be avoided if evaluation and reporting is based on a variety of sources and forms of assessment that fairly represent the entire spectrum of curricular goals.

Reliability and Validity

Criterion-referenced tests must also be both reliable and valid. If repeated administrations produce wildly fluctuating scores, the test is unreliable. The test must also be valid — that is, it must measure what it actually says it measures. Some tests require children to read out isolated words, with the score determined by the number correctly pronounced. Such scores are converted into a "reading age" and taken as a general indicator of the children's reading ability. Dunkeld (1970) has shown that these types of tests are poor predictors of a first grade student's ability to comprehend a written text, and are even less reliable for older grades.

INSTRUCTIONAL UNIT TESTS

Unit testing should be fully incorporated into the preparation, presentation and postmortem cycle of unit and lesson planning.

The following model was developed around a unit testing program, although it could also be modified to fit other forms of assessment. We've used it only with older students.

Review

At the end of the unit we asked the students to offer suggestions as to topics that had been covered. These we wrote randomly on the chalkboard; then we established conceptual connections. After we'd put the topics into major categories we reviewed our teaching notes to ensure that all major ones had been included and added any we felt were important. We then established and circulated a definitive list of topics with the guarantee that all questions on the test would be drawn from that list.

If we wanted to include creative extensions or applications of course content to new situations, we made the students familiar with the type of extension required and the characteristics of adequate or superior responses.

Preparation for Private Study

We made plain the form or forms the questions would take and offered guidance on how to address each form. We provided specimen answers — superior, adequate and inferior — together with an explanation of the grade each answer would receive, drawn where possible from actual answers offered by previous students.

We wanted the students to have a clear understanding of what would be assessed, why particular answers were good, and how to apply concepts derived from instruction to the formulation of acceptable answers.

Independent Study

We offered the students guidance on how to study, modeling strategies such as rereading, highlighting, diagramming, and self-testing. Then we discussed and practiced them in class before assigning independent practice.

Test Administration

We administered the test exactly as negotiated with the students during the preparation period, without surprises with regard to content, form or timing.

Postmortem

We returned the test papers with some explanatory commentary regarding the grades awarded. Most concerns were met by a general oral review, with written comments on individual papers used only where absolutely necessary.

We assured the students they had the right to question the validity and consistency of our judgments. We were prepared to revise our judgment if we'd misinterpreted something or made arithmetic errors.

Implications for Instruction

The results of a unit test have diagnostic implications for both the program and the students. It's reasonable to assume that any consistent pattern in the answers can be attributed to instruction, any idiosyncratic responses to the individuality of the students.

Where we observe consistent patterns of strength or weakness we review the relevant portions of the unit for some explanation. If questions based on the assigned reading of a textbook are poorly answered, we review our teaching procedures to see if closer supervision, modeling, greater structure, etc., might improve the situation. If questions based on a problem-solving project, for instance, are particularly well answered, we note the effectiveness of the approach and note it for inclusion in future units.

The responses of individual students also offer diagnostic information. If high achievers do well on self-directed study, while less able students require more direct supervision, then those differences can be planned for in future units. If the class as a whole answers text-based questions reasonably well but a few students clearly have difficulty, then some direct coaching of the individuals concerned may be appropriate.

Actual details will vary with each instructional setting. The general point is that the assessment/instruction cycle must be a closed, recursive loop. All factors in the instructional setting are modifiable. To achieve optimal learning we must be prepared to consider change in any area, including our personal beliefs. Lack of appropriate learning doesn't necessarily mean that "bad" students have failed to benefit from "perfect" instruction.

General Application

The preceding model, with appropriate modifications, can be applied to standardized testing, examination of student products, student interviews, self-evaluation by students or teacher observation of classroom behavior. Each setting will produce information that can be fed back into the instruction/assessment cycle. In all cases the point is to be as open as possible so students understand what's being done, how it's being done and why it's being done — sharing with them as much of the information gained as possible and helping them understand how it will be used so they continue to be effective learners.

Educational assessment should be open, not a secret ritual conducted over the heads of students or behind their backs. Nor should the results or subsequent evaluations be withheld from either students or parents. Everyone who is touched by the assessment procedures should be kept as fully informed as possible.

WRITTEN COMMENTS ON CHILDREN'S WRITTEN WORK

Many teachers spend long, reluctant hours "marking" children's work, making evaluative comments, suggesting changes and noting grammar and spelling errors, all in the hope of improving the writing. Hillocks (1986) suggests that this practice is ineffective, that such comments don't have any beneficial effect on writing ability. He refers to this as "somewhat discouraging"; we find it monumental. Pessimistically it suggests that the hundreds of thousands of hours expended by hundreds of thousands of teachers have been wasted. Optimistically it suggests that we no longer need burden ourselves with this unnecessary chore.

Why have we persisted so conscientiously with a practice that appears to be ineffective? Perhaps because in our attempts to improve the present written *product* we've presumed our comments would improve the student's writing *process,* that errors corrected on product A will not be repeated on products B, C, D, etc. But Hillocks' research review suggests that such is not the case.

Another factor is that our comments are too frequently made on final drafts. Even if the students have gone through one or more preliminary drafts, what we mark is regarded as "finished." So our remarks arrive too late. Students are likely to view suggestions for needed change as persecution rather than assistance. We'd prefer to confine written comments on a child's paper to preliminary drafts. During the drafting stage the paper is still in flux, the ideas in process of formulation, and the young writer is much more open to and receptive of wise counsel.

However, we are growing increasingly sensitive to Graves' cautions regarding ownership of a piece of writing (1983). If we cover their papers with directives for change, then ownership starts to slip from them to us. We've adopted a policy: we don't hold a pencil during writing conferences, the children do. They, and not we, make the decisions for a change. But we've been surprised and shocked at how difficult it is for us to follow this simple dictum. Even when working with mature graduate students we still have the impulse to take hold of the correcting pencil .

Unfortunately there's never enough time for sustained conferences with each child for every piece of writing. Figure 5.4 contains our recommendations for comments on preliminary drafts, in descending order of value. Figure 5.5 contains our suggestions for comments on final drafts.

OBSERVATION

This is the richest source of data. But how do you record? And how do you make sure to include everyone?

Recording

Recording becomes difficult when you plan a series of teacher-centered lessons. While you are developing the content and keeping the children on task you can't also

1. **Practice:** Provide explicit and informative comments.
   Example: "I thought your description of the boat as a 'tarry old scow' was really good. I could see its battered sides were all black and gummy."
   Principle: The writer must know where and how s/he succeeded.

2. **Practice:** Ask questions.
   Example: "Can you think of a way to describe how the dog went down the road?"
   Principle: Questions imply a need for improvement and suggest a structure but leave the decision to change with the author.

3. **Practice:** Make suggestions.
   Example: "I think you need to explain how Andrea was able to escape from the cave."
   Principle: Direct suggestions should be made only when you cannot frame a question that will lead the author towards productive revision.

4. **Practice** Indicate grammatical and spelling errors.
   Example: "The boy's coats were missing.
   Principle: The location but not the nature of the error is noted. The author must decide on the correction required.

5. **Practice:** Provide vague and unsubstantiated evaluations.
   Examples: A+ Good work! You must try harder. 6/10
   Principle: Remarks such as these tell the author only how the teacher feels about the piece. They fail to explain how the writer wrought the effect.

6. **Practice:** Correct grammatical and spelling errors.
   Example: The boat was abowt to sink. (corrected: about)
   Principle: The correction of errors is a long and arduous task. It should be undertaken only by those who have long evenings bereft of anything better to do. The correction of errors may have a beneficial effect on the teacher's writing.

Figure 5.4 Suggestions for written comments on students' preliminary drafts

Practice:	Direct remarks on final drafts to the reader rather than the author.
Examples:	"Notice how David builds the tension as the rescue attempt is made. As readers we can guess who it is before the hero does."
	"Emily has tried really hard to get you to see, hear and feel what it was like on the beach."
Principle:	Make a positive comment on some successful aspect of the piece or on an attempt to achieve a particular effect.

Figure 5.5 Suggestions for written comments on students' final drafts

systematically observe individual children. However, if you have an abundance of independent and small-group work listed on your timetable, there will be times when every child is productively engaged without needing direct supervision. You may be tempted to draw together a small group for personal attention, and by all means do that. But some of that time should regularly be allocated to observation.

You may want to supplement these observations by notes jotted down at recess, lunch or immediately after school. However, other matters may demand your attention at those times; besides, notes based on selective (and fallible) memory may not be as revealing as records made at the time of the observation.

Systematizing the Survey

Figure 5.6 on the next page is an example of a chart that will help ensure each child comes under your scrutiny. As you record notes on significant behaviors the sheet will alert you to pay special attention to the children whose spots are still blank.

You could cut up these charts to incorporate the information in each child's cumulative record. Remember to date each square or the information will lose much of its value.

Observational notes are likely to record behavior rather than evidence of conceptual mastery. You can see if the child appears to be on task, for example, but you can't see if anything is being learned.

The kinds of information that might be recorded include:

Read silently for ______ minutes.
Wrote continuously for ______ minutes.
Sought help from ______.
Offered help to ______.
Consulted dictionary.
Participated in discussion.
Left desk to socialize ______ times in ______ minutes.

Of course you are the final judge on what actual information you collect, based on who you are, what your program is and which aspects of behavior bear on your current curricular objectives.

While observation will provide a rich source of information on which to base an evaluation, a word of caution is in order. We teachers aren't immune to the "halo" effect. If for whatever reason we *think* a child is pleasant, cooperative, intelligent or curious, then we tend to notice behaviors that confirm this attitude and ignore or discount those that may conflict with it. Negative halos are equally possible. Observations must be truly representative of a child's behavior. A second opinion from a trusted colleague is always worthwhile.

John Date____	*Jessica* Date____	*Ravinda* Date____	*Sameer* Date____	*Paul* Date____
Toby Date____	*Roesmary* Date____	*Allen* Date____	*David* Date____	*Ken* Date____
Claude Date____	*Horatio* Date____	*Alexander* Date____	*Wilbur* Date____	*Samantha* Date____
Templeton Date____	*Siddartha* Date____	*Tensing* Date____	*Hilary* Date____	*Manuel* Date____
Andreyus Date____	*Rachel* Date____	*Paula* Date____	*Nick* Date____	*Daniel* Date____
Tamara Date____	*Robin* Date____	*Colin* Date____	*Linden* Date____	*Kelly* Date____

Figure 5.6 An at-a-glance record sheet arranged according to a traditional class seating plan

CHECKLISTS

Checklists help you to systematize and record observations efficiently. They should reflect those behaviors you believe indicate productive learning strategies. The example in figure 5.7, based on the shared reading experience, lists behaviors we feel a child who is benefiting from the instruction will exhibit.

However, checklists can also act as blinkers, causing you to notice only the behaviors listed and overlook others that may be significant.

Checklists also won't remind you of the development that occurs within a given category. Take, for example, *Names words framed by teacher* in figure 5.7. Particular children may be able to name some words during the first week of their first year in school. Gradually the number of words, the speed of their response and the number of associations they can make for a given word will increase, while they also add more

	June P.	Mohir K.	Alan D.	Adolf H.
Tracks as teacher traces print.				
Names story or poem				
Names line framed by teacher				
Frames line on request				
Names phrases framed by teacher				
Frames phrases on request				
Names words framed by teacher				
Frames words on request				
Uses context to identify words				
Self-corrects				
Decodes using initial letter				
Recognises familiar words in new context				

Figure 5.7 A checklist of behaviors for shared reading

and more abstract words. None of these developments is readily recorded by a simple tick on a checklist.

You can record that kind of development within a given category by combining checklists and rating scales (see figure 5.8 on the next page).

CONFERENCES

Meeting with children individually to hear them read or to discuss their writing is expensive of time but richly rewarding. Many classrooms have adopted both types of conferences. The checklist in figure 5.8. can be used to record observations made during reading conferences, the list in figure 5.9 during writing conferences. If these are allowed to accumulate through the year, a detailed record of the children's progress will develop.

Figure 5.9 lists only general characteristics of process, purpose, and mechanics. Characteristics listed under product apply only to story. Alternative lists for report writing and poetry would need to be developed. More comprehensive and detailed lists of writing skills which you may find useful in developing criterion tests or checklists are available (for example, in Wilkinson, Barnsley, Hannah and Swan, 1980).

You may also want to consider interviewing the children regarding their responses to particular items on standardized tests. The children's explanations of their choices are often quite revealing.

Name Reading Skills	Grade Level 1	2	3	4	5	6	7	8
• **Vocabulary**								
Sight Vocabulary								
Decoding								
Meaning Vocabulary								
Context								
Decoding/Context								
• **Comprehension**								
Literal								
Central Idea								
Sequence								
Prediction								
Imagery								
Inference								
Cause and Effect								
Conclusions								
Judgment								
Substantiation								
Integration								
Prior Knowledge								
Metaphor								

***Figure 5.8** Checklist and rating scale combined (the full meaning of each term is discussed in the Skills Analysis section in the next chapter)*

Writing Checklist **Process**	**Attempted**	**Used Well**
Generates ideas from experience		
Collects information		
Organizes information		
Revises for content		
Revises for mechanics		
Accepts criticism		
Purpose Sense of audience		
Product: stories Plot:		
Setting		
Problem		
Attempt		
Climax		
Resolution		
Character development		
Description		
Action		
Speech		
Thoughts		
Speech of others		
Thoughts of others		
Mood		
Pace		
Imagery		
Point of view		

Figure 5.9 A writing skills checklist

WRITING FOLDERS

Writing folders are a simple and impressive way of keeping track of children's progress. One striking method of reporting that progress is to highlight and compare a piece of writing from the beginning of the year, one or two from during the year and one from near the end. Explanatory comments regarding growth in clarity, originality, length, vocabulary size, spelling and letter formation could be added, but such things are usually self-evident as Michael's writing in figure 5.10 shows.

Remember to date *all* samples. It may be useful to add a note regarding the circumstances surrounding the writing. For example, you may want to show the drafts a particular piece went through. Each draft should be dated and labeled.

Writing folders store information that is both easy to gather and easy to interpret. The series of examples in figure 5.10 (A and B) gives a good impression of the child's progress. More detailed analyses require more work but may show progress more dramatically. Figure 5.11 (next page) shows the words Michael spelled correctly at three points in the school year. Verbal commendations or letter grades are quite superfluous.

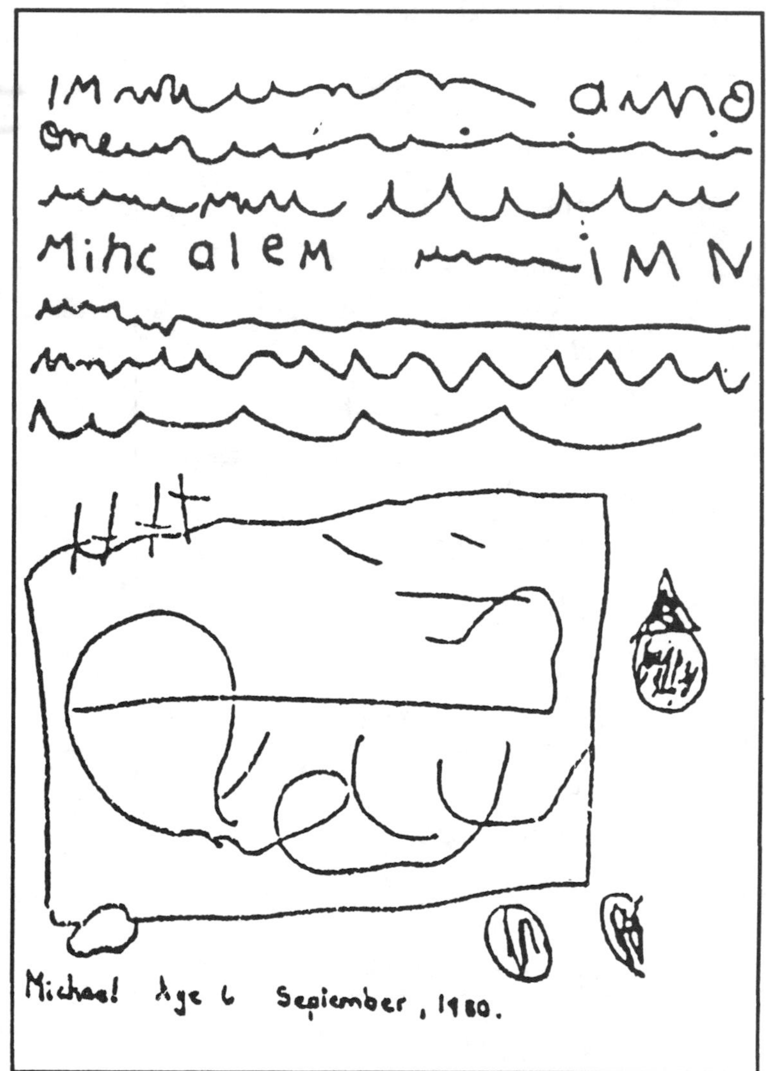

Illustrations courtesy of Gail Heald-Taylor

Figure 5.10 (A) A sample of Michael's writing during his first month in school

October 1980

My Nme is Michael M
Dear Santa Merry Christmas
please
me a
and a

December 1980

I got two 'Cyclopedias
and I got one chocolate
bunny. I got 36 eggs.
David waz running on
he hert his foot.
are baby brother got
the most eggs he had
29. an David got
46 eggs.

Michael Age 6. March, 1980

March 1981

The big goast

One day a big goast came
I got vairy skaird I ran aroan
but the goast got up to me.
every time I ran right in my
house. My mom told me
to go owtside But but
what if thair is a goast
owtside oh oh rily, a goast
But thair is a goast owtside
you go owt side you will
see a goast. I wil but I wil
not see a goast. So my mom
went owtside. I saw a goast
but it wil go alway at night
and it did. and never came
back.

Michael Age 6. May, 1980.

May 1981

Illustrations courtesy of Gail Heald-Taylor

Figure 5.10 (B) Changes in Michael's writing during his first nine months of school

ATTITUDE

Many language arts curricula claim that they promote positive attitudes towards language, literature and literacy. Attitude assessment is really a measure of customer satisfaction. However, when student report cards include items on attitude they present them as characteristics of the learners, not the program ("John's attitude towards poetry must improve").

Attitude scales are relatively easy to prepare and administer. They should be kept short, simple and specific. Thirty children responding to a 30-item questionnaire generate 900 pieces of data! A question such as "Indicate how you feel about reading" could be interpreted as reading library books, reading aloud in class, completing workbook exercises or the lesson called reading. Figure 5.12 shows specific questions that are much more valuable in modifying future practice.

Term	Actual words spelled correctly					
First	spook	ghost				*Total—2*
Second	my Santa me got she made we it	am games they is merry a an could	cake had at nice eat are Michael Christmas	and take get with the was like fruit	dear please I to too Mum ate love	good play people *Total—43*
Third	March boy eggs his brother bike snail house lot snake stay room every hiding	worm everyone about votes right last least break two David foot most broke named	ghosts will help kill lived sick corner door stay that leave told school visits	went chocolate running girls leg head then bats dinosaur ran but happy going jumped	hot crow back town came pass reptile friends bunny he baby when went time	once lizard store air never then place day were something big birthday toy salamander *Total—84*

***Figure 5.11** Correct spellings by Michael, age 6, during his first year of school*

MEDIA

Tape recorders are useful for recording speech development and oral reading. Some teachers have purchased a cheap cassette for each child and regularly record their speech and oral reading, showing progress as it has occurred throughout the year.

Cameras, particularly Polaroid cameras, can be very useful for capturing transient products such as block buildings, displays, costumes and Plasticine models. Such products often demonstrate a depth of knowledge on a topic that is far beyond the child's capacity for written expression.

SECOND OPINIONS

You should not feel that you are the sole source of information pertinent to the evaluation of the children in your class. Parents, other teachers, the principal, the

How do you feel when the teacher tells you that it is now a 40 minute reading period in which you may continue reading a story of your own choice? +2 +1 0 -1 -2	Do you enjoy listening to other students' ideas about the story? +2 +1 0 -1 -2 How do you feel about making up a word web about part of the story? +2 +1 0 -1 -2
How do you feel when the teacher tells you that it is now time to continue with the unit based on *The Secret of NIMH?* +2 +1 0 -1 -2	How do you feel about drawing maps of various parts of the story? +2 +1 0 -1 -2 +2 = I am very pleased +1 = I am quite pleased 0 = I feel all right -1 = I am mildly displeased -2 = I am very displeased

***Figure 5.12 Examples of questions from an attitude scale related to a literature unit based on* The Secret of NIMH**

school nurse, a school psychologist and a teacher-librarian may all be able to contribute to a fuller picture of individuals. Consultation might be no more than a brief chat over coffee.

Parents

Parents are enormous untapped sources of information and are experts on their own children. Figure 5.13 shows a letter one of our colleagues sends; responses are warm, witty and replete with sound advice.

GRADING

Grading must be rationally tied to the decisions that are made about students. A 12-point grading scale (A+ to D) serves no purpose in the go/no-go system in most primary schools. Passing on to a higher grade with an A+, a B, etc. serves little purpose. Reports need say only that a particular child is or is not ready for a particular program.

Language Arts Information Sheet

Prior to finalizing my long range plans for Grade 5 Language Arts, I would appreciate information from you regarding your child's perceived strengths and weaknesses.

As parents you are in the best position to evaluate your child's use of language skills (such as reading and writing) in "the real world." I would appreciate your consideration of the following questions and your careful appraisal of your child's skills.

Thank you,

We/I would like our child to learn ________ this year. We/I would like our child to be exposed to ____________________________
and ____________________________
He/She is also able to ____________________
easily. However, in spite of ______ talents, ____ needs lots of assistance to ______________
________ and ______________________

In general, a perfect Language Arts program for ______________ would ______________
____
____

If you ever want ____________'s undivided attention you just have to mention ________ or ________________. Whatever you do, don't ever ____________________________!

Good luck in your endeavors! Sincerely,

______________'s parents

Figure 5.13 A letter sent to parents at the beginning of the school year

In schools where "promotion" is automatic, no symbolic grading is necessary either. A prose description of the child's strengths and areas where support is needed is sufficient.

The defense of letter grades that rests on the desire of parents merely raises the question of educational leadership. Who will determine evaluation practices: professionals or parents?

RANKING

Reporting each child's relative rank in the class should be done only in those schools and school districts where the relative merit of each teacher and administrator is ranked and published each month in the local news media.

The practice assaults self-esteem. Someone has to come "bottom" and that child is destroyed. The purpose of education is to provide all children with sufficient skills and knowledge to enable them to lead happy and productive lives. Most of the material presented in school can be learned to a reasonable level by the majority of the population. Schools don't have a mandate to rank, stream or apply publicly accessible badges of relative merit to its clients.

REPORTING

Reporting always involves summarization based on a file full of anecdotal observations and checklists, a folder of the child's work, test data, tape recordings and photographs. These raw materials become the evidence to support any evaluative comment or judgment that may be called into question. Such a rich source of information can't be meaningfully reduced to a rank, percentile or letter grade. Each child is worthy of at least a prose description and a teacher-parent interview.

EVALUATION: SUMMARY

Evaluation should not be equated with testing. Testing should not be equated with the administration of standardized tests. Each individual is an amazing complex of varied abilities. Each is worthy of being described with at least a prose description. We are not in the meat packaging business. Our "products" can't be graded along a single, universally agreed continuum or described by a number, a letter or a rank.

The prose description should be framed in reference to the goals of the curriculum. It should be of assistance to those who will continue to have dealings with the child: parents and subsequent teachers. It should summarize the child's strengths and indicate areas where the child is still in need of guidance. It should be based on a wide variety of data gathered from several different sources over a sustained period of time.

The United States has probably suffered the most among English-speaking countries from the overuse and misuse of standardized tests. Many administrators have sought to control teacher behavior through extensive testing programs. In 1977 the International Association for Childhood Education and the National Association of Elementary School Principals called for a moratorium on the use of standardized tests because of the deleterious effects on children and programs (Jeffrey, Hall, Meister and Provonost, 1985). But at the time of writing such appeals appear to have fallen on deaf ears.

CHAPTER SIX

DEVELOPING A LITERACY CURRICULUM

AN ACTIVITY-CENTERED, LITERATURE-BASED LITERACY CURRICULUM

By the time they reached the third grade, children in a certain school had been presented with the same rather mediocre big book by four different teachers. Each teacher was unaware of the actions of the other three. While rampant repetition is disturbing enough, the consequent omissions in the literary experience of those children are of even greater concern. What literacy experiences did they miss? What literacy experiences might have been substituted that would have been equally effective in promoting skill development, but considerably more enriching than these unplanned and unnecessary repetitions? In figure 6.1 we outline a year-long curriculum for year three, one that gives us a handle on addressing the concerns. Each unit is designed to last three to four weeks and can easily be modified.

DEVELOPMENTAL SEQUENCES

The proposed curriculum has several developmental features. We use the word "developmental" not in the North American sense that would have us accept an invariant sequence of skills to be mastered, which eventually leads to the production of lock-step programs. Rather, we simply affirm our belief that children feel comfortable with and eager about tasks they understand and that are within their range. They also become more accomplished as they grow up. For us "developmental learning" is like "natural learning."

Given what we said about repetition, you will find that:

- Each unit introduces new routines.
- Subsequent units reuse familiar routines.
- Simple routines precede more complex ones. For example, *Clues* and *Find It* in Unit I use single clues while *Countdown* in Unit II uses a coordinated set of clues.
- The number of routines in later units increases since the reuse of familiar procedures will require much less instructional time than the introduction of new ones.
- *Free Choice* is introduced after the children develop a repertoire of approaches. By the end of Unit IV they will be familiar with 11 ways of responding to books.
- The year begins with collections of picture books and concludes with simple chapter books.

Year 3 Language Arts Curriculum

Page numbers refer to this book.
Numbers preceded by LTL refer to sections in *Literacy through Literature* by Johnson and Louis (1985).

Unit I. Home is Best: the circular story

- Bureaucratic forms (LTL 3.9)
- Clues (LTL 2.5)
- Find it (p. 112)

Unit II. The problems of getting there: the linear story

- Maps (LTL 3.6)
- Find it (p.112)
- Countdown (LTL 3.4.1)

Unit III. Monsters: human horrors, fabulous beasts and fearsome animals

- Bureaucratic forms (LTL 3.9)
- Interview (LTL 3.17)
- Posters (LTL 3.10)
- Rating scales (LTL 3.3)
- Sociogram (LTL 3.14)

Unit IV. Growing up

- Countdown (LTL 3.4)
- Interviews (LTL 3.17)
- Rating scales (LTL 3.3)
- Book bingo (p. 53)
- Word webbing (p. 40)
- Free choice

Unit V. Quests: kin, treasure, kingdom, self

- Maps (LTL 3.6)
- Plot profile (LTL 3.16)
- Sociogram (LTL 3.14)
- Book bingo (p. 53)
- Free choice

Unit VI. Poetry: pleasure and pain

- Cloze (p. 57)
- Disturbed poems (p. 58)
- Pattern writing (LTL 3.18.2)
- Word webbing (p. 40)
- Free Choice

Unit VII. Novel study: Charlotte's Web

- Plot profile (LTL 3.16)
- Sociogram (LTL3.14)
- Word webbing (p. 40)
- Burgess summary (LTL 3.1)
- Interviews (LTL 3.17)
- Posters (LTL3.10)
- Rating scales (LTL 3.3)
- Free choice

Unit VIII. Novel study: The Lion, the Witch and the Wardrobe (Lewis 1961)

- Interviews (LTL 3.17)
- Plot profile (LTL 3.16)
- Sociogram (LTL 3.14)
- Burgess summary (LTL 3.1)
- Posters (LTL 3.10)
- Rating scales (LTL 3.3)
- Story completion (LTL 3.18.2)
- Character grid (LTL 3.3.2)

Unit IX. Novel study: The Boundary Riders (Phipson, 1965)

- Story grammar (p. 74)
- Rating scale (LTL 3.3)
- Book bingo (p. 53)
- Word webs (p. 40)
- Countdown (LTL 3.4.1)
- Maps (LTL 3.6)

Unit X. Novel study: I Own the Racecourse (Wrightson, 1968)

- Bureaucratic forms (LTL 3.9)
- Find it (p. 112)
- Posters(LTL 3.10)
- Rating scales (LTL 3.3)
- Story completion (LTL 3.18.2)
- Book bingo (p. 53)
- Word webs (p. 40)
- Readers' theater (p. 82)

Figure 6.1 A year-long literature-based literacy curriculum

SKILLS ANALYSIS

Figure 6.3 presents an analysis of our proposed curriculum. The routines are listed in the left-hand column. The skills are shown across the top. A brief explanation of each skill is given in figure 6.2. If a given activity requires a given skill to become the focus of the learner's attention, it receives a check mark. If the skill is used but not directly addressed, it receives a dot.

Comprehension

- *Prior knowledge*. The ability to apply appropriate prior knowledge to a given text. This ability is not a skill in the sense that there exist alternative routes to comprehension. The application of prior knowledge is the process of comprehension. However, a reader may have relevant knowledge but fail to invoke it in trying to understand a particular text.
- *Literal information*. The ability to identify, state or paraphrase information stated explicitly in the text.
- *Gist*. The ability to identify, state or paraphrase the central idea of a text.
- Inference. The ability to perceive relationships not made explicit in the text.
- *Imagery*. The ability to form sensory images from the text: visual, tactile, auditory, gustatory and olfactory.
- *Sequence*. The ability to recall or restructure events into a rational sequence: temporal, causal, spatial.
- *Prediction*. The ability to predict outcomes based on incomplete textual knowledge.
- *Cause and effect*. The ability to determine cause and effect.
- *Conclusions*. The ability to draw rational conconclusions based on specified literal, inferential and extra-textual information.
- *Substantiation*. The ability to identify textual and non-textual information to support a conclusion or judgment.
- *Judgment*. The ability to make value judgments based on explicitly stated facts, conclusions and standards.
- *Integration*. The ability to compare, contrast, relate and integrate information from two or more sources: within a single text; across several texts; extra-textual information.

Vocabulary

- *Sight vocabulary*. Words that are immediately visually familiar and part of the reader's oral and meaning vocabulary.
- *Decoding*. The approximation or possible pronunciation of the sound value of sub-word units to assist in the identification and/or pronunciation of a word.
- *Meaning vocabulary*. Words for which a meaning or range of potential meanings is known.
- *Denotation/connotation*. The ability to state the literal meaning of a word in a given context; the ability to state the associations commonly carried by the word; and the ability to distinguish between the denotative and connotative aspects of the word.
- *Decoding/context*. The ability to use minimal decoding cues in combination with context to identify an unknown word.
- *Metaphor*. The ability to note that a given expression is metaphorical; the ability to state the two concepts compared; the ability to state the connotation of a given metaphor.

Figure 6.2 General reading skills

Figure 6.3

A skills analysis of a year-long literature-based literacy curriculum

	Comprehension													Vocabulary						
	Prior knowledge	Literal information	Gist	Inference	Imagery	Sequence	Prediction	Cause and effect	Conclusions	Substantiation	Judgement	Integration	Coherence	Sight vocabulary	Decoding	Meaning vocabulary	Denotation/connotation	Context	Decoding/context	Metaphor
Unit I																				
Bureaucratic Forms	✓	✓	✓	✓				✓	✓	✓	✓	✓	•	✓	•	✓	•	•	•	•
Clues	✓	✓		✓			✓	✓	✓	✓	✓	✓	✓	✓	•	✓	•	•	•	•
Find it	✓	✓		✓			✓	✓	✓	✓	✓	✓	✓	✓	•	✓	•	•	•	•
Unit II																				
Maps	✓	✓	✓	✓	✓	✓		•	✓	✓	✓	✓	•	•	•	✓	•	•	•	•
Find it	✓	✓		✓			✓	✓	✓	✓	✓	✓	•	✓	•	✓	•	•	•	•
Countdown	✓	✓	✓	✓	✓	✓	✓	✓	✓	✓	✓	✓	•	✓	•	✓	•	•	•	•
Unit III																				
Bureaucratic forms	✓	✓	✓	✓				✓	✓	✓	✓	✓	•	✓	•	✓	•	•	•	•
Interviews	✓	✓	✓	✓	✓	✓		✓	✓	✓	✓	✓	•	✓	•	✓	•	•	•	•
Posters	✓	✓	✓	✓	✓	•		✓	✓	✓	✓	✓	•	✓	•	✓	•	•	•	•
Rating scales	✓	✓	✓	✓	✓	•	✓	✓	✓	✓	✓	✓	•	✓	•	✓	•	•	•	•
Sociogram	✓	✓	✓	✓	✓	•		✓	✓	✓	✓	✓	✓	✓	•	✓	✓	•	•	•
Unit IV																				
Countdown	✓	✓	✓	✓	✓	✓	✓	✓	✓	✓	✓	✓	•	✓	•	✓	•	•	•	•
Interviews	✓	✓	✓	✓	✓	✓		✓	✓	✓	✓	✓	•	✓	•	✓	•	•	•	•
Rating sclaes	✓	✓	✓	✓	✓	•		✓	✓	✓	✓	✓	•	✓	•	✓	•	•	•	•
Book bingo	✓	✓	✓	✓	✓	•	✓	✓	✓	✓	✓	✓	•	✓	•	✓	•	•	•	•
Word webbing	✓	✓	✓	✓	✓				✓	✓	✓	✓	•	✓	•	✓	✓	✓	•	•

Figure 6.3 (cont.)	Comprehension													Vocabulary						
	Prior knowledge	Literal information	Gist	Inference	Imagery	Sequence	Prediction	Cause and effect	Conclusions	Substantiation	Judgement	Integration	Coherence	Sight vocabulary	Decoding	Meaning vocabulary	Denotation/connotation	Context	Decoding/context	Metaphor
Unit V																				
Maps	✓	✓	✓	✓	✓	✓		•	✓	✓	✓	✓	•	✓	•	✓	•	•	•	•
Plot profile	✓	✓	✓	✓	•	✓	✓	✓	✓	✓	✓	✓	✓	✓	•	•	•	•	•	•
Sociogram	✓	✓	✓	✓	✓		✓	✓	✓	✓	✓	✓	✓	✓	•	✓	•	•	•	•
Book bingo	✓	✓	✓	✓	✓	•	✓	✓	✓	✓	✓	✓	•	✓	•	✓	•	•	•	•
Unit VI																				
Cloze	✓	✓	✓	✓	✓	✓	✓	✓	✓	✓	✓	✓	✓	✓	✓	✓	✓	✓	✓	✓
Disturbed poems	✓	✓	✓	✓	✓	✓	✓	✓	✓	✓	✓	✓	✓	✓	✓	✓	✓	✓	✓	✓
Pattern writing	✓	✓	✓	✓	✓	✓	✓	✓	✓	✓	✓	✓	✓	✓	•	✓	•	•	•	•
Word webbing	✓	✓	✓	✓	✓				✓	✓	✓	✓	•	✓	•	✓	✓	✓	•	•
Unit VII																				
Plot profile	✓	✓	✓	✓	•	✓	✓	✓	✓	✓	✓	✓	✓	✓	•	•	•	•	•	•
Sociogram	✓	✓	✓	✓	✓		✓	✓	✓	✓	✓	✓	✓	✓	•	✓	•	•	•	•
Word webbing	✓	✓	✓	✓	✓				✓	✓	✓	✓	•	✓	•	✓	✓	✓	•	•
Summary cloze	✓	✓	✓	✓	✓	✓	✓	✓	✓	✓	✓	✓	✓	✓	✓	✓	•	✓	✓	•
Interviews	✓	✓	✓	✓	✓	✓		✓	✓	✓	✓	✓	•	✓	•	✓	•	•	•	•
Posters	✓	✓	✓	✓	✓	•		✓	✓	✓	✓	✓	•	✓	•	✓	•	•	•	•

Figure 6.3 (cont.)	Comprehension													Vocabulary						
	Prior knowledge	Literal information	Gist	Inference	Imagery	Sequence	Prediction	Cause and effect	Conclusions	Substantiation	Judgement	Integration	Coherence	Sight vocabulary	Decoding	Meaning vocabulary	Denotation/connotation	Context	Decoding/context	Metaphor
Unit VIII																				
Interviews	✓	✓	✓	✓	✓	✓		✓	✓	✓	✓	✓	•	✓	•	✓	•	•	•	•
Plot profile	✓	✓	✓	✓	•	✓	✓	✓	✓	✓	✓	✓	✓	✓	•	•	•	•	•	•
Sociogram	✓	✓	✓	✓	✓		✓	✓	✓	✓	✓	✓	✓	✓	•	✓	•	•	•	•
Summary cloze	✓	✓	✓	✓	✓	✓	✓	✓	✓	✓	✓	✓	✓	✓	✓	✓	•	✓	✓	•
Posters	✓	✓	✓	✓	✓	•		✓	✓	✓	✓	✓	•	✓	•	✓	•	•	•	•
Rating scales	✓	✓	✓	✓	✓	•		✓	✓	✓	✓	✓	•	✓	•	✓	•	•	•	•
Story completion	✓	✓	✓	✓	✓	✓	✓	✓	✓	✓	✓	✓	✓	✓	•	✓	•	•	•	•
Character grid	✓	✓	✓	✓	•	✓		✓	✓	✓	✓	✓	✓	✓	•	•	✓	•	•	•
Unit IX																				
Story grammar	✓	✓	✓	✓	✓	✓	✓	✓	✓	✓	✓	✓	✓	✓	•	✓	•	•	•	•
Rating scales	✓	✓	✓	✓	✓	•		✓	✓	✓	✓	✓	•	✓	•	✓	•	•	•	•
Book bingo	✓	✓	✓	✓	✓	•	✓	✓	✓	✓	✓	✓	•	✓	•	✓	•	•	•	•
Word webs	✓	✓	✓	✓	✓				✓	✓	✓	✓	•	✓	•	✓	✓	✓	•	•
Countdown	✓	✓	✓	✓	✓	✓	✓	✓	✓	✓	✓	✓	•	✓	•	✓	•	•	•	•
Maps	✓	✓	✓	✓	✓	✓		•	✓	✓	✓	✓	•	✓	•	✓	•	•	•	•
Unit X																				
Bureaucratic forms	✓	✓	✓	✓				✓	✓	✓	✓	✓	•	✓	•	✓	•	•	•	•
Find it	✓	✓		✓			✓	✓	✓	✓	✓	✓	•	✓	•	✓	•	•	•	•
Posters	✓	✓	✓	✓	✓	•		✓	✓	✓	✓	✓	•	✓	•	✓	•	•	•	•
Rating scales	✓	✓	✓	✓	✓	•		✓	✓	✓	✓	✓	•	✓	•	✓	•	•	•	•
Story completion	✓	✓	✓	✓	✓	✓	✓	✓	✓	✓	✓	✓	✓	✓	•	✓	•	•	•	•
Book bingo	✓	✓	✓	✓	✓	•	✓	✓	✓	✓	✓	✓	•	✓	•	✓	•	•	•	•
Readers' theatre	✓	✓	✓	✓	✓	✓	•	✓	✓	✓	✓	✓	✓	✓	•	✓	✓	•	•	•

There's a subjective element in determining whether certain activities bring a given skill to the focus of attention. Some forms of the activity may require the skill directly; other forms of the same activity may use the skill only tacitly.

None of the skills is a discrete entity. All are highly interrelated and work in dynamic harmony. Each label covers a variety of activities which vary with the text, the social context in which the text is read, and the purpose for reading. For example, identifying the main idea in a fable, in a short story, in a chapter in a novel and in an expository text involves quite different operations.

The skills are called general because they apply to a wide variety of texts. We haven't included the special skills that are required when reading narratives, expository texts or poetry.

Numerous skills are covered, many of them several times. It's clear that some skills (such as decoding and metaphor) are rarely addressed directly. A teacher or curriculum committee that decides that a proposed program needs to be strengthened in particular areas could modify it so that certain skills are brought more directly to the attention of the learners. It's our belief that low order skills, such as decoding, should be incorporated in the service of higher goals rather than being made the focus of attention. Metaphor is a pervasive aspect of language and probably deserves more careful attention.

The goal of the curriculum is not that skills be *taught* but that they be *learned*. Unfortunately teaching can be mandated while learning can't. If skills are to be learned, then instruction must be provided. But instruction need not be narrowly defined as exercises that require the repeated use of an isolated skill. Effective instruction can be conceived of as an activity, game, discussion, project or exploration, all of which deploy a range of skills. The skills may be used unconsciously to attain a broader objective; the fact that they aren't brought to the conscious level of the teacher or learner doesn't mean they aren't there.

We feel that an integrated approach to literacy not only addresses the skills demanded by a skills approach but teaches the learner how to orchestrate those skills to achieve some relevant and interesting goal.

A WRITING CURRICULUM

Writing Instruction

For quite a while our attitude towards writing has been heavily influenced by the work of Donald Graves, especially by his notion that children should be able to select their own topics and pursue their own writing inclinations. However, a recent review of research on written composition (Hillocks, 1986) indicates that the free writing aspect of the approach advocated by Graves, while twice as effective as traditional skills-based methods, is only half as effective as the *environmental approach* Hillocks advocates.

Hillocks' work doesn't question Graves' recommendation of the process approach which involves the progressive refinement of a text through editing and revision. It's the "choose your own topics" aspect of Graves' work (Hillocks calls it "free writing") he criticizes.

A Free Approach to Writing

Hillocks criticizes free writing on several grounds. He doesn't agree with the assumption that growth in writing is part of a child's genetic makeup and that it requires only a nurturing, kindly environment to unfold. He also claims that free writing rests on three further unwarranted assumptions, each of which relegates the teacher's role to that of mere reactor:

- Children will invent written forms to express their meanings.
- If it's necessary to know something about writing, such knowledge is best gained from peers.
- Imagination is best served by freedom of choice and inhibited by structure.

Hillocks, in his endorsement of an environmental mode of instruction, advocates that the teacher take on much more of a leadership role.

An Environmental Approach to Writing

The environmental approach is characterized by:

- Clear and specific objectives.
- Specific materials and concrete, short-term problems for students to solve. The problems are selected to promote the exercise and development of a specified writing process such as narration, definition or explanation.
- Activities in which small group problem-solving sessions precede individual written responses.

One of the most effective writing programs reviewed by Hillocks was a study by Troyka (1974) in which first-year college students engaged in a series of simulation games. It has not been determined if such an approach would be as effective at lower levels. Materials based on this study are published in Troyka and Nudelman (1975).

Sentence Combining, Scales and Inquiry

Hillocks identifies several other aspects of instruction in written composition that research has shown to be highly effective.

Sentence combining. Having students build complex sentences from simple ones has been shown repeatedly to have a significantly beneficial effect on writing performance.

Scales. Providing students with evaluative scales against which the writing of others, and their own, may be judged has a strong positive effect on the quality of written products (Sager, 1973). We see a kinship between scales and our "rules" described in A General Teaching Model, pages 30-31.

Inquiry. Situations which require students to examine sets of data, develop explanations, analyze situations and propose solutions were found by Hillocks to be nearly four times as effective in the improvement of writing as a free approach.

Interaction

It isn't clear whether a program that incorporated all these factors into a single instructional mode would have the combined benefit of each. However, the prospects for improved methods of instruction in writing look very exciting indeed.

We would tentatively suggest that a Graves-style approach of free writing be adopted for the first two years of school. Increasingly thereafter the children should be set in problem-solving situations which demand writing in an increasing variety of forms. Models should be examined and characteristics of good performance elucidated from such models. One consistent aspect of revision would be the combining of simple sentences into longer and more complex structures.

The Genrists

Genrists Martin and Rothery (1986) have pointed out that we express our meanings in a finite set of socially determined forms or genres. They feel that teachers need to take an active role in showing children how meaning can be expressed within these genres. While their suggestions have the merit of pointing towards the basis of a writing curriculum, they could easily lead back to the dark days of the five paragraph essay and the writing of *Engfish* (Macrorie, 1976).

The Significance of Audience

Both Graves' freedom writers and the genrists pay insufficient attention to the purpose for writing. In the world beyond the classroom writing is addressed to a specified audience for a particular purpose. Such writing is contextually determined — that is, once audience and purpose have been identified, the form (or genre) is mandatory. This necessary relationship between audience, purpose and form is but one manifestation of the dictum: form follows function (Nystrand, 1982).

Prowess Writing

In the classroom most writing is done for the purpose of demonstrating the author's prowess. Children say that in school they write for the teacher who will evaluate what they produce (Tamburri, Willig and Butler, 1984).

Functional school writing programs must include writing activities that are done with genuine communicative intent. Children must be helped to write real messages about real topics that are of real concern to both the writer and the intended audience.

THEORETICAL REFLECTIONS

Developmental literacy

The development of skills

It is clear that from birth to maturity human beings increase their control over both oral and written language. It is also evident that an accomplished language user has a repertoire of language skills. For a long time we assumed that we could identify basic skills which are easy for the inexperienced learner to acquire and which will provide the foundation for learning more demanding skills. We also assumed that these skills could be sequenced developmentally.

Literacy learning does not appear to proceed in a linear additive manner, however. Instead, processes of assimilation and accommodation seem to create an increasingly rich associative net. The *process* of increasing the number and complexity of associative connections is general, but the making of specific associations is peculiar to each individual. While we can say in general terms what children must do to become literate, we cannot specify what any given individual needs to do on a given day. Programs that arrange instructional activities in rigid, predetermined sequences are in conflict with the natural learning proclivities of the child. Learning happens without the learner being aware of it, and without it being directly evident to an observer.

Reading development

Acceptance of an associative network view of literacy calls many traditional assumptions and practices into question: controlled vocabulary, for example. We do not know, and will never know, which words in which order a given child is ready to learn to read. Nor do we know the rate at which new vocabulary should be introduced, nor the number of repetitions each child needs for each word. We heard an eminent scholar boast that some kindergarten children had learned to read "marshmallow" by acting out a poem that used the word. Marshmallow, he reminded us, is not a kindergarten word. And why not? What committee is authorized to allocate particular words to particular grades?

Equally we can question predetermined skill sequences and the very concept of a discrete reading skill. Breaking reading down into skills involves a process of intellectual abstraction, but does not necessarily result in a description of reading that has any psychological reality.

The reductionism involved in detailed skills analysis is like studying rabbits by looking at molecules or atoms. Those tiny particles do not behave in any way that will tell us much about bunnies. Texts, like rabbits, are dynamic structures. Each word in a given text derives some of its meaning and function from its association with other words in the text. If we reduce the text to single, separate words the nature of each word changes. We can learn little about a text by the close examination of each word in isolation.

With respect to the readability, we can refer to the level of difficulty of a text only in the broadest terms. A third grader with an obsessive interest in a given topic may be able to read books on that topic at a much higher level. Readability assessments that report levels of difficulty to one or two decimal places are figments of a hand calculator's imagination. At best we can say that a book with a readability level of 5.0, for example, can normally be read by children with average reading abilities sometime between grades four and six.

It is much better to select materials intuitively, guided by the content and a presentation that seems to appeal to the children for whom they are intended, rather than some observable linguistic characteristic which is believed to be appropriate for a learner at a given level. We can identify stories and poems that are suitable for children in a given year but we simply cannot justify a fixed, predetermined order in which those materials shall be presented.

We select activities on the same intuitive basis. By and large we know the kinds of activities six-year-old children like. We know some changes we would make if we were planning to teach 9-, 14- or 27-year-olds. We could not, however, defend a particular sequenced set of activities. Almost any activity that requires children to interact meaningfully with written language will serve our purpose. Many activities do not fit into a developmental paradigm (suitable for one age but not for another). People sing, chant, write, perform and discuss at almost any age. The level of maturity and complexity of such activities will increase over time but such progressive changes are, in many cases, under the control of the learner rather than the teacher.

The notion that there are limits to the specificity with which we can describe language development has *instructional* implications. Instruction should parallel our knowledge of the learning process. If we can specify the general level of the child's present capacity for language processing and can generally predict the direction in which it will develop, then our instructional procedures should reflect that generality. Instruction should not pretend that we know that today Jessica *must* learn the "ng" digraph, while Joshua *must* work on the appreciation of symbol. Or, as is more likely, today is the day that the children are all "ready" to use three-syllable words or to pay attention to medial vowels. All we can really say is that there are certain things that readers need to be able to do: use context, for example. We might then use an activity that requires children to identify the meaning of nonsense words embedded in the summary of a story since it will encourage the use of context. We can offer children general guidance on how to approach the task but the specific tactics and specific learnings that result are under the control of each individual child.

Development and Progress

Is change necessarily progress? There are developmental changes in the child's behavior that may look like regressions. The child who used *went* correctly at two years of age may say *wented* at the age of three. But such a change can be perceived as regressive only by taking a limited view of the child's language. The appearance of *wented* signals that the child has begun to note how past tense is regularly formed and has erroneously applied it to the verb "to go." Later the child will come to understand regularities and their exceptions. In reading, beginners may read/recite a familiar text fluently but begin to read more haltingly when they realize the one-to-one correspondence between written and spoken words. Such "regressions" are in fact signs of progress. Raising them to support the argument that change is not necessarily progress confuses the issue. Children may, through poor instruction, come to mistrust their linguistic instincts and artificially reconstruct their vocabularies, but by and large the language of children changes in the direction of the adult speech community in which they live.

This is not to suggest that the language of children is inherently inferior to the language of adults. We value the speech of a three-year-old as appropriate for her age. But we would not value the same language if it were expressed by a seven-year-old. We would label it as "immature" and feel that some intervention would be required. If a teenager used such language, we would suspect a limited mental capacity. We have an expectation that children's language will progress toward adult norms. We value such changes since they indicate that progress is taking place.

The Development of Writing Ability

Writing develops analogously to reading, in that the writer must learn the conventions associated with written expression: letter formation, spelling, selection and sequencing of words on the page, sentence formation, grammar and appropriate usages. Learners must also learn to express themselves within the constraints of the numerous forms of written expression: stories, poems, plays, letters, posters, memos, shopping lists, forms, expository texts, editorials, political pamphlets, travel brochures, directions, rules, and warnings. Each form has numerous subcategories. Within narration, for example, the child must learn about chronology and the permissible ways in which linear time sequences may be manipulated through flashbacks and parallel plot construction.

The procedure involved in writing, like reading, can be placed on a continuum between deep structure and surface realization (see page 91). Deep structure includes the act of creation or inspiration, which is ineffable and uncommunicable. The learning of surface structure is largely tacit. Most speakers and writers are unaware of most of the rules that govern their selection and ordering of words. We believe that writing instruction, like reading instruction, should be approached through a range of mid-level strategies which are readily available to the conscious mind and which may be demonstrated, analyzed, discussed, and modified.

We can illustrate our point of view with a discussion of a contemporary debate about the learning of writing.

The early writing of young children, like much of their other behavior, is egocentric. Graves has documented some of the changes towards increased conventionality that occur as the children, realizing that others cannot understand all that they have written, proceed to make the necessary elaborations (Graves, 1981).

Increased elaboration is brought about, in part, through more complex T-units/sentences. A T-unit is a written construction that an adult writer would have punctuated as a sentence. Hunt (1965) and O'Donnell, Griffin and Morris (1967) have demonstrated that T-units increase in length and complexity as the writer matures.

But further research casts up an interesting anomaly. The developmental data suggest that longer T-units are characteristic of better writing. However, Martinez San Jose (1973), Stewart and Grobe (1979) and Jurgens and Griffin (1970) found little or no relationship between the T-unit length and ratings of quality. These three studies cover writers from grade four to grade eleven.

Thus, on the one hand we have growth in writing associated with maturity in syntactic complexity. On the other we find that syntactic complexity is not associated with improved quality.

We would like to suggest a resolution to this apparent anomaly. The young writer's initial task is to gain control over the basic procedures listed above. The nature of the task then changes. Armed with a repertoire of basic skills the writer takes on the task of becoming familiar with a wide variety of written forms. Such knowledge is gained, initially, by listening, and later, by reading. However, learning to compose within the constraints of a given form remains a major accomplishment for the novice.

Perhaps this understanding of the developmental change in the nature of the task will help to resolve the dispute between Graves (1983) and Hillocks (1986). Graves advocates a free writing approach. Hillocks presents research which shows that a free writing approach is less effective than several other kinds of intervention. Graves' research is based on work conducted with children in the early primary grades.

Hillocks' research review deals with studies which employ upper elementary children, high school students, and adults. Since Graves' subjects are in the process of mastering basic writing skills it matters little what the topic or form of the writing assumes. During this phase the child's two major preoccupations are the creative act of composition (which is not accessible) and rules governing surface structure (which are learned for the most part tacitly). Thus there is little left for the teacher to do other than encourage children in their exploration. The reactive role advocated by Graves is appropriate for those who teach the very young. A more active leadership role may become more appropriate as the writer is introduced to the variety of written forms. As Hillocks demonstrates, some active interventions with older students appear to have highly beneficial effects on the development of writing ability.

Donaldson (1978) reviews studies which indicate that young children are capable of producing more complex language when functioning within the meaningful flow of everyday events than when "disembedded" language demands are placed upon them. A two-year-old child was unable to repeat to an investigator sentences that the child himself had produced the day before. Donaldson argues that children's capacity for language is supported by their understanding of the situations in which a speech act occurs. When this support is withdrawn, the child's linguistic competence is reduced. Thus any situation which requires children to deal with decontextualized language ensures that the children are practicing at a level which is below their level of capacity. If this line of reasoning applies to older children and to written forms of language then the implications for instruction in the classroom are enormous. It suggests that any activity or exercise which requires the child to examine and manipulate decontextualized language actually depresses opportunities for linguistic growth. It would seem that children rise to the demands placed upon them by real communicative situations. Such occasions would appear to be the times when growth in language occurs. If such situations are displaced by disembedded language activities then potential learning opportunities are lost.

In practical terms the argument suggests that having children write real letters to real people for real reasons is better than learning the form of a contrived letter to an imaginary person for no good reason. Writing a story for someone who genuinely wants to read it is better than writing for a teacher who will regard the task of "marking" it as onerous.

Our extension of Donaldson's argument to writing suggests why the teaching of grammar is an ineffective means of developing writing and why an environmental approach has such positive effects (Hillocks, 1986). The teaching of grammar necessarily involves the decontextualization of language. An environmental approach creates situations where genuine written communication is required.

CHAPTER SEVEN

PARENTS AND READING

INTEGRATING HOME AND SCHOOL

Teachers who speak of integration usually think in terms of the school day and school-based activities. Most of this book is devoted to that limited interpretation as well. However, children spend only a minor portion of their waking hours at school. True integration must include consideration of the time spent and activities completed at home.

A standard piece of advice suggests that parents act as good models and read to their children. Goldfield and Snow (1984) review studies that document the home factors that are positively associated with reading achievement: access to reading materials and reading aloud to children. However, neither of these factors has any direct or self-evident explanatory power. Simply having books in the home won't ensure that children will become readers. Reading aloud to them may provide some children with the opportunity to learn by imitation. However, there are numerous cases of children who have been read to who didn't learn to read easily. It's significant that being read to wasn't one of the factors associated with success in learning to read in Tizard, Schofield and Hewison's Dagenham project (Topping and Wolfenden, 1985).

Factors such as the presence of the books in the home and frequent reading to children bespeak a positive attitude toward reading. The actual mechanism by which children acquire the knowledge that makes it easy to learn to read is, presumably, the interaction that occurs between parent and child in relation to books. Ninio and Bruner (1978), Ninio (1979), Snow and Goldfield (1981), Doake (1982, 1988) and Anderson, Teale and Estrado (1980) have all documented very carefully the transactions that occur among the parent, the child and the book. The parents adjust what is said about the book to the maturity of the children. Simple labeling is superseded by more complex discussions involving explanations and motives. Some parents draw the children's attention to the function of words or letters.

A child who shares a book with an adult for 15 minutes each evening from ages one to six may have had 455 hours of individual reading instruction before they enter school. A child who isn't read to may have had none. What the child has learned during those hours may not be precisely the things the teacher is planning to teach, but they will certainly be things that will complement the learning the school will require. The child will know that most books contain stories; that stories are organized according to a particular pattern; that one is expected to remember what occurs; that one must sometimes infer from one's own experience what isn't specified in the story; that a story reread regularly reproduces a verbal ritual of words that rapidly becomes predictable. Some children will go on to develop a sight vocabulary. Some will begin to note the sound significance of certain spelling patterns. All of these learnings will be of enormous benefit when the child enters school and "begins" to learn to read.

PARENTAL INVOLVEMENT PROGRAMS

Parental Influence

Educators have only recently begun to appreciate the potency of parents in the teaching of reading. The time-honored practice of sending books home has usually been regarded as somewhat peripheral to the real and important classroom actions. Simple arithmetic should have alerted us to the truth of the matter. Twelve years of 180 six-hour school days provide 12,960 instructional hours. Allowing plenty of time for sleeping, eating and maintenance, this still constitutes only 16.4% of the child's potentially educative time (Grave, Weinstein and Walberg, 1983). What, then, does the child do and learn during the remaining 83.6% of the time?

Topping (1985) has pointed out that, relative to the teacher, the parent is a more powerful model, can offer more regular practice, can provide more immediate feedback, and can confer more highly valued reinforcement. It's easier for children to disregard a teacher they spend only a year with than the parent they grow up with.

A great deal of interest in parental involvement has been sparked by the remarkable success of the very simple Haringay project (Tizard, Schofield and Hewison, 1982), extensively emulated in England, Australia, Canada and the United States. Teachers merely sent books home regularly with a request that the children read to their parents. No complex and expensive elaborations, no training sessions, no home visits and follow-up sessions by educational psychologists. Instead, just what we also would advocate when developing parental involvement: simplicity and long-term maintenance.

Simplicity

The Haringay project asked the parents to listen to the children read for a few minutes each evening. No direction regarding the role of the parents or the nature of the interaction was offered.

Even if there's reason to believe that some parents may impose harsh or overly demanding standards of performance, or over-stress attention to the sound-symbol associations, we continue to invoke our principle of simplicity. If guidance is to be offered it should be clear and easy to apply. One remarkably effective routine is paired reading.

Paired reading

This involves two phases. In the first phase parent and child read the text aloud together. The parent adjusts the pace to suit the child. The child is expected to read all words aloud and correctly. If there are miscues the parent rereads the appropriate portion of the text correctly and has the child repeat it.

In the second phase, whenever the child feels able to proceed alone, he signals the parent by means of a tap or some other gesture. The parent then remains silent. The parent praises the child for trying and continues to offer liberal praise as the reading proceeds. If the child miscues, the parent reads correctly the sentence or phrase containing the miscue and has the child repeat it. If the child hesitates over a word for more than four seconds the parent reads it and has the child repeat it.

Miller, Robson and Bushnell (1985), Bush (1985) and Jungnitz (1985) offer statistical evidence that this simple intervention, if sustained over one or more years, provides immediate and long-lasting improvements in reading ability.

Maintenance

Almost any innovation, given enough hoopla and enthusiastic implementation, will produce temporary gains. However, once the excitement of the moment has passed things seem to settle down. Innovations that require sustained extra effort tend to be abandoned and teachers slip back into old, less exciting but sustainable patterns. Education has suffered from a series of such fads. In schools, inevitably, any innovation will become regularized and systematized. Significant and beneficial innovations must be robust enough to withstand the press of institutionalism.

Read with Me Club 25

Here's how it works!

- Each child reads and/or is read to for 10 minutes a night.
- Parent dates and initials on the appropriate space below. One signature a day maximum please.
- When child has accumulated 25 signatures, he/she returns record sheet to class and becomes a member of Sidney School's *Read With Me* Club and receives an award!
- Your child can then try to become a member of the *Read With Me* Club 50 Night. (You'll have a twenty-five night head start!)

As few as 10 minutes a day reading to or with your child *can* make a tremendous difference in that child's development. Set the 10 minutes aside each day and make it a firm commitment. We all can find 10 minutes . . . even in the busiest schedules. It will be time well spent, time which is priceless, time which cannot be recaptured if we let it pass.

	Date/initials		Date/initials
1		14	
2		15	
3		16	
4		17	
5		18	
6		19	
7		20	
8		21	
9		22	
10		23	
11		24	
12		25	
13			☆ *Congratulations!*

It's a good idea to put this in a visible spot (maybe on the fridge)

Figure 7.1 A circular sent from the school, explaining to the parents how the "Read With Me" program works

Along with simplicity, our main defense against the rigors of "routinization" is easy maintenance, especially for parental involvement programs. We know of a program that requires the children to answer a simple quiz about a book before receiving credit for having read it. Each book in the program therefore had to have a quiz prepared and copies kept on file. Someone had to check the children's answers and record the fact that the test had been passed. Less than satisfactory scores required retaking the test and further bureaucratic machinery.

By contrast, a second school used the "Read With Me" program. The teacher simply sent home a piece of paper with 25 lines on it (figure 7.1). The parents were asked to listen to the children read for 10-15 minutes each day and sign one of the lines to indicate the reading had occurred. When the paper was full it was returned to the school and filed and the children were given a second sheet of paper. At one point per line they could earn certificates worth 25, 50, 75 or 100 points. Suitably impressive certificates (figure 7.2) were presented with some ceremony on Awards Day. Those children who earned 100 points also received a paperback book. This program was so successful that the local public library phoned the school to find out what was going on — the program had had a noticeable effect on the number of books being borrowed.

It seems to us that the second program is much more likely to be sustained over a long period of time than the first. Figures7.3 and 7.4 show some simple

Read With Me

CLUB 25 AWARD

Congratulations to

____

Signed ________________ **Date** ______

Figure 7.2 A certificate awarded to a child for reading aloud at home

Checklist for *Read With Me* parents

How are you doing?

- ☐ I read something every day.
- ☐ I have a library card and visit the library.
- ☐ I take my child to the library often.
- ☐ I read stories to my child frequently.
- ☐ I listen to my child share the day's events.
- ☐ I encourage my child to write notes, letters, lists.
- ☐ I expose my child to different reading experiences in the community.
- ☐ We play word and listening games.
- ☐ I buy books as gifts for my child.
- ☐ I praise my child for efforts and accomplishments without comparing him/her to others.

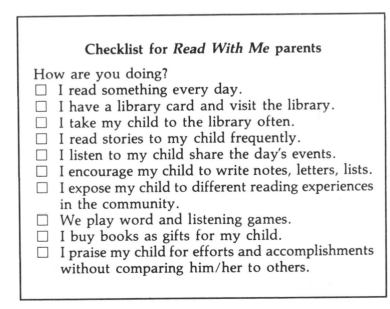

Figure 7.3 A checklist for "Read With Me" parents

advice sent to parents participating in the program, to help them work with their children most effectively.

Introducing Parental Involvement Programs

Since these programs touch teachers, children and parents, all three need to be involved in planning and accepting the idea — and all three need to appreciate that there will be some personal benefit in it for them. Planning meetings need to stress the benefits that will accrue to each group:

Children

- It's fun.
- You'll enjoy the stories.
- You'll become a better reader.
- You'll get a special private time with your mom or dad.

Parents

- It's fun.
- You'll enjoy the stories.
- You can watch your child grow in independence.
- You'll get a special private time with your child. The benefits of that time will affect other areas of your relationship.

How to go about it

- Have your child read aloud to you.
- Read aloud to your child.
- Read one page each, taking turns.
- Share the reading time by sitting together without distractions.
- Either parent, or both, can be a reading partner. What about a grandparent? Aunt or uncle?
- At the end of 10 minutes, if your child wants to continue reading, by all means encourage the child to do so.
- Have fun. Keep the atmosphere positive.

Tips for parents as reading partners

Establish the right atmosphere:

- Make reading an enjoyable experience.
- Have books and reading materials in visible spots.
- Use the *Five Finger* method of choosing a book suitable for your child to read aloud. Choose any page, have the child begin to read it aloud. For each word the child doesn't know, hold up a finger. By the end of the page, you should have 5 or less fingers up. If more, the book is usually too difficult for the child to read aloud. *Success is important.*

Create excitement:

- Make a story come to life by using a puppet to tell the story.
- Begin reading a story and stop before it's finished. Have the child finish the story. Read together to see how the author finished it.
- Read with expression. Change your voice for different characters and vary your voice volume and speed.

Offer positive comments:

- Build confidence by praising any reading your child does. Each and every bit of reading makes your child a better reader. Please remember that there is a difference between encouragement and pressure. Each child needs to experience success.
- Never use reading as a punishment.

Figure 7.4 Advice to "Read With Me" parents

Teachers

- It will reduce or eliminate some of your instructional problems.
- You'll get to know your students' parents better.
- Your students' reading scores will go up and the world will admire you.

Many of the projects described in Topping and Wolfenden (1985) involved the use of readers from basal reading series. We would prefer library books, as long as the teacher is aware of the need to provide a rough match between the difficulty of the books and the ability of the children.

Why Do Parental Involvement Programs Work?

We have estimated the amount of personal attention an individual child might receive in school and at home — although the figures in any given situation may vary widely. If you make heavy use of learning centers and/or aides, you may be able to increase the amount of individual attention. You should be able to estimate the average amount of time for each child in your particular teaching situation.

Personal attention in school

If each school day allocates five hours per day for instruction for 200 days per year, then the total instructional time is 1000 hours per year. Deducting 20% for classroom routine and maintenance leaves 800 hours. If 50% of that time is used for whole-class instruction, there will be 400 hours left to distribute among 30 children, for 13.3 hours of personal attention per child per year. However, the elementary teacher must give attention to math, social studies, science, physical education, art and music. If language arts makes up 50% of the timetable, individual attention to that part of the timetable drops to 6.65 hours per year.

Personal attention at home

If parent and child pursue the "Read With Me" program and earn a 100-point award, they will have spent 100 15-minute sessions together for a total of 25 hours, almost four times the amount of individual classroom attention.

Quality of attention

We can think of no reasons to assert that the things teachers say and do with children are so superior to the parent-child interaction that they overcome the diluting effect of the teacher-child ratio.

Whole-class instruction

We are strong proponents of appropriately deployed whole-class teaching. But its greatest virtue is the introduction of new ways of looking at and dealing with the world. Once such information has been presented, the children need supportive guidance for their early and inexpert attempts to apply the newly acquired knowledge themselves. Such guidance can be provided much more effectively in one-to-one situations.

CHAPTER EIGHT

A TEACHER'S GUIDE FOR *The Secret of NIMH*

CRITICAL REVIEW

Robert O'Brien bases this fantasy (original title: *Mrs. Frisby and the Rats of NIMH*) on the not-too-impossible concept of a breed of rats rendered exceptionally intelligent, strong and long-lived through a series of injections at NIMH (National Institute for Mental Health) who learn to read, escape and set up a colony with all modern conveniences, such as electricity and running water.

Beside the story of the rats is the story of Mrs. Frisby, a mouse who because of a sick son is driven to seek the rats' aid — which seems "a rather ordinary 'outer' story" (Townsend, 1974). Although Townsend says "the construction is awkward, and there is a lack of memorable characters," the novel begins to become absorbing with a flashback that describes the capture of the rats and their subsequent history. It retains its momentum as Mrs. Frisby is caught by a small boy and overhears news that leads to the exciting climax: the attempted recapture of the rats by the researchers from NIMH.

Details of plot and setting are well imagined and described in careful prose, but the book's greatest strength lies in its ideas. O'Brien himself, explaining the origins of the book, said: "I . . . am concerned over the seeming tendency of the human race to exterminate itself . . . I have wondered: If we should vanish from the earth, who might survive us?" (O'Brien, 1972). By exploring the predicament of the "civilized" rats who no longer wish to steal or to eat garbage, the novel generates thought about ourselves, our society and its values, and our relationship to other species. Their great "Plan" involves escape to a place where they will be free of man's influence; there is "no slick ending, but something of a question mark," as one reviewer has commented.

ANALYSIS: LITERARY SOCIOGRAM

General Analysis

The story of *The Secret of NIMH* deals with four groups that are linked in many complex ways: the Frisby family, the rats and mice, the Fitzgibbon family and the scientists at NIMH. The groups are linked by a series of minor characters: the Toy Tinker, Dragon, Jeremy and the owl; an object: the tractor; and two settings: the rosebush and the Boniface Estate. The story starts on a tiny scale with Mrs. Frisby's concerns about food. The problem soon widens to embrace moving day, Jeremy and the owl. The Frisby family has been represented as very small but central to the action of the story.

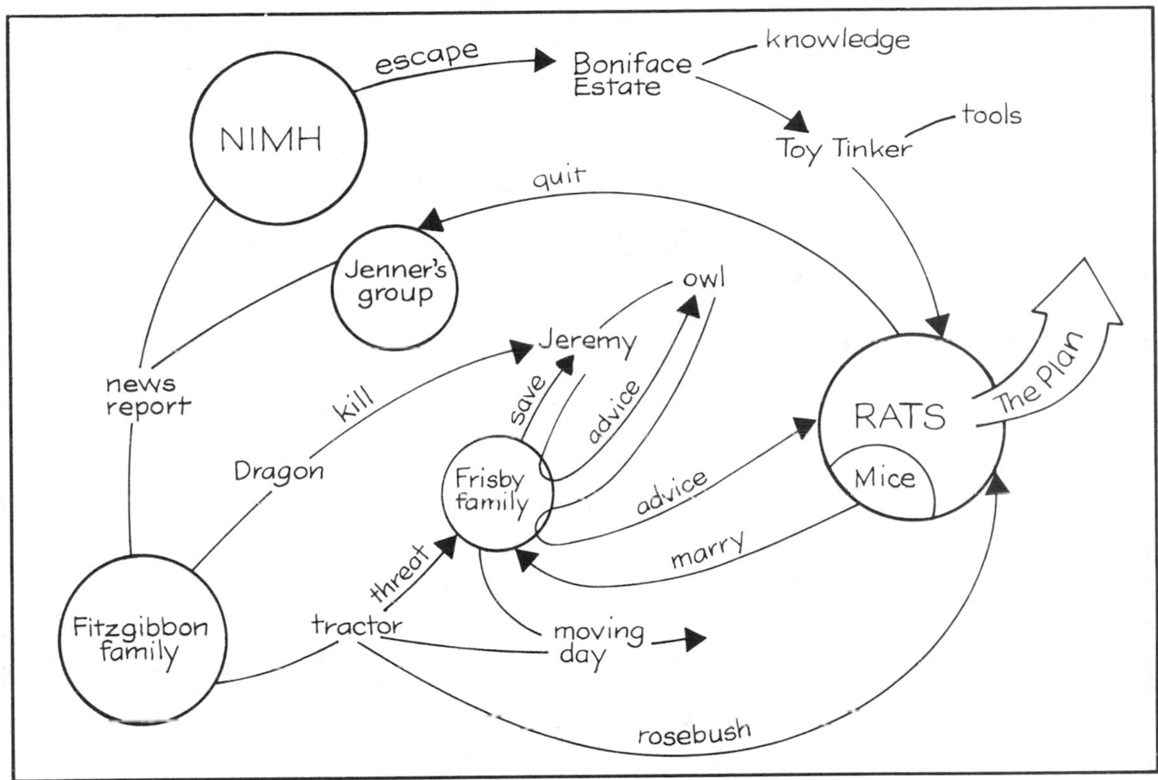

Figure 8.1 A general overview of **The Secret of NIMH**

The Frisbys are linked to the Fitzgibbons through both Dragon and the tractor. Dragon, who represents the archetypal monster after which he is named, is an ever-present danger to all the animals. It's because of Dragon that Mrs. Frisby meets Jeremy who, via the owl, leads her to the rats. The tractor represents the first outside threat to the Frisby family and remains as a sinister symbol of destruction as Mrs. Frisby searches for a solution to her problem.

Through the medium of an extended flashback we learn about the connections between the rats and NIMH. At NIMH the rats become intelligent and long-lived, and they learn to read. During the long march to freedom they obtain knowledge from the Boniface Estate Library and tools from the Toy Tinker. We also learn how the mice are connected to the Frisby family and why Mrs. Frisby's name produces such a remarkable effect on the owl and the rats.

The Fitzgibbons are linked both to NIMH and to the rats through the tractor. The necessary repair of the tractor gives Mrs. Frisby a little breathing space but results in Mr. Fitzgibbon's trip to town, where he hears of the death of some mechanized rats. His conversation with Health Department officials brings about the final confrontation between Dr. Schultz, the head scientist at NIMH, and the rats. The tractor is used as the engine of destruction. This close brush with the real world is sufficient to cause the rats to activate their Plan and retreat to their remote valley. A general overview of the novel, arranged as a sociogram, appears in figure 8.1.

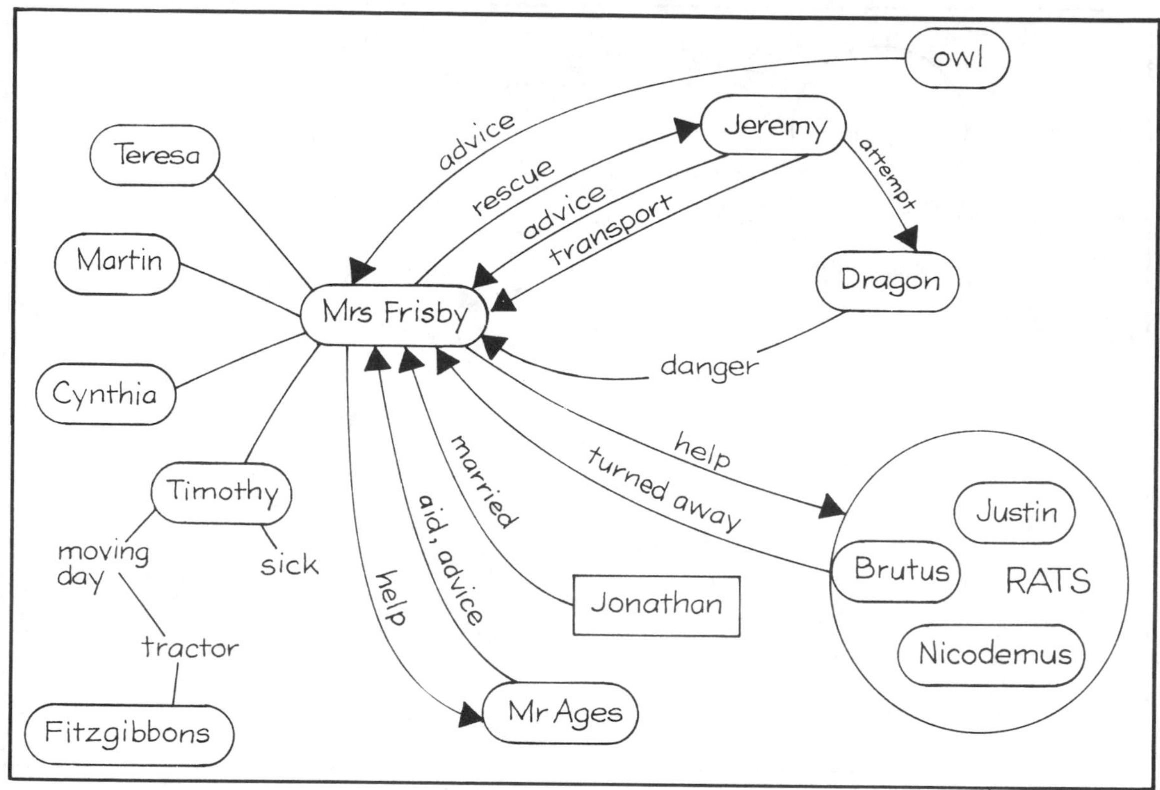

Figure 8.2 An example of a detailed analysis based on pages 1-71 of the novel

Example of a Detailed Analysis

Each group is made up of several individuals and detailed representations of internal group relationships is possible (see figure 8.2):

> Timothy, one of Mrs. Frisby's four children, is sick. If he's moved, he'll die. But if the family doesn't leave on Moving Day they'll die under the blade of the plow. Mr. Ages provides some aid and advice. While foraging for food Mrs. Frisby rescues Jeremy the crow from Dragon. Jeremy leads her to the owl, who recommends that she seek help from the rats. It's from the owl that Mrs. Frisby learns that her dead husband's name has some mysterious significance. She's told to ask for Justin and Nicodemus. But when she goes to the rat colony she's turned back by a young guard, Brutus, who is quite unresponsive to the name of the late Jonathan Frisby (p.71).

Similar internal analyses of other groups are possible.

Note that all page references in this chapter refer to the Apple Paperbacks (Scholastic) edition of *The Secret of NIMH.*

Teaching Suggestions

The thinking required to produce literary sociograms like those in figures 8.1 and 8.2 is more valuable than the final product. The children should be actively involved in their development, rather than simply receiving ones you've completed.

One productive use of sociograms is to develop them intermittently as the story unfolds. Chapter breaks make natural occasions for constructing them, but developing one after every chapter would render an interesting technique tiresome. If you do a very simple diagram after the first chapter, including only Mrs. Frisby and her children, you might want to leave it on an unused section of the chalkboard and further develop or review it as new story information becomes available.

If a chalkboard coated with metallic paint is available, you can put the names and/or pictures of the characters, places and objects in the story on cards held in place by small magnets. Then you can move the story items around into tentative arrangements until a satisfactory constellation results. This ability to manipulate items permits easy reorganization so competing arrangements can be presented. It also permits reorganization as the story develops and situations change. Attempts to represent, share and defend various constellations can lead to highly involved discussions.

PREREADING DISCUSSION

Three issues raised in the story are:

- the use of animals as experimental subjects
- stealing
- the reaction of mankind to an alien intelligence.

The questions below are designed to stimulate discussion on these issues and challenge some of the students' initial attitudes. The introductory question is designed to elicit those attitudes, the elaboration section to suggest situations that preclude superficial, blanket judgments.

Stealing

Introduction

Most religions say it's wrong to steal, and stealing is against the law in most countries. Is it ever right to steal?

Elaboration

- If our country were at war with another country would it be all right to steal from the enemy?
- Is it all right for a poor person to steal from a rich person?
- Would it be all right for a starving person to steal food from someone who had more food than he could eat?

- If a student took the following things from school without permission, which would you consider as stealing?

  a typewriter
  a paper clip
  $100
  a small piece of used chalk
  a full stick of brand new chalk
  1¢
  10 pieces of drawing paper that have been used on one side only

- Which of the following would you regard as stealing?

  a farmer taking milk from cows
  a child taking eggs from a robin's nest
  the same child taking eggs from the family hen
  birds taking grain from a farmer's field

Alien Intelligence

Introduction

If an alien spaceship landed beside you and an alien stepped out, how would you feel and what would you do? (The alien can speak English, or communicate perfectly through telepathy.)

Elaboration

How would you feel and what would you do if:

- The alien is completely human in appearance, tall with light brown skin and long golden hair.
- The alien looks like a giant beetle covered in green slime. It smells like a dead fish.
- The alien is short and furry. It has large brown eyes and makes soft purring sounds.
- The alien is completely human but only about four inches (10 cm) high.
- The alien is a cloud of insects with a group mind.

In each case say how you think the human race would respond to the aliens. Here are some possibilities:

- attack and kill them
- greet them as friends and learn about them
- capture them and study them
- ignore them
- eat them
- capture them and use them as slaves
- teach them about human beings and the world

Animal Experimentation

Introduction

Animals are frequently made to suffer pain, injury and death in experiments conducted by human beings. How do you feel about this practice? Is it right or wrong?

Elaboration

- *Fact:* Doctors use animals to test out new drugs to see if they have any harmful side effects. The animals often suffer great pain and discomfort. Many of them die in pain.

Question: Should animal experiments to discover and test new medicines that may help to cure human diseases be permitted?

- *Fact:* Some army officers want to use animals as targets to test new kinds of guns and bullets. The results can be used to make improved weapons so the army can defend the country better.

Question: Should animals be used to test out new weapons?

- *Fact:* Some cosmetic firms that make things like eye shadow or lipstick try out new products on animals to see if there are any harmful side effects. Some animals experience great discomfort.

Question: Should animals be used to test out cosmetics?

- *Fact:* Most major cities around the world keep wild animals in zoos so people can look at them.

Question: Should wild animals be kept in zoos?

Recording Attitudes

Record the students' attitudes on stealing, alien intelligence and animal experimentation until each issue is raised in the story. Then review the recorded attitudes, taking the story information into consideration.

PREREADING ACTIVITIES

Surviving in a New Land

Imagine that because of sudden severe changes in the climate it has become impossible to live in North America any longer. Fortunately all the ice in the Arctic has melted and new forests, full of wildlife, have sprung up there. However, there are no roads, buildings or electricity.

Because of limited space, each family can take only as much as will fit in a car trailer. Assuming that your family has to take care of itself entirely, make a list of things you think you will need in order to survive.

From the things listed below choose ten you would like to take. Explain why you would or wouldn't take each item.

color TV
gun and ammunition
box of vegetable seeds
artist's painting equipment
record player and records
photograph album
stamp collection
$10 000
jewelry
box of canned food
carton of cigarettes
medical supplies
box of books dealing with plumbing, carpentry, cooking and medicine
religious books
piano
guitar
family dog
family cat
fishing equipment
aquarium
box of chocolates
video game
box of woodworking tools
sewing machine
box of pictures and ornaments
box of story books

Note: You might invite the children to compare their preparations with those made by the rats when that portion of the story is covered.

Developing a New Community

Imagine that the climate in your new community is mild, with wet winters and warm, dry summers.

Describe the things you'd like in your new community. You can make up your own rules. For example, under *Schools* you might say, "School will be held from 8:00 a.m. until 12:00 noon. In the afternoon children will be expected to help their parents in the community."

Consider the following topics:

Shelter: What sort of houses?
Warmth: What sort of fuel?
Lighting: How will it be provided?
Clothing: Who will make it? From what?
School: Where? What for? How long?
Food: What kind? Who produces it? How?
Law: What laws? Who enforces them? What happens if the law is broken?
Entertainment: What kind? When? Will entertainers be paid?
Community: Where will the houses be built? Where will the work be done? Where will public meetings be held?

You may find that maps, pictures or diagrams will help you explain what you'd like.

Note: You might invite the children to draw up a similar plan for a Rat Utopia once the rats' Plan has been revealed.

Background Information

In the story you'll meet the following creatures:

rats	a crow
field mice	a shrew
an owl	a house cat

Pick one of these animals and do some research on it. Try to find out the following information:

size	behavior during the day and night
description	life cycle
habitat	living patterns (group, alone?)
diet	

Note: You should make books that provide information on these topics available to the children.

ANTICIPATING OUTCOMES

The anticipation of the outcome of a story is an excellent means for establishing a purpose for reading or listening, and thus for promoting comprehension. However, the anticipation technique works well only when the readers or listeners are genuinely ignorant of the outcome of the story. In order to ensure that the children don't know what's going to happen, you would have to prohibit them from proceeding past a certain point. That's difficult to enforce. In general we've found that anticipating outcomes with a complete novel works best when the story is being read aloud.

Answers to anticipatory questions are, by their very nature, speculative and free ranging. Oral responses will be fuller and more readily elicited than written ones.

The following questions assume that you are reading the book aloud to the whole class and that responses take the form of an oral discussion.

Chapter and page numbers for the novel have been added in this guide to aid location of the relevant portions of text.

End of Chapter 5: "Five Days" (p. 39)

- What do you think was wrong with Dragon? Why did he not attack Mrs. Frisby?
- Why do you think the rats were carrying a piece of electrical cable? What might they use it for?

While these questions don't appear to be future-oriented, the story will reveal the solutions.

End of Chapter 8: "Go to the Rats" (p. 62)

- Why do you think the owl was so impressed by the name Jonathan Frisby?
- Why did the owl recommend that Mrs. Frisby go to the rats?
- What are the "things" the rats have?
- How might the rats solve Mrs. Frisby's problem?
- What does "in the lee of the stone" have to do with Mrs. Frisby's problem?

End of Chapter 15: "In the Cage" (p. 115)

- How could the injections change their whole lives?

You might have the students compare the capabilities of the rats when they were caught with their capabilities at the time Nicodemus is telling his story. For example:

When captured	*Now*
wild	intelligent
living off garbage	know about tools
could not read	use electricity
	live in an organized community

End of Chapter 16: "The Maze" (p. 124)

- What might Justin have learned?
- We know that the rats will escape. How do you think they might do it?

End of Chapter 20: "The Main Hall" (p. 167)

- We have heard of the Plan several times. What do you think it is?

You might want to have the class review what they've learned about the Plan up to this point. For example:

live without stealing
two-year supply of seeds
making of plows
working on a schedule

End of Chapter 24: "Seven Dead Rats" (p. 206)

- How can Mrs. Frisby warn the rats of the danger they are in?

Classroom procedure

You may want to have predictions recorded and reviewed and revised periodically as new information becomes available.

RELATED ACTIVITIES

These activities have been designed to follow the completion of the portion of text listed. Since they assume familiarity with the story up to the point described and ignorance beyond that point, they will be most effective if and when the reader arrives at the place indicated.

Chapters 1–3: "The Sickness of Timothy Frisby" to "The Crow and the Cat," pp. 1–26 (clues)

Try to work out who or what is referred to in each of the following clues:

1. It is slightly damaged, with two oval holes through it.
2. I've been dead almost a year when the story starts.
3. It's somewhat larger than a shoe box and resembles the house of a hermit.
4. It's silver in color and may have been used on a Christmas package.
5. It's the time when the Frisby family leave their winter home and go to their summer home.

Answers:

1. The cinder block.
2. Mrs. Frisby's husband.
3. Mr. Ages' house.
4. The string Jeremy was entangled in.
5. Moving Day.

Make up one clue about each of the following and try them out on a friend.

1. Mr. Fitzgibbon's tractor.
2. Jeremy.
3. Cynthia.
4. The abandoned supply of food that Mrs. Frisby found.
5. Timothy's house.

Choose five more items from the story and make up clues about them. Try them out on a friend.

You might want to have the clues copied out onto clue cards. A pack of these can then become a game to be played by small groups during free choice activity periods.

Chapters 4–5: "Mr. Fitzgibbon's Plow" to "Five Days," pp. 27–39 (summary cloze)

Fill each blank with a word that makes sense, looking back through the book if you wish. Only one word is missing from each space.

One of Mrs. Frisby's children, ______ [1], is sick and can't be moved. If he is, he will ______ [2]. Unfortunately, the spring has come and the Frisby family must move out of their ______ [3] home. If they do not, their house will be crushed under the blade of Mr. Fitzgibbon's ______ [4] and they will all be killed. Mrs. Frisby is worried when she hears Mr. Fitzgibbon's ______ [5] start up. She overhears a conversation between Mr. Fitzgibbon and his son, Paul. She learns that the plow is in need of repair but that it needs only ______ [6] days to have it fixed. Mr. Ages had said Timothy must not be moved for ______ [7] weeks.

While she is worrying about her problem, she almost walks into ______ [8], the cat. Miraculously, the cat does not attack her. She escapes and climbs a dead asparagus plant. From there, she sees a line of ______ [9] carrying an ______ [10] cable. They disappear into a rosebush. All this time Dragon sleeps on.

Answers:

1. Timothy
2. die
3. winter
4. plow
5. tractor
6. five
7. three
8. Dragon
9. rats
10. electric

Retell part of the story up to this point, in your own words. If your summary is about 50 words long, knock out about ten important words. Try it out on a friend.

Chapters 6–9: "A Favor from Jeremy" to "In the Rosebush," pp. 40–69

Mrs. Frisby is being considered for the "Good Citizen of the Month Award." Rate Mrs. Frisby on each of the scales (figure 8.3, next page) and then decide whether or not she deserves the award. Give a reason for each rating. For example, you might rate her as Very Brave and write, "I think Mrs Frisby was very brave because she dared to enter the home of an owl." The first one has been done for you.

Copy out the scales in figure 8.3 and rate Jeremy, Dragon and Timothy. Remember to give a reason for each rating. Timothy is being considered as "Wimp of the Week." Dragon has been arrested for molesting birds and small woodland creatures. Jeremy is to be considered for the "Airhead of the Air Award."

Make up a rating scale of your own using new pairs of adjectives. You might use pairs of words like: *Strong–Weak, Active–Quiet, Determined–Irresolute, Happy–Sad* or *Thoughtful–Brainless.* Choose three other characters from the story so far and have a friend rate them. See if you agree. Think of some reward or punishment each character is to be considered for.

Character						
	Very	Quite	Neutral	Quite	Very	
1. **Good**	x					**Bad**
Reason:	*I think Mrs Frisby is very good because she cared for her children.*					
2. **Powerful**						**Weak**
Reason:						
3. **Content**						**Worried**
Reason:						
4. **Brave**						**Cowardly**
Reason:						
5. **Harmless**						**Dangerous**
Reason:						

Final Decision: *Worthy of Award?* Yes/No *Circle one.*

Figure 8.3 Character rating sheet: Mrs. Frisby

Chapters 10–12: "Brutus" to "Isabella," pp. 70–92

Find information to support or contradict each of the following statements. Say whether you think the statement is true or false.

1. Brutus is a small, weak mouse. True? False?
   Support/Contradiction ____________
2. Mr. Ages would have difficulty trying to escape from Dragon. True? False?
   Support/Contradiction____________
3. Mrs Frisby loves Timothy. True? False?
   Support/Contradiction____________
4. The rats are working on a mysterious plan. True? False?
   Support/Contradiction ____________
5. The rats know how to use tools and electricity. True? False?
   Support/Contradiction____________
6. The rats never steal. True? False?
   Support/Contradiction ____________
7. Mrs. Frisby is familiar with elevators. True? False?
   Support/Contradiction____________
8. Jonathan Frisby was better educated than his wife. True? False?
   Support/Contradiction____________
9. Isabella is a scatterbrain. True? False?
   Support/Contradiction ____________
10. Jenner is one of the rats' heroes. True? False?
    Support/Contradiction____________

Specimen answers. Others are possible:

1. *False.* Brutus is a large rat with powerful muscles. He is almost a match for Dragon.
2. *True.* He moves very slowly because one of his legs is injured. It's wrapped in splints and bandaged.
3. *True.* To find help for Timothy, Mrs. Frisby enters the home of an owl and tries to get to see the rats.
4. *True.* Justin pronounces "Plan" with a capital P. Information about the Plan is written on the chalkboard. The Plan must be kept secret.
5. *True.* Their home is lit with electric lights. The elevator runs on electricity. The building of an elevator would require the use of tools.
6. *False.* The rats stole the light bulbs.
7. *False.* She is startled when it starts to descend.
8. *True.* He knew how to read. He also knew about electricity.
9. *True.* She drops her papers. She doesn't explain herself very well.
10. *False.*Jenner deserts the group. Isabella says they don't like Jenner.

Description

Name: ____________ Age: ______ Height or Length: ______
Weight: ________ Body covering: ________ Species: ____

Previous experience

Decisions you have made:

1. ____________________
2. ____________________

Exciting or interesting incidents in which you have been involved:

1. ____________________
2. ____________________

Character description

2 = Very 1 = Quite 0 = Neutral −1 = Barely −2 = None

				My most outstanding characteristics are:
Goodness	_____	Determination	_____	
Strength	_____	Sensitivity	_____	1. ____________
Intelligence	_____	Aggressiveness	_____	____________
Agility	_____	Bravery	_____	____________
Creativity	_____	Beauty	_____	2. ____________
Cunning	_____	Ingenuity	_____	____________
Friendliness	_____	Loveability	_____	____________

Position desired

Please indicate the type of position you would like to take up.

Character Type Preferred:

A = Highly preferred B = Acceptable C = Unacceptable

Villain	_____
Hero	_____
Heroine	_____
Fool	_____
Trickster	_____
Lone Survivor	_____
Wise Person	_____
Healer	_____
Wicked Enchanter	_____

Please indicate in your own words the kind of work you would like to do.

____
____
____
____
____
____

Figure 8.4 Job application form for a book character

Chapters 13–18: "A Powder for Dragon" to "The Air Ducts," pp. 93–149 (a lesson in reading: job application forms)

Imagine you are one of the characters in the story. You have enjoyed being in *The Secret of NIMH* but now you'd like a change. You want to be considered for a job in another book. Fill out an application form to the editor of a publishing company and try to persuade him or her that you are an interesting and useful character (see figure 8.4).

We've provided an example in figure 8.5, a form filled out by Dr. Schultz. As far as possible we've used information from the story, but where the story doesn't give the information we've made up answers that fit with what we know about the character. For example, we guessed that the scientist might be quite old, so we made him 56. We also made up his first name.

DESCRIPTION

Name: Ivor Schultz Age: 56 yrs Height or Length 170 c.m.

Weight: 70 kg Body covering: Skin and clothing Species: Human

PREVIOUS EXPERIENCE

Decisions you have made:

1. I decided to catch wild rats for my experiments.
2. I decided to try and teach them to read.

Exciting or interesting incidents in which you have been involved:

1. Chasing the rats with nets at night was quite exciting.
2. It was exciting to see the rats and mice become more intelligent.

CHARACTER DESCRIPTION

2 = Very 1 = Quite 0 = Neutral -1 = Barely -2 = None

Goodness	-1	Determination	+2
Strength	0	Sensitivity	-2
Intelligence	+2	Aggressiveness	+1
Agility	-1	Bravery	0
Creativity	+2	Beauty	0
Cunning	+2	Ingenuity	+2
Friendliness	0	Loveability	0

My most outstanding characteristics are:

1. I am very intelligent and very good at experiments.
2. I am not very sensitive. I am willing to do things that make others uncomfortable.

POSITION DESIRED

Please indicate the type of position you would like to take up.

Character Type Preferred:

A = Highly preferred B = Acceptable C = Unacceptable

Villain	B
Hero	A
Heroine	C
Fool	C
Trickster	B
Lone Survivor	B
Wise Person	A
Healer	A
Wicked Enchanter	B

Please indicate in your own words the kind of work you would like to do.

I wouldn't mind being a villain again as long as I could use my intelligence and have lots of power. But I would like to be a hero for a change. I wouldn't mind re-capturing the rats and showing them how to help humans.

Ivor Schultz, M.D.

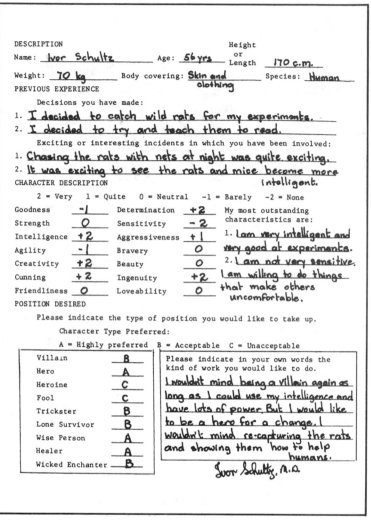

Figure 8.5 A completed job application form

Chapters 19–22: "The Boniface Estates" to "Thorn Valley," pp. 150–188 (map making)

Copy the map (figure 8.6) and add to it the following places and routes:

Places	*Routes*
Boniface Estate	The rats' journey from NIMH to the Fitzgibbon's farm.
Toy Tinker's van	Schultz's journey after capturing the wild rats.
The owl's tree	Mrs. Frisby's flight on Jeremy's back.
Thorn Valley	
The river	

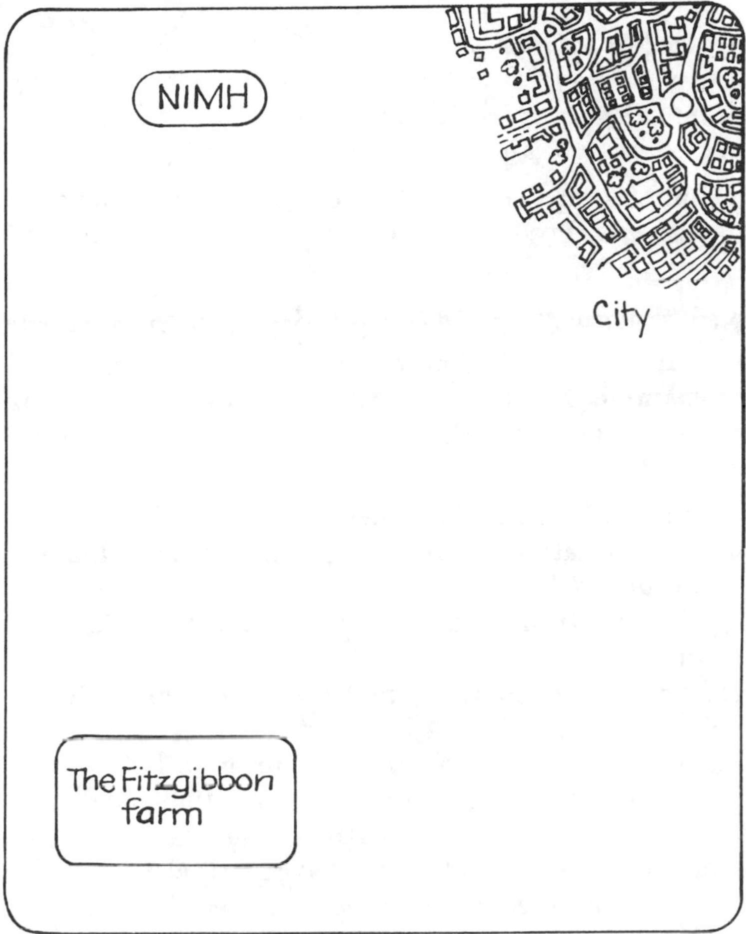

Figure 8.6 Incomplete story map

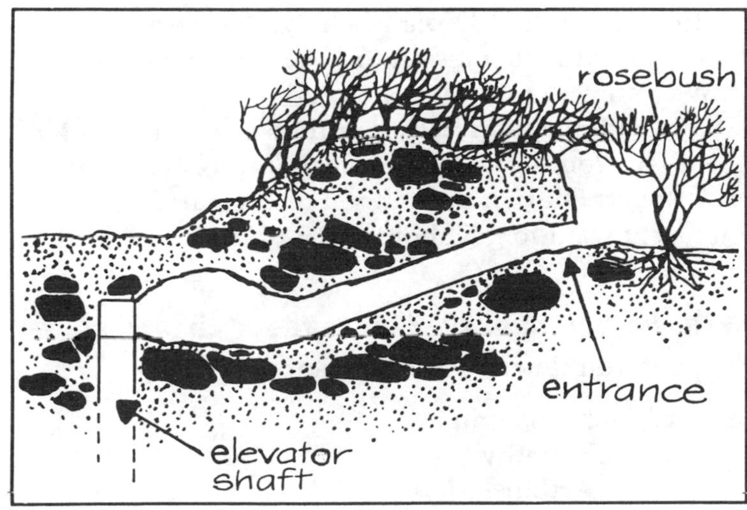

Figure 8.7 A cross-section map

Make sure your map fits the story. For example, the Boniface Estates must be somewhere between NIMH and the Fitzgibbon farm. The rats' journey must include a stop at the Toy Tinker's van.

Make a more detailed map of the Fitzgibbon farm. Include the following items:

- the Fitzgibbons' farm house
- the Fitzgibbons' barn and tractor shed
- the garden
- the rock in the garden
- the Frisby's cinder block
- the owl's tree
- Mrs. Frisby's hollow fence post
- the rosebush
- the place where Jeremy became entangled
- Mr. Ages' house

Be sure your map fits the story. For example, Mrs. Frisby watched Mr. Fitzgibbon examine the tractor from a fence post at the edge of the garden. This means that the fence post must be quite close to the tractor shed.

Make a map of the rats' colony. You may find that a cross section will help (see figure 8.7).

You'll find it useful to reread chapters 10 to 12 (pp. 70–92) and 20 (p. 158). Here are some clues that may help:

- *the tunnel led gently downward*
- *Ahead of her stretched a long, well-lit hallway*
- *the hall widened into a large oval chamber*
- *Justin opened the door. It led into a square room that looked like a closet . . . Mrs Frisby . . . had never been in an elevator before.*

If you reread the suggested chapters carefully you'll find many other hints as to what should be included. For example, your map should show the library and Nicodemus' office.

Chapters 23–25: "Captured" to "Escape," pp. 189–218 (filling in the spaces)

When an author writes a story, he or she tells you many things that happen. But many things are left out too. For example, we know that Mr. Ages hurt his leg trying to drug Dragon, but the author doesn't tell us the details of what happened. Choose one of the suggestions below and fill in some of the spaces left by Robert O'Brien.

- Tell the story of how Mr. Ages came to hurt his leg while trying to drug Dragon. Be sure to use all the information about getting into the house that's presented in Chapter 23: "Captured."
- Tell the story of Mrs. Frisby's rescue from Justin's point of view. You might want to imagine you are Justin.
- Tell the story of Mrs. Frisby's capture from Billy's point of view. You might want to imagine you are Billy.
- Imagine you are Jenner. Only six rats died. You are the sole survivor. Tell the story of how it all happened. Begin at the point where you all left the rat colony.
- Imagine you are the reporter, Fred Smith, who wrote the article about the dead rats. Copy down the headline MECHANIZED RATS INVADE HARDWARE STORE and then write the complete article. Explain why you used the word "mechanized" to describe seven (six?) dead rats around an electric motor.
- Imagine you are Dr. Schultz and it was you Mr. Fitzgibbon talked to at Henderson's store. Tell the story of that day. Explain why you were at Henderson's store, report what Mr. Fitzgibbon said to you, describe your plans and your suspicions. Why are you pursuing the rats?
- Retell the escape from NIMH from Jonathan Frisby's point of view. You might want to imagine you are Jonathan. You'll find a good deal of information in Chapter 18, "The Air Ducts." Robert O'Brien doesn't tell us the names of the mice who were lost but you might want to tell about some of the individual mice who died.

Chapter 26, "At the Meeting" to the end, pp. 219–249 (readers' theater)

Present this chapter as a radio play. You'll need speaking voices for:

a narrator	an unnamed rat	Nicodemus
Brutus	Teresa	Timothy
Justin	Isabella	Arthur
Mrs. Frisby	Cynthia	

Assign parts and have the players practice their lines privately. When they are all ready, have them sit in a circle and read directly from the book. There's no need for costumes or movement. You may want to consider sound effects.

You might present the play on an audio tape over the school speaker system, or live before an audience. If you do it live it's helpful to have the actors sitting in a semicircle facing the audience. Provide each player with the name of his of her character on a card that is clearly visible to the audience. These will help the listeners to know who's speaking and to follow the dialogue more easily.

There are several other parts of the story that can readily be turned into plays. Here are some suggestions:

- *Chapter 24: "Seven Dead Rats."* The conversation in the Fitzgibbons' kitchen.
- *Chapter 25: "Escape."* Justin's rescue of Mrs. Frisby and the defense of Mrs. Frisby's house by the shrew.
- *Epilogue:* The family's conversation about what had happened.

DEVELOPING INSIGHT

This activity, designed for use when the story is finished, requires your participation. The rating system is a bit complex and many students will need help.

Robert O'Brien's attitudes towards males and females

How do you think the author, Robert O'Brien, regards males and females? Is he a male chauvinist or a women's liberationist or neither? Does he treat males and females equally?

Say how you feel about each of the following statements. Be prepared to mention something from the story to support your choice.

[+2] = Strongly Agree
[+1] = Agree
[0] = Neutral
[-1] = Disagree
[-2] = Strongly Disagree

O'Brien's book suggests that men are more important than women.
[+2]   [+1]   [0]   [-1]   [-2]

O'Brien's book suggests that men are leaders and women are followers.
[+2]   [+1]   [0]   [-1]   [-2]

O'Brien's book treats males and females equally.
[+2]   [+1]   [0]   [-1]   [-2]

Rating Statements

Each statement listed below is a true and accurate observation about the story. Read each statement and rate it as pro-male, anti-male, pro-female or anti-female. Rate pro statements as positive and anti statements as negative. If you feel a statement is very negative, give it a -3. If you feel a statement is moderately positive, give it a +2. If you feel a statement is mildly negative, give it a -1. Use figure 8.8 to help you.

	Male		Female	
Positive	Strong Moderate Mild	+3 +2 +1	Strong Moderate Mild	+3 +2 +1
Negative	Strong Moderate Mild	−3 −2 −1	Strong Moderate Mild	−3 −2 −1

Figure 8.8 Rating statements about males and females

The first two have been done for you. Statement number 1 is rated as being moderately positive for males. Statement number 2 is rated as being strongly positive for females.

	Male				Female		
1.The story has many more male characters than female characters.	±3	±2	±1	0	±1	±2	±3
2. The central character, Mrs. Frisby, is a female.	±3	±2	±1	0	±1	±2	±3
3. Whenever Mrs. Frisby gets into trouble she is helped by a male.	±3	±2	±1	0	±1	±2	±3
4. Jeremy, a male, is presented as a bit stupid.	±3	±2	±1	0	±1	±2	±3
5. The female rats do not usually attend meetings about the Plan.	±3	±2	±1	0	±1	±2	±3
6. Isabella is presented as a silly creature.	±3	±2	±1	0	±1	±2	±3

	Male				Female		
7. All the rat leaders are male.	±3	±2	±1	0	±1	±2	±3
8. The wise old owl is a male.	±3	±2	±1	0	±1	±2	±3
9. Mr. Ages, the wise healer, is male.	±3	±2	±1	0	±1	±2	±3
10. Schultz, the head scientist, is male.	±3	±2	±1	0	±1	±2	±3
11. Julie, the research assistant, is presented as soft-hearted.	±3	±2	±1	0	±1	±2	±3
12. Mrs. Frisby is shown as wise and courageous.	±3	±2	±1	0	±1	±2	±3
13. The lady shrew holds 20 rats back from Mrs. Frisby's house.	±3	±2	±1	0	±1	±2	±3
14. Jonathan Frisby is presented as wise and brave.	±3	±2	±1	0	±1	±2	±3
15. Mrs. Frisby receives help when her husband's name is mentioned.	±3	±2	±1	0	±1	±2	±3
16. Of the rats and mice that escape from NIMH, only males are mentioned by name.	±3	±2	±1	0	±1	±2	±3

Make four more true observations about the story that deal with males or females. Rate each statement.

Classify the 20 ratings under these headings:

Pro-Male
Anti-Male
Pro-Female
Anti-Female

How Do You Feel Now?

Add up each column in the ratings and think again about O'Brien's attitudes towards males and females. You might add all the pro-male points and all the anti-male points and then subtract the anti-male score from the pro-male score. Do the same thing with the female points.

Final Judgment

Which of the following statements do you agree with most?

1. O'Brien favors males.

2.O'Brien favors females.

3. O'Brien treats males and females equally.

4. O'Brien shows strengths and weaknesses in both males and females, but favors males.

5. O'Brien shows strengths and weaknesses in both males and females, but favors females.

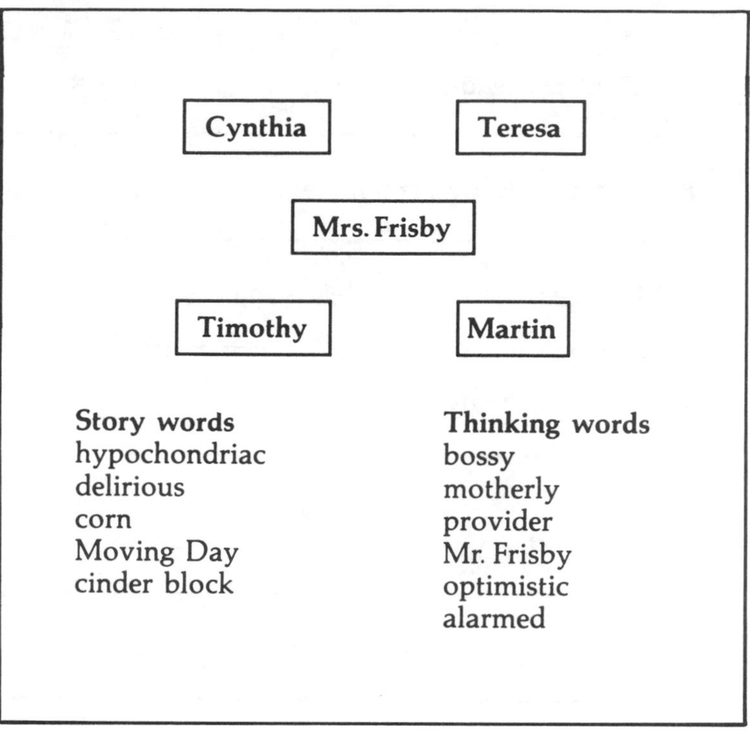

Figure 8.9

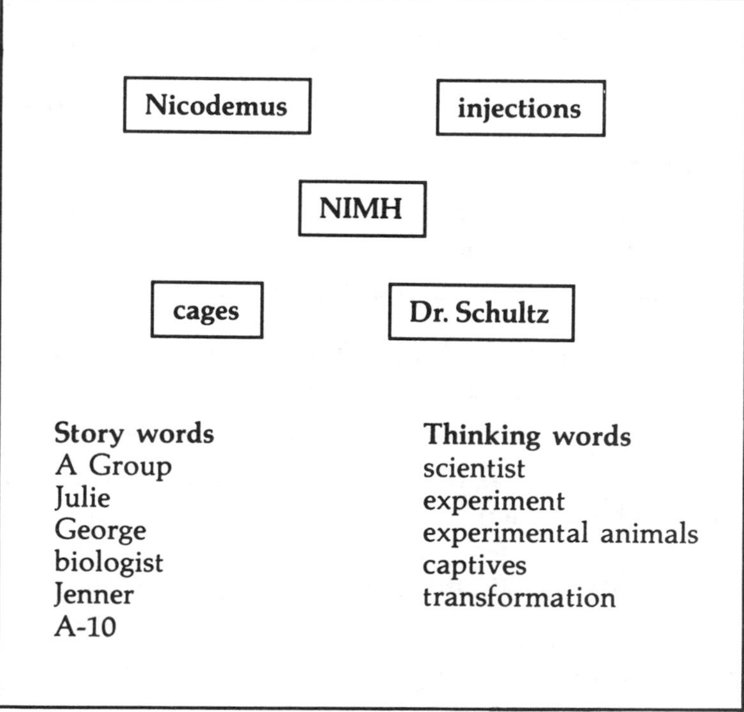

Figure 8.10

VOCABULARY DEVELOPMENT

Word Webs

Complete the word webs in figures 8.9 and 8.10 by attaching the story and thinking words or phrases in the diagram to the concepts in the boxes.

Make up a word web for one of the following:

- Inside Mr. Ages' house (pp. 15–18)
- Mrs. Frisby's house (pp. 1–3)
- Mrs. Frisby's family (pp. 6–9)
- Jeremy (pp. 21–26, 41–45)
- The owl's house (pp. 51–53)
- The dead rats in Henderson's store (pp. 202–204)
- Moving Mrs. Frisby's house (pp. 215–218)

Choose a person, place, thing or activity from the story and make a word web, using pictures as well as words if you wish.

Using Context to Work Out the Meaning of Difficult Words

On page 196 the story says, *Thus admonished, she crept forward again until she was near the edge of the cabinet.* See if you can figure out what *admonished* means.

Reread paragraphs three and four on page 196 and answer these questions:

Who is *she*?
Someone *admonishes* her. Who is it?
What actually happens when she is *admonished*?
Admonish probably means:

- talk to yourself
- give advice
- warn or scold *Answer: to warn or scold*

On page 89 it says, *It was quite incomprehensible.* See if you can use the words nearby to figure out what *incomprehensible* means.

Reread the paragraph following the list of plows on page 76 and answer the following questions:

What is *It*?
Who is *she*?
What does *trying to make head or tail of it* mean?
Does Mrs. Frisby understand what is written on the chalkboard?
Incomprehensible probably means:

- can't be understood
- can't be held in the hand
- not complete *Answer: can't be understood*

On page 3 it says, *She climbed up the tunnel, emerging whiskers first, and looked around warily.* See if you can work out what *warily* means. Reread page 3 and answer these questions:

Who is *she*?
What is she leaving?
What is she about to enter?
What danger has just been mentioned?
Which word could best be used instead of *warily: happily, fearfully* or *cautiously*?

Warily probably means:

- being hungry and afraid
- being tired
- being watchful for danger

Answer: being watchful for danger

Use the context (the sentences nearby) to help you work out the meaning of the words below. Don't consult a dictionary until after you've written out what you think the word means:

abandoned (p. 5)
relentlessly (p. 12)
muttering (p. 32)
filtered (p. 68)
adjourned (p.77)
consternation (p. 142)

Making Meanings

A Rat Encyclopedia

One of the things the rats might do when they get to Thorn Valley is make up a Rat Encyclopedia. Listed below are some items that might appear in an encyclopedia written by the rats of NIMH. The explanations are written from a rat's point of view.

maze. A series of corridors that seem to lead to freedom but actually lead nowhere. The floors are fitted with electric shocks. This cruel device is used by humans to measure the intelligence of rats.

NIMH. A large white building used by human beings for experiments on rats and mice. It was at NIMH that rats first developed their intelligence.

human beings. The only other known species of animal that can talk, read and write. Human beings regard rats as dirty and disease-ridden. They will try to kill rats whenever they can. Being slow and clumsy, they are easy to avoid, but should be regarded as extremely dangerous.

Read the following rat definitions and see if you can match them to the correct words from the answer list.

A. A series of dark tunnels used in NIMH to bring fresh air to the rooms. Extremely dangerous, particularly to mice.

B. A kind of hollow brick used by human beings and mice for building.

C. A large and dangerous hunting animal — very strong and quick, with sharp claws. Its low intelligence makes it easy to outwit.

Answers (out of order): 1. cat 2. air ducts 3. cinder block

Answers: A = 2, B = 3, C = 1

Make up rat definitions for five of the following:

tractor	Thorn Valley	schedule
plow	injection	rat race
garden	cage	reading
the Plan		

Find five more words or phrases from the story and make up rat definitions for them, using illustrations to help you if you wish.

BOARD GAME: "PURSUIT!"

The Board and Game Design

Design. The game board of "Pursuit!" (figure 8.11) presents the sequence of major events in the order in which they actually happened, rather than the order in which they are encountered in the story.

The game reflects the interwoven plot lines of Mrs. Frisby's story and the rats' story. The rats' story begins at *City Life* and ends at *Departure*. Mrs. Frisby's story starts out independently but joins up with the rats' after her visit to them.

Objectives. There are four counters representing the rats, Mrs. Frisby, Dr. Schultz and the plow. The object of the game is to get Mrs. Frisby and the rats along the track to the safety of Departure before they are caught by Dr. Schultz or the plow. All four counters are used regardless of the number of players.

Counters. The counter representing the rats is placed on *City Life* and follows the track to *Departure*. Note that the rats move from *Thorn Valley and the Plan* to *Entering Fitzgibbons' Kitchen*.

The counter representing Mrs. Frisby begins at *Shortage of food* and follows the inner circuit until it joins with the rats' track at *Entering Fitzgibbons' kitchen*.

The counter representing Dr. Schultz pursues the rats. The counter representing the plow pursues Mrs. Frisby.

Movement. Movement forward is controlled by the numbers [in square brackets] that accompany the answers to the question cards in figure 8.12. If the question is

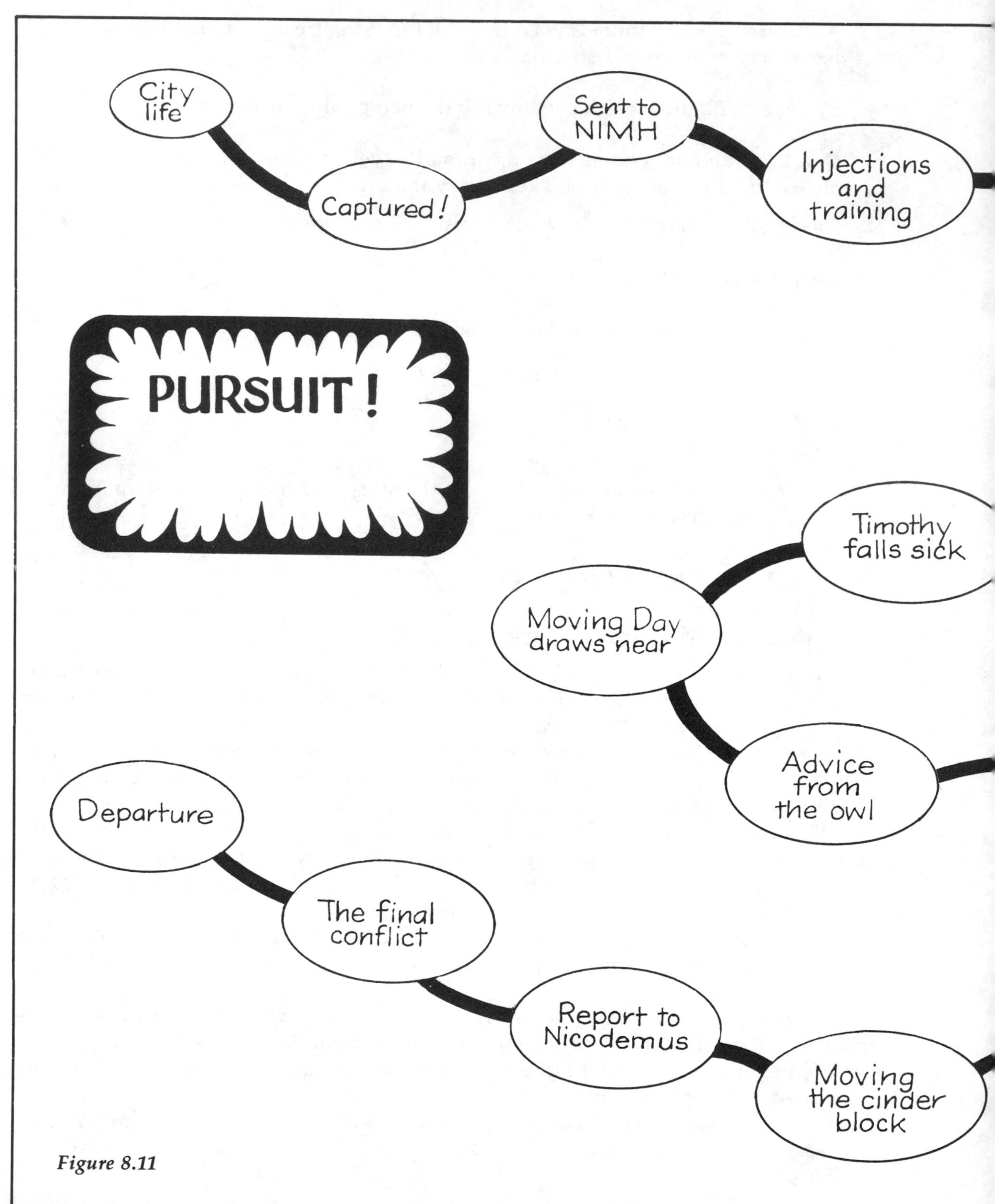
City life
Captured!
Sent to NIMH
Injections and training
PURSUIT!
Timothy falls sick
Moving Day draws near
Advice from the owl
Departure
The final conflict
Report to Nicodemus
Moving the cinder block

Figure 8.11

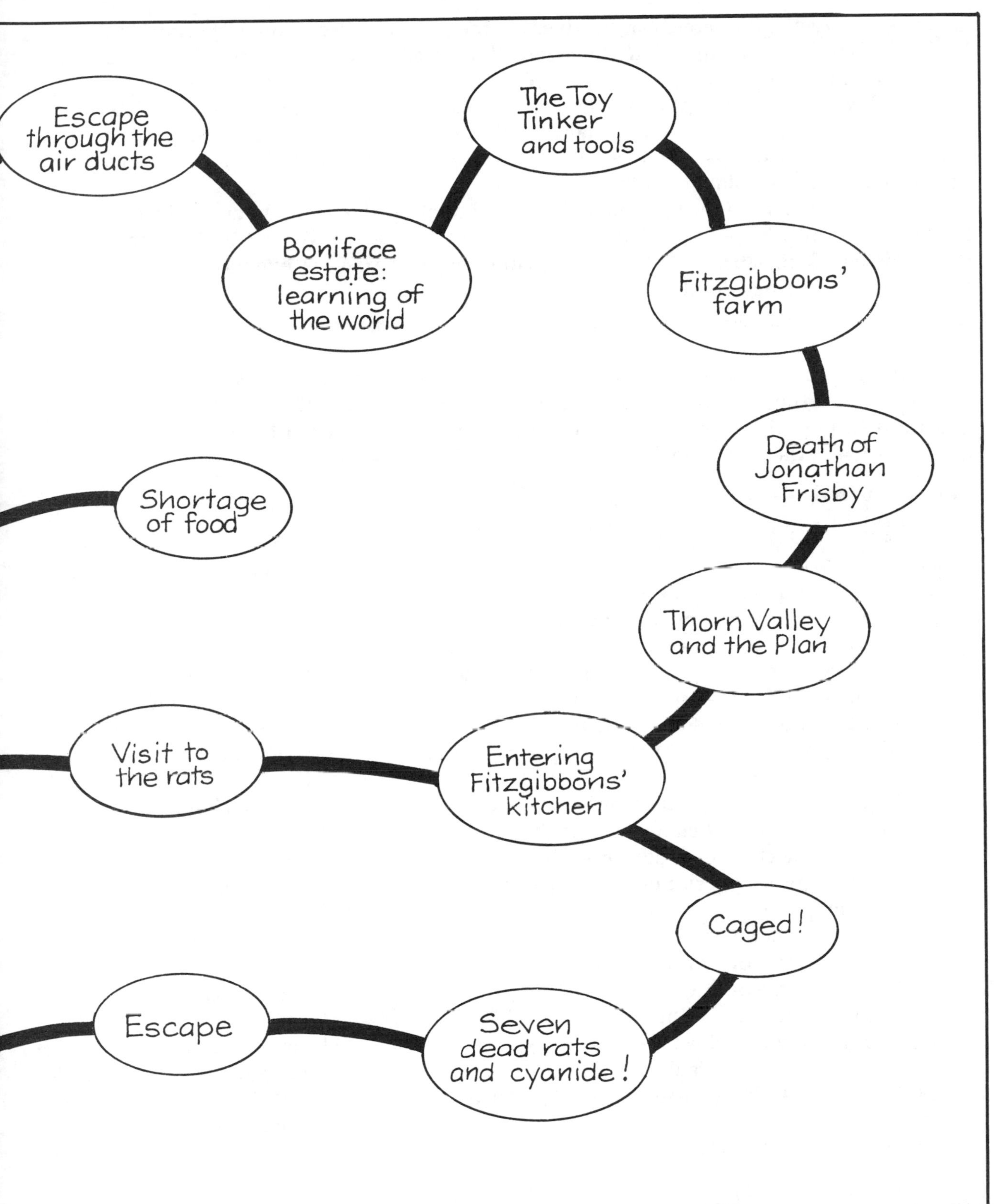
Escape through the air ducts
Boniface estate: learning of the world
The Toy Tinker and tools
Fitzgibbons' farm
Death of Jonathan Frisby
Thorn Valley and the Plan
Shortage of food
Visit to the rats
Entering Fitzgibbons' kitchen
Caged!
Seven dead rats and cyanide!
Escape

answered correctly, the move can be given, at the player's discretion, either to Mrs. Frisby or to the rats. If a question is answered incorrectly, the move is given either to Dr. Schultz or to the plow.

The players. The group playing the game works cooperatively to ensure the safety of the rats and Mrs. Frisby. Individuals should take turns answering questions but may receive help from other players if they encounter difficulties. The game works best with two to four players.

Materials preparation. For convenient reproduction the game board is in two halves, which may be photocopied and mounted on cardboard. When fitted together they form a playing surface. Colors and illustrations of characters, events and objects from the story can be added if you wish.

Question Cards

These questions are representative of the range of literature skills that can be developed and the variety of formats that might be used. But there aren't enough questions to play the game for very long. Encourage the children to create further questions using these as models.

Skills covered

The skills covered in the set of questions in figure 8.12 include:

Q.	*Skill*	*Format*
1.	Identify important aspects of character.	Rating scale
2.	Identify causes for the behavior of a character.	Mini-cloze
3.	Identify changes in character.	Lie
4.	Identify causes of changes in character behavior.	Multiple choice
5.	Identify the feelings of a character.	Mini-countdown
6.	Identify the cause of an incident.	Clue
7.	Identify the passage of time for a given incident.	Mini-cloze
8.	Identify setting.	Lie
9.	Identify how setting affects mood.	Multiple choice
10.	Identify the central character's problem.	Literary sociogram
11.	Identify the climax of the story.	Plot profile
12.	Relate significant prior events to present circumstances.	Sociogram
13.	Identify archetypes.	Supporting evidence
14.	Recognize use of symbol.	Plot profile
15.	Recognize use of dilemma.	Question (dilemma)
16.	Recognize use of conflict.	Character grid
17.	Identify point of view.	Mini-countdown
18.	Recognize use of flashback.	Story sequence
19.	Recognize authentic use of speech patterns of characters.	Rating scale
20.	Note narrator's voice.	Lie

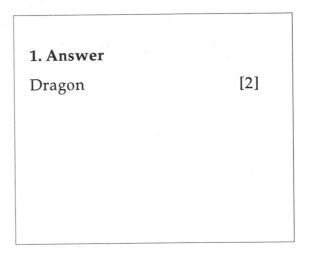

1. Rating Scale: Who is it?

Powerful	_ x _ _ _	Weak
Quick	x _ _ _ _	Slow
Intelligent	_ _ _ x _	Dull
Friendly	_ _ _ _ x	Unfriendly
Human	_ x	Animal

1. Answer

Dragon [2]

2. Mini-cloze: Who? What?

__(a)__ and his friends leave the group because they don't agree with the __(b)__ .

2. Answers

(a) Jenner [1]

(b) Plan [1]

3. A Lie: What's wrong? Put it right.

At first Mrs. Frisby was eager to fly on Jeremy's back. Later in the story she is too frightened to drug Dragon.

3. Answers

- *eager:* afraid or reluctant [1]
- *too frightened:* willing or ready [1]

Figure 8.12

4. Multiple choice: Pick the right one

At first Mrs. Frisby is cautious and afraid but later she grows brave enough to enter the home of an owl. This change in her courage occurs because:

a) she is growing into a more mature person.

b) she overcomes her fear to save her son.

c) she doesn't realize that owls hunt mice.

4. Answer

b) She overcomes her fear to save her son. [2]

5. Mini-countdown

Who is speaking and what is he speaking about? Guess after each clue.

3. I never got used to the feeling.

2. My muscles cramped, my eyes blurred and I became dizzy.

1. It's not exactly pain but it is unbearable.

Bonus clue: read page 99.

5. Answer

Nicodemus speaking about electric shock

If it took one clue: [3]

If it took two clues: [2]

If it took three clues: [1]

6. Clue: What is it:

A tractor was used to destroy this plant so that Dr. Shultz could get at the rats' home.

6. Answer

Rosebush [2]

7. Mini-cloze: How long?

Mrs. Frisby was trapped in the birdcage for about ___ hours.

a) 5

b) 12

c) 24

7. Answer

a) 5 hours. She was captured about 6 p.m. and rescued about 11 p.m. [2]

8. Lie: Tell the truth!

The setting for Mrs. Frisby's conversation with the owl is full of gloom and doom. This feeling is produced because the conversation takes place <u>beside a clear running stream.</u>

8. Answer

In an old dead tree [2]

9. Meaning in context

At the bottom of page 3 to the top of page 4 the author describes the world covered in thick white frost with no sign of greenery. This description gives you a feeling of:

a) happiness and hope

b) coldness and death

c) courage and effort

9. Answer

b) coldness and death [2]

10. Literary sociogram

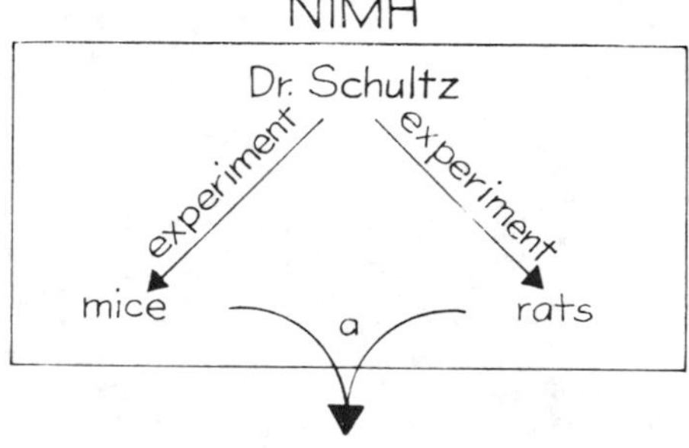

When Dr. Schultz has the rats and mice in NIMH he experiments with them. What do the rats and mice want to do? How would you label the arrow marked "a"?

10. Answer

a = Escape [2]

11. Plot profile: How does the story work?

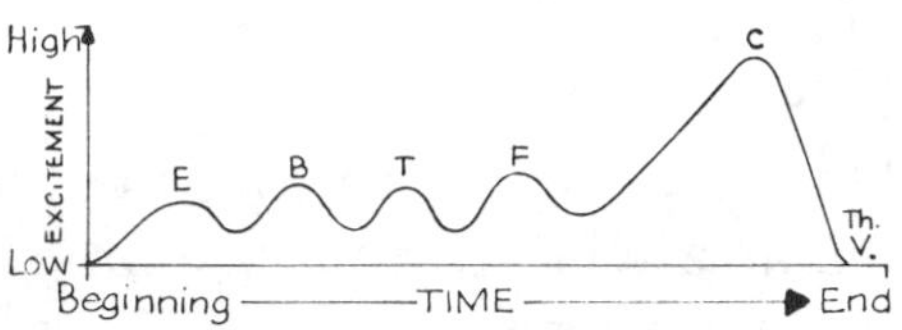

E = Escape from NIMH
T = Toy Tinker
F = Fitzgibbons' farm
Th.V = Thorn Valley
C = Climax
B = Boniface Estate

The climax of the rats' story is:
a) moving Mrs. Frisby's house
b) learning about Jenner
c) escaping the cyanide gas

11. Answer

c) escaping the cyanide gas [2]

12. Sociogram

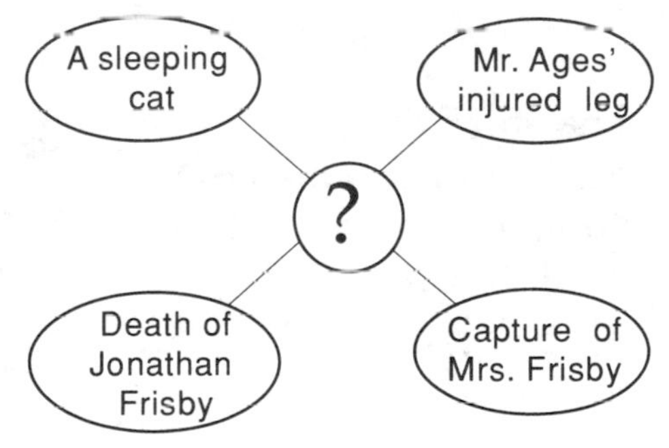

These four incidents are all caused by trying to do something. What is it?

12. Answer

Drugging Dragon *or*

Putting the cat to sleep *or*

Putting sleeping powder in the cat's food *or*

anything that means the same thing. [2]

13. Supporting evidence

Mr. Ages is somewhat like a wizard in fairy tales. Tell three things about Mr. Ages that make him seem like a wizard.

13. Answers

He is old
He is wise
He uses powders to cure people
He has a wise-sounding name
He lives alone.

Other reasons may be added.

[1] for each correct answer

[3] maximum.

14. Plot profile

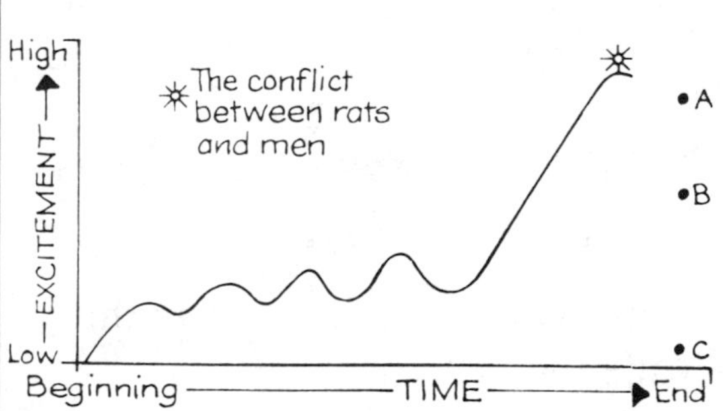

The story ends with the setting of the sun, which suggests that the plot line showing the level of excitement should go to: A, B, or C?

14. Answer

C. The story ends with a feeling of peace and calm, so the excitement level is low. [2]

15. Dilemma

A dilemma is a situation where something bad will happen no matter what the character decides to do. In Chapter 5, "Five Days," Mrs. Frisby has a dilemma. She must stay in the house or move out. If she moves, Timothy may die. What will happen if she stays?

15. Answer

The whole family will die. [2]

16. Character grid

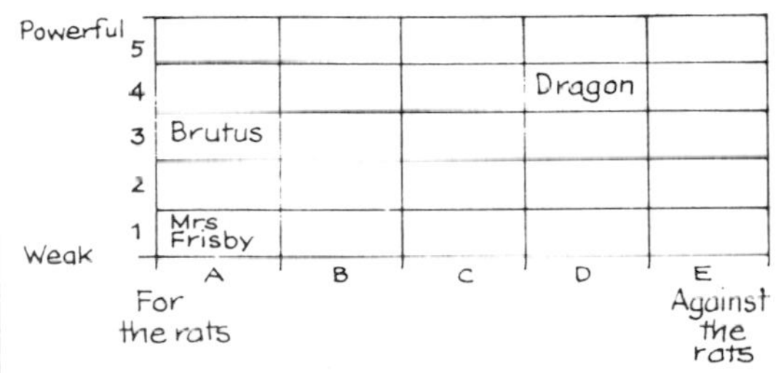

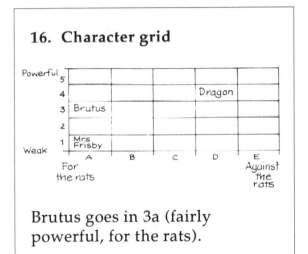

Brutus goes in 3a (fairly powerful, for the rats).

Dragon goes in 4d (more powerful than Brutus, against the rats).

In which box would you put Dr. Schultz?

16. Answers

5e = [2]

5d = [1]

3d = [1]

4e = [1]

4d = [1]

Everything else = [0]

17. Mini-countdown

Guess after each clue.

3. I sat high up
2. I am human
1. I caught a mouse with a colander.

17. Answer

Billy

[3] If you guessed correctly after the first clue

[2] If you guessed correctly after the second clue

[1] If you guessed correctly after the third clue.

18. Story sequence

We learn about these events in this order:

1. The death of Jonathan Frisby
2. Moving Day
3. Escape from NIMH.

In what order do they actually happen?

18. Answer

3 → 1 → 2 [3]

19. Rating scale: Why?

Uses long words	X ___ ___	Uses short words
Uses long sentences	X ___ ___	Uses short sentences
Hard to understand	X ___ ___	Easy to understand
Cold	X ___ ___	Warm
Intelligent	X ___ ___	Dull

19. Answer

Dr. Schultz [2]

20. A lie! Tell the truth

On page 116 it says, "During the days that followed, our lives fell into a pattern, and the reason for our captivity became clear." These words are spoken by Jenner to Timothy Frisby.

20. Answers

Jenner → Nicodemus [1]

Timothy Frisby → Mrs. Frisby [1]

Format

The questions have been set out to facilitate reproduction: you can photocopy each page and mount individual questions on 7 x 10 cm cards with the questions on one side and the answers on the other.

RELATED READING

Books with a Similar Theme: The Oppressed

One idea that is developed in *The Secret of NIMH* is the survival of a group of (relatively) physically weak characters in a hostile environment. First we learn how Mrs. Frisby provides for her family. Later the story broadens and we find how the rats learned to live in a human world. The books listed below share the common theme of small creatures surviving in a dangerous world.

A second aspect that intrigues the reader is the use that small creatures make of human artifacts. Several of the books listed also address this idea. An animal's view of humans, human practices and artifacts permits the author to help the young reader look at human society from a fresh vantage point and perhaps question assumptions that might otherwise go unexamined.

Adams, Richard. *Watership Down.* Penguin, 1974.

A human housing development forces a group of rabbits to search for a new home. The enforced journey brings trials and terrors but, also, brings out a growing sense of accomplishment. The new warren is threatened by the monstrous General Woundwort. A daring raid brings about the final conflict. The history and folklore of the rabbits contributes to the plausibility of the secondary world. The fantasy element is deftly handled. The story occurs in the real world and, apart from speech, the rabbits are limited to lapine abilities. The human world brushes the fantasy world but human society is seen as distant and alien by the protagonists. A long story that rewards the effort invested in it. Somewhat more difficult than *The Secret of NIMH.*

Dann, Colin. *The Animals of Farthing Wood.* Heinemann, 1979.

A motley collection of animals are driven out of their home by urban development. In their search for a haven they are threatened by farmers, fire, flood, hunters, traffic and pesticides. Most but not all of them make it safely. The story is episodic and it is difficult to see why such incidents as the disruption of a human wedding were included. As in *Black Beauty,* the animals are endowed with a higher morality than most human beings — indeed the author's didacticism becomes more pronounced as the story develops. Characters are not well developed and the author takes on more of them than he can handle. Thus some, such as Tawny Owl and Weasel, seem to fade in and out of the story. Two incidents of quite unnecessary anthropomorphic male chauvinism occur: two females, a vixen and a heron, are selected as mates, purely on the basis of their physical appearance.

Title / *Elements*	The Voyage of QV 66 Lively	The Kremlin Cat Babington	The Animals of Farthing Wood Dann	Watership Down Adams	The Borrowers Norton	**The Secret of NIMH** O'Brien
Small creatures	A group of assorted animals (not all small)	Feliski and mice	Assorted wood-land creatures	Rabbits	15 cm high humans	Rats and mice
band together and	become friends and	reject spy role and work for peace.	take an oath not to harm one another and	living in a warren	Clock family	trained at NIMH
go on a mission	search for Stanley's identity. They travel to London	Feliski spies on Washington conference in Bali.	search for a new home.	are forced to search for a new home.		escape and search for a home.
in hostile territory.	avoiding hostile dogs and crows.	All animal activities avoid human attention.	They pass through fire, flood and human habitation	Dogs, foxes, humans and machines are avoided.	Cat, weasels, terriers, humans are hostile.	Scientists, cats, farmers and machines threaten them.
They make use of human artifacts.	They examine, use and wonder about artifacts left by human beings.	Animals are trained by humans to spy and use tools. Weapons are used in disarmament.			Borrowers live off items borrowed from humans.	The rats steal electricity, light bulbs, carpets. Mrs Frisby lives in a cinder block.
Events build to a conflict/climax.	Pansy the cat is rescued from crows.	U.S. and Soviet governments held hostage.	Foxhunt? Motorway? Wedding?	Battle between heroes and Woundwart.	Rat catcher smokes out the Borrowers.	Dr Schultz attacks rat colony.
Negative commentary on human values.	Animals parody pointless human activities, such as bureaucracy.	Futility of the arms race.	Detrimental effects of human practices on wildlife: hunting, pesticides, urban development.		Pod suggests animals avoid humans since no good ever came from knowing one.	Cruelty of experimentation on animals. Human "rat" race discussed.

Figure 8.13 A book comparison grid: The Oppressed

The fantasy element is not handled well. The story takes place in the real world and the animals are endowed with their natural abilities except that they can talk and reason. Their knowledge of human affairs seems inconsistent. They exhibit familiarity with such things as traffic problems on a motorway, circuses and the habits of naturalists. But they seem ignorant of churches and the use of pesticides.

The story does not have a clearly defined climax — at least not one that has any unifying or resolving capacity. Excitement and tension are engendered in three incidents near the end of the book (the fox hunt, crossing the motorway and escaping the church) abut none of these have any cohesive power. Somewhat more difficult than *The Secret of NIMH*. Despite its weaknesses, the similarity of treatment to *The Secret of NIMH* makes it worthwhile for comparison.

Babinton, K. G. *The Kremlin Cat*. Oriel Press, 1983.

A communist cat and a group of capitalist mice, trained to spy, discover the futility of the arms race and plot to bring about involuntary world disarmament. The mature reader will appreciate the satirical treatment of East-West political tensions. Younger readers will enjoy the swift-paced story. The climax presents a consummation devoutly desired by millions of people throughout the world. The book is likely to appeal to the idealism of youth. Somewhat more difficult than *The Secret of NIMH*. A group that was reading *The Secret of NIMH* for themselves might benefit from listening to *The Kremlin Cat* read aloud and discussed.

Lively, Penelope. *The Voyage of QV66*. Dalton, 1979.

In an England devoid of people, a group of assorted talking beasts set out to discover the identity of one-of-a-kind Stanley. Inexplicably, all the animals have the power of speech and some can read. The creatures are repeatedly puzzled or shocked by the record of pointlessness or cruelty of human behavior recorded in the artifacts left behind by the departed humans. Episodes thinly strung together by an unlikely quest which reaches a climax in the rescue of one of the band from being sacrificed at Stonehenge. Easier than *The Secret of NIMH*.

Norton, Mary. *The Borrowers*. Harcourt, Brace and World, 1952.

Tiny people live off human households. Arrietty's friendship with a boy brings great riches and then disaster. The housekeeper, Mrs Driver, discovers the Borrowers' home and brings in the rat catcher to drive them out. The borrowers escape through a broken grill.

Excellent characterization, although Arrietty somehow manages to speak in a "proper" fashion, while her parents use working class speech.

In addition to the elements listed in figure 8.13, these books have several other points in common: female central character, confinement and urge for freedom, use of toys for daily living, cat as hostile predator, humans as antagonists, escape and flight out into the country, ambiguous and unresolved ending.

Other Works by O'Brien

O'Brien, Robert C. *The Silver Crown.* Atheneum,1968

Ellen, a girl of ten, wakes up to find a silver crown on her pillow. A series of mysterious and violent events, including the apparent death of her entire family, sets her off on a journey to reach a distant aunt. She is joined by a young boy. Both are pursued by a fearsome stranger. They enter a black castle, where a plot for world domination, the true fate of her family, and the secret of the silver crown, are revealed.

A careful comparison of this book and *The Secret of NIMH* would be rewarding, since they match on several points: central character is female, mysterious events lead to a wider conflict, characters are taken to a large building for the purpose of experimentation, previous mysteries are explained by the sustained retelling of even earlier events, a plan is revealed, the villain is an academic; the story starts out as fantasy and slips into science fiction. *The Silver Crown* is not nearly as convincing as *The Secret of NIMH* but the differences between the two show interesting changes in the growth of O'Brien's writing ability.

O'Brien, Robert C. *Z for Zachariah.* Heinemann, 1978.

The story of a teenage girl's attempt to survive after a nuclear holocaust. The mood of the story is much more somber than *The Secret of NIMH* and the theme less optimistic. Sexual subthemes are implied but not addressed directly.

BIBLIOGRAPHIES

Professional Books

Applebee, A. M. (1978). *The Child's Concept of Story: Ages Two to Seventeen.* University of Chicago Press.

Atwell, Nancy (1987). *In the Middle: Writing, reading, and learning with adolescents.* Heinemann.

Baker, L. and A. Brown (1984)."Metacognitive Skills and Readings." In P. D. Pearson (ed.) *Handbook of Reading Research* (pp. 353-394). Longman.

Barrett, Frank. (1988). *A Teacher's Guide to Shared Reading.* Scholastic.

Baskwill, J. and P. Whitman. (1986). *Whole Language Sourcebook.* Scholastic.

Baskwill, J. and P. Whitman. (1989). *Evaluation: Whole Language, Whole Child.* Scholastic.

Baskwill, J.and P. Whitman. (1988). *A Guide to Classroom Publishing.* Scholastic.

Berliner, D.C. and R.V. Rosenshine. (1977). "The Acquisition of Knowledge in the Classroom." In R.C. Anderson, R. Spiro, and M. Montague (eds.), *Schooling and the Acquisition of Knowledge* (p. 384). Lawrence Erlbaum.

Bissex, G. (1980). *GNYS AT WRK: A child learns to read and write.* Harvard University Press.

Boomer, G. (1984). "Piggy Nick — That's a Good Word." In J. Britton (ed.), *English Teaching: An International Exchange.* Heinemann.

Britton, J. (1970). *Language and Learning.* Allen Lane, The Penguin Press.

Buncombe, F. and A. Peetoom. (1988). *Literature-Based Learning: One School's Journey.* Scholastic.

Calkins, L. M. (1983). *The Art of Teaching Writing.* Heinemann.

Calkins, L. M. (1983). *Lessons from a Child: On the Teaching and Learning of Writing.* Heinemann.

Cambourne, B. (1989) *The Whole Story: Natural Learning and the Acquisition of Literacy in the Classroom.* Ashton Scholastic.

Carnine, D., and T. Silbert. (1979). *Direct Instruction Reading*. Charles E. Merrill.

Carpenter, H. and M. Prichard. (1984). *The Oxford Companion to Children's Literature* (pp.529-531). Oxford University Press.

Cashdan, A. (1986). *Literacy: Teaching and Learning Language Skills.*Oxford

Clay, M. M. (1979). *Reading: the Patterning of Complex Behavior*. Heinemann.

Cohen, S. Alan. (1988). *Tests: Marked for Life?* Scholastic.

Cullinan, B. E. (Ed., 1987). *Children's Literature in the Reading Program.* IRA.

Dakos, K. D. (1989). *What's There to Write About?* Scholastic.

de la Mare, Walter (1970). *The Complete Poems of Walter de la Mare.* Holt.

Doake, David B. (1988). *Reading Begins at Birth.* Scholastic-TAB.

Donaldson, Margaret (1978). *Children's Minds.* Fontana.

Downing, J. and C. K. Leong. (1982). *Psychology of Reading.* Collier Macmillan.

Dunkeld, C.G. (1970). *The Validity of the Informal Reading Inventory for the Designation of Instructional Reading Levels: a Study of Relationships between Children's Gains in Reading Achievement and the Difficulty of Instructional Materials* Unpublished doctoral dissertation, University of Illinois.

Durkin, D. (1978-79). "What Classroom Observations Reveal about Reading Comprehension Instruction." *Reading Research Quarterly,*14(4), 481-533.

Fox, G., andM. Benton. (1986).*Teaching Literature: 9 to 14*. Oxford.

Fry, D. *Children Talk about Books: Seeing themselves as readers.* Milton Keynes.

Gentry, J. Richard. (1987). *Spel . . . Is a Four Letter Word.* Scholastic. (Also available from Heinemann in the United States).

Goodlad, J. I. (1984). *A Place called School: Prospects for the Future.* McGraw Hill.

Goodman, K. (1986). *What's Whole in Whole Language.* Scholastic. (Also available from Heinemann in the United States).

Goodman, Kenneth S., Yetta M. Goodman and Wendy J. Hood (1989). *The Whole Language Evaluation Book.* Heinemann.

Grave, M.E., T. Weinstein, and H.J. Walbert. (1983). "School-based Home Instruction and Learning: a Quantitative Synthesis." *Journal of Educational Research,* 76(6), 351-360.

Graves, D.H. (1981). "Patterns of Control of the Writing Process." in *A Case Study Observing the Development of Primary Children's Composing, Spelling, and Motor Be-*

haviors During the Writing Process. Final Report. M.I.E. Grant No. G-78-0174. Edited by D.H. Graves, University of New Hampshire. ED 218 653.

Graves, D. H. (1983). *Writing: Teachers and Children at Work.* Heinemann.

Hansen, J., T. Newkirk and D. Graves. (1985). *Breaking Ground: Teachers Relate Reading and Writing in the Elementary School.* Irwin.

Harste, J. C., B. Woodward and C. L. Burke (1984). *Language Stories and Literacy Lessons.* Heinemann.

Hart-Hewins, Linda and Jan Wells. (1988). *Borrow-a-Book: Your Classroom Library Goes Home.* Scholastic.

Heath, S. B. (1983). *Ways with Words: Language, life and work in communities and classrooms.* Cambridge University Press.

Hill, Susan. *Literature-Based Programs at Work in the Classroom.* Heinemann. (Available in Canada from Scholastic.)

Hillocks, G., Jr. (1986). *Research on Written Composition: New Directions for Teaching.* National Conference on Research in English, ERIC Clearinghouse on Reading and Communication Skills, National Institute of Education.

Holdaway, D. (1979). *Foundations of Literacy.* Ashton Scholastic.

Hunt, K.W. (1965). "Grammatical Structures Written at Three Grade Levels." NCTE *Research Report No. 3*, NCTE ED 113 735.

Jackson, D. (1983). *Encounters with Books: Teaching Fiction 11-16.* Methuen.

Jeffrey, S., Hall, J., Meister, S., and Pronovost, J. (1986). *Evaluation Techniques: a Handbook for Teachers.* British Columbia Teachers Association.

Johnson, Terry D. *Unriddling the World.* Foundation for Research in Literacy. In press.

Johnson, T. and D. Louis. (1987). *Literacy through Literature.* Scholastic. (Available in the United States from Heinemann.)

Jurgens, J.M. and W.J. Griffin. (1970). *Relationships Between Overall Quality and Seven Language Features in Composition Written in Grades Seven, Nine and Eleven.* George Peabody College for Teachers, Institute on School Learning and Individual Differences. ED 046 932.

Karlsen, B., R. Madden, and E.F. Gardner. (1976). *Stanford Diagnostic Reading Test.* Harcourt, Brace, Jovanovich.

Lynch, Priscilla (1986). *Using Big Books and Predictable Books.* Scholastic. (Also available in the United States from Heinemann.)

Lynn, R. N. (1983). *Fantasy for Children* (2nd ed.). Bowker.

Macrorie, Ken (1976). *Telling Writing.* Hayden.

Malam, C. (1930). *Upper Pasture.* Holt.

Mallick, D. (1984). *How Tall is this Ghost, John?* AATE.

Mandler, J.M., and N.S. Johnson. (1977). "Remembrance of Things Parsed: Story Structure and Recall." In *Cognitive Psychology, 9*, 111-151

Martin, J.R. and J. Rothery. (1986). *Writing Project Report: Working Papers in Linguistics, No. 4.* Linguistics Department, University of Sydney.

Martinez, San Jose, C.P. (1973). "Grammatical Structures in four Modes of Writing at Fourth-grade level." *Dissertation Abstracts International* 33. 5411-A.

Murray, D. (1984). *Write to Learn.* Holt, Rinehart and Winston.

Newman, Judith. (1984). *The Craft of Children's Writing.* Scholastic. (Also available from Heinemann in the United States).

Nystrand, Martin (1982). "Rhetoric's 'Audience' and Linguistic's 'Speech Community': Implications for Understanding Writing, Reading and Text. In Martin Nystrand (ed.). *What Writers Know: The language, process and structure of written discourse.* Academic Press.

O'Donnell, R.C., W.J. Griffin, and R.C. Morris. (1967). "Syntax of Kindergarten and Elementary School Children: a Transformational Analysis." *NCTE Research Report No. 8.* NCTE. ED 017 508

Page, M. (1986). *Towards an Alternative Approach to the Teaching of Children's Literature and Literacy.* Unpublished M. Ed. project, Faculty of Education, University of Victoria, Victoria, British Columbia, Canada.

Park, Louise. (1989). *Art Attack: Programmed Art for the Frenzied Teacher.* Ashton Scholastic.

Pearson, P. D. and D. Johnson. (1978). *Teaching Reading Comprehension.* Holt, Rinehart and Winston.

Phinney, Margaret. (1988) *Reading With the Troubled Reader.* Scholastic. (Available in the United States from Heinemann.)

Peetoom, Adrian. (1986). *Shared Reading: Safe Risks With Whole Books.* Scholastic.

Quigg, P. (1985) *The Emergence of Literacy.* Unpublished M.Ed. thesis, Faculty of Education, University of Victoria, British Columbia.

Rico, G. L. (1983). *Writing the Natural Way.* J. P. Tarcher Inc.

Rosen, Michael. (1989). *Did I Hear You Write?* Scholastic.

Rosenblatt, L. (1968). *Literature as Exploration.* Noble and Noble.

Rosenblatt, L. (1978). *The Teacher, the Text and the Poem: the Transactional Theory of the Literacy Work.* Southern Illinois Press.

Sager, C. (1973). "Improving the Quality of Written Composition of Pupil Use of Rating Scale." Paper, Annual Meeting of NCTE. ED 089 304

Shulevitz, Uri (1985). *Writing with Pictures: How to Write and Illustrate Children's Books.* Watson-Guptill.

Smith, F. (1971). *Understanding Reading.* Holt, Rinehart and Winston.

Stewart, M.F. and C.H. Grobe. (1979). "Syntactic Maturity, Mechanics of Writing, and Teachers' Quality Ratings." *Research in the Teaching of English.* 13, 207-215.

Stott, J. C. (1978). "Running Away to Home — A Story Pattern in Children's Literature." Language Arts, 55(4), April, pp. 473-477.

Tamburri, Joan, James Willig and Clive Butler (1984). *Children's Concepts of Writing.* Croom Helm.

Taylor, Denny and Dorothy S. Strickland. (1986). *Family Storybook Reading.* Heinemann (Available in Canada from Scholastic).

Thomas, R. and A. Perry. (1984). *Introductory Book: 101 Literature Activities for the Classroom.* Oxford.

Thompson, Gare. (1988). *Classroom Drama: Act it Out.* Scholastic.

Tolkien, J. R. R. (1964). "On Fairy Stories." In *Tree By Leaf.* Unwin.

Topping, K. (1985). "Parental Involvement in Reading: Theoretical and Empirical Background." In K. Topping and S. Wolfenden, *Parental Involvement in Children's Reading* (pp. 17-31). Croom Helm.

Troyka, L.Q. (1974). "A Study of the Effect of Simulation-gaming on Expository Prose Competence of College Remedial English Composition Students." *Dissertation Abstracts Intarnational,* 4092-A. ED 090 541.

Troyka, L. Q. and J. Nudelman. (1975). *Taking Action: Writing, Reading, Speaking and Listening through Simulation-games.* Prentice-Hall.

Van Manen, Max. (1987). *The Tone of Teaching.* Scholastic. (Also available from Heinemann in the United States).

Vaughan, J. L. and T. H. Estes (1986). *Reading and Reasoning beyond the Primary Grades.* Allyn and Bacon.

Villiers, Una. (1989). *Luk Mume Luk Dade I Kan Rit.* Scholastic.

Walshe, R.D. (1981). *Every Child Can Write!* Primary English Teachers Association.

Watson, Dorothy, Carolyn Burke and Jerome Harste. (1989). *Whole Language: Inquiring Voices.* Scholastic.

Weaver, Constance. (1988). *Reading Process and Practice: From socio-psycholinguistics to whole language.* Heinemann.

Wells, G. (1986). *The Meaning Makers.* Heinemann.

Wilkinson, A., G. Bamsley, P. Hanna, and M. Swan. (1980). *Assessing Language Development.* Oxford.

Children's Books

Aardema, V. (1975). *Why Mosquitoes Buzz in People's Ears.* Illustrated by L. and D. Dillon. Dial.

Adams, R. (1974). *Watership Down.* Macmillan.

Alexander, L. (1964). *The Book of Three.* Holt.

Arkhurst, J.C. (1964). *The Adventures of Spider.* Illustrated by J. Pinkney. Scholastic.

Arno, E. *The Gingerbread Man.* (1967). Scholastic.

Asbjornsen, P.C. (1908). *Popular Tales from the Norse.* Translated by G.W. Dasent. Putnam.

Asbjornsen, P.C., and Moe, J.E. "The Husband who Had to Mind the House." Reprinted in Saxby, M. and Smith, G. (1986). *Just Imagine!.* Methuen Australia.

Asbjornsen, P.C. and Jorgen, M. (1957). *The Three Billy Goats Gruff.* Illustrated by M. Brown. Harcourt.

Bond, M. (1960). *A Bear Called Paddington.* Illustrated by P. Fortnum. Houghton Mifflin.

Brown, M. (1980). *Arthur's Valentine.* Atlantic Little, Brown.

Burnett, F. H. (1962). *The Secret Garden.* Scholastic.

"The Creature in the Forest." *In Great Myths and Legends.* Childcraft Annual, Worldbook, 1984. (105-115)

Defoe, D. (1954). *Robinson Crusoe.* Silver.
Eastman, P. D. (1960). *Are You my Mother?* Beginner Books.
Farmer, P. (1972). *Charlotte Sometimes.* Penguin.
Flack, M. (1933/1961). *The Story about Ping.* Illustrated by K. Wiese. Penguin.
Freeman, D. (1976). *Corduroy.* Puffin, Penguin.
Grimm, J., and Grimm, W. (1968/1805). *Grimm's Fairy Tales.* Based on the Frances Jenkins Olcott edition of the English translation by Margaret Hunt. Follett.
Hoban, R. (1974). *How Tom Beat Captain Najork & his Hired Sportsmen.* Macmillan.
Holm. A. (1980). *I am David.* Methuen.
Kuskin, K. (1982). *Alexander Soames: his Poems.* Harper & Row.
Le Guin, U. (1968). *A Wizard of Earthsea.* Parnassus.
L'Engle, M. (1962). *A Wrinkle in Time.* Farrar, Straus, Giroux.
Lewis, C.S. (1961). *The Lion, the Witch and the Wardrobe.* Macmillan.
Lionni, L. C. (1975). *Pezzettino.* Pantheon.
Littledale, F. (1975). *The Elves and the Shoemaker.* Illustrated by B. Turkle. Scholastic.
Littledale, F. (1966, 1985). *The Magic Fish.* Illustrated by Winslow Pinney Pels. Scholastic.
Lobel, A. (1971). *Frog and Toad.* Harper & Row.
Lobel, A. (1970). *Frog and Toad are Friends.* Scholastic.
Lunn, J.L.S. (1983). *The Root Cellar.* Macmillan.
McCloskey, R. (1968). *Make Way for Ducklings.* Scholastic.
Majorian, M. (1981). *Goodnight, Mr. Tom.* Kestrel Books, Harper & Row.
Mark, Jan. (1980). *Nothing to be Afraid Of.* Harper & Row.
Milne, A.A. (1926). *The House at Pooh Corner.* Illustrated by E. Shepard. Dell.
Montgomery, L.M. (1908). *Anne of Green Gables.* Putnam.
Morrison, L. (1977). *The Sidewalk Racer.* Lothrop, Lee & Shepard.
O'Brien, R.C. (1972). Newbery Medal Acceptance Speech, *The Horn Book Magazine,* Vol. XLVIII, No.4 (August 1972), p.344.
O'Brien, Robert C. (1974). *The Secret of NIMH.* Scholastic. Also published as *Mrs. Frisby and the Rats of NIMH.* (video) United Artists.
O'Neill, M. (1969). *My Fingers Are Always Bringing Me News.* Doubleday.
Park, R. (1980). *Playing Beatie Bow.* Macmillan.
Parkes, B., and Smith, J., 1986. *The Three Billy Goats Gruff.* Scholastic.
Pearce, P. (1959). *Tom's Midnight Garden.* Dell.
Peet, B. (1971). *The Caboose Who Got Loose.* Houghton Mifflin.
Phipson, J. (1965). *The Boundary Riders.* Angus & Robertson, 1962, Puffin.
Ransome, A. (1981). *Swallows and Amazons.* Merrimack.
Roethke, T. (1938). *The Collected Poems of Theodore Roethke.* U. of Wash. Press.
Rosetti, C. (1924). *Sing-song, a Nursery Rhyme Book for Children.* Dover.
Sendak, M. (1968). *Where the Wild Things Are.* Scholastic.
Silverstein, S. (1974). *Where the Sidewalk Ends.* Harper & Row.
Sperry, A. (1963). *Call it Courage.* Also published as *The Boy Who Was Afraid.* Macmillan, 1940.
Spyri, J. (1962/1884) *Heidi.* Illustrated by G. Elgaard. Scholastic.